A WORLD BANK COUNTRY STUDY

Afghanistan—State Building, Sustaining Growth, and Reducing Poverty

THE WORLD BANK
Washington, D.C.

Manufactured in the United States of America
First Printing: February 2005

printed on recycled paper

1 2 3 4 5 07 06 05

World Bank Country Studies are among the many reports originally prepared for internal use as part of the continuing analysis by the Bank of the economic and related conditions of its developing member countries and to facilitate its dialogues with the governments. Some of the reports are published in this series with the least possible delay for the use of governments, and the academic, business, financial, and development communities. The manuscript of this paper therefore has not been prepared in accordance with the procedures appropriate to formally-edited texts. Some sources cited in this paper may be informal documents that are not readily available.

The findings, interpretations, and conclusions expressed herein are those of the author(s) and do not necessarily reflect the views of the International Bank for Reconstruction and Development/The World Bank and its affiliated organizations, or those of the Executive Directors of The World Bank or the governments they represent.

The World Bank does not guarantee the accuracy of the data included in this work. The boundaries, colors, denominations, and other information shown on any map in this work do not imply and judgment on the part of The World Bank of the legal status of any territory or the endorsement or acceptance of such boundaries.

ISBN-10: 0-8213-6095-7 ISBN-13: 987-0-8213-6095-8
eISBN: 0-8213-6096-5
ISSN: 0253-2123

Library of Congress Cataloging-in-Publication Data has been requested.

Contents

List of Tables

List of Figures

List of Boxes

Abstract

Afghanistan has come a long way since emerging from major conflict in late 2001. Important political milestones mandated by the Bonn Agreement (two Loya Jirgas, a new Constitution, recently the Presidential election) have been achieved. The economy has recovered strongly, growing by nearly 50 percent cumulatively in the last two years (not including drugs). Some three million internally- and externally-displaced Afghans have returned to their country/home. More than four million children, a third of them girls, are in school, and immunization campaigns have achieved considerable success. The Government has supported good economic performance by following prudent macroeconomic policies; it has begun to build capacity and has developed the nationally-led budget process and made the budget into its central instrument of reform; and it has made extraordinary efforts to develop key national programs (for example public-works employment programs and community development programs) and to revive social services like education and health.

Nevertheless Afghanistan remains one of the poorest countries in the world in terms of both per capita incomes and social indicators, with large gender gaps. The difficult challenge of poverty reduction is made even more difficult by continuing insecurity, weak rule of law, and narcotics. Worsening security in many parts of the country threatens to derail reconstruction, undermine state building efforts, delay parliamentary elections and adversely affect other aspects of political normalization, reduce private sector activity, and keep it in the informal/illicit economy. The burgeoning revival and spread of opium production during the last two years (opium accounted for about a third of the Afghan economy and three-quarters of global illicit opium production in 2003, even more in 2004, and is now found in all 34 of Afghanistan's provinces) has fueled insecurity and funded anti-government interests. Drugs, insecurity, "capture" of large parts of the country by regional powerbrokers, and the weak capacity of the state (including difficulties in centralizing revenue) all contribute to a self-reinforcing "vicious circle" that would keep Afghanistan insecure, fragmented politically, weakly governed, poor, dominated by the informal/illicit economy, and a hostage to the drug industry.

Afghanistan, with robust support from the international community, has to break out of this vicious circle—and move toward a "virtuous circle" whereby improving security, state capacity building, revenue mobilization, formal private sector development, and sensible, coordinated actions against drugs all reinforce each other and put Afghanistan on a path of sustained economic growth and poverty reduction. This will require simultaneous progress on several key fronts; actions in any one area alone will not be effective given the strong interests working to maintain the current status quo. On the other hand limited resources and capacity dictate that the Government prioritize core reforms that will enhance governance, focusing on the implementation of ongoing tasks rather than going for a large number of new initiatives. As the report discusses in detail, the essential elements for a breakthrough in the next one or two years include:

- *Enhancing security and rule of law* through vigorous security sector reform and capacity building (especially the Afghan National Army, police force, and justice system), combined with external security assistance including outside of Kabul.

- *State building* through increasing capacity and intensifying public administration reforms, with a focus on enhancing center-periphery relations (with provincial and district administrations), revenue mobilization, and service delivery (national programs, social services, basic infrastructure).
- *Further political normalization,* focused on making key institutions (cabinet, legislative bodies, judiciary) work effectively, with neutralization of warlords and other illegitimate powerbrokers.
- *Maintaining economic growth* with macroeconomic stability, and *pro-actively pursuing private sector development* through a good enabling environment, support services, and capacity building within the private sector.
- *Meaningful, coordinated actions against drugs,* consistent with the overall state building, security, and development strategy.
- *Enhancing the effectiveness and efficiency of international assistance,* focusing on the attainment of core reforms and enhancing donor alignment with the national budget.

This is a daunting agenda, which will require strong commitment, actions, and persistence on the part of the Government. In each area listed above sustained, coordinated assistance from the international community will be required. Moreover, the international community can support Afghanistan's state building and reconstruction agenda by (i) maximizing assistance that goes through government budget channels and moving toward programmatic support; (ii) maximizing use of coordinated Government-led technical assistance mechanisms, and coordinating pay policy with the Government; (iii) stopping payments and other support to non-legitimate regional authorities; and (iv) standing ready to respond to macroeconomic shocks (such as drought) by accelerating and adjusting assistance as needed.

Acknowledgments

This report was prepared by a team led by William Byrd and including Deepak Ahluwalia, Christine Allison, David Atkin, Philippe Auffret, Anne Evans, Stephane Guimbert, Syed Mahmood, Nick Manning, Peter Middlebrook, Asta Olesen, Arlene Reyes, Shalini Saksena, Juliet Teodosio, and Renos Vakis.

Valuable comments and advice were received from the Peer Reviewers for this task, Barnett Rubin (External Peer Reviewer) and Ian Bannon. The report benefited from guidance provided by Ijaz Nabi, and from comments by participants at the review meeting on the concept note, held on January 20, 2004, and at the review meeting on the draft report, held on June 24, 2004. The report was prepared under the overall supervision of Sadiq Ahmed and Alastair McKechnie.

The report benefitted greatly from very useful dialog at an informal seminar with Afghan Government leaders, held in Kabul on May 27, 2004, at which some of the main themes emerging from the task were presented and discussed, and from numerous individual meetings on specific topics with Government officials, whose insights and support are gratefully acknowledged. The draft report was shared and discussed with the Government, including at a high-level meeting on August 21, 2004; with donor and UN representatives; with NGO representatives; and with professors and students of Kabul University. Comments received at these meetings were taken into account in finalizing the report. More generally, the report takes as a foundation the vision for Afghanistan set forth in the Government's *National Development Framework* (April 2002), articulated into a detailed program of investments, policies, and reforms in the more recent Government document *Securing Afghanistan's Future: Accomplishments and the Strategic Path Forward* (March 2004).

Acronyms and Abbreviations

ACD	Afghan Customs Department
ADB	Asian Development Bank
AFMIS	Afghan Financial Management Information System
AIHRC	Afghan Independent Human Rights Commission
AISA	Afghanistan Investment Support Agency
AMF	Afghanistan Militia Forces
ANBP	Afghanistan New Beginnings Program
AREU	Afghanistan Research and Evaluation Unit
ARTF	Afghan Reconstruction Trust Fund
ASP	Afghanistan Stabilisation Program
BCM	Billion Cubic Meters
BPHS	Basic Package of Health Services
CAO	Control and Audit Office
CND	Counter-Narcotics Directorate
CSO	Central Statistics Office
DAB	Da Afghanistan Bank
DDR	Disarmament, Demobilization, and Reintegration
EC	European Commission
EU	European Union
FAO	UN Food and Agriculture Programme
GDP	Gross Domestic Product
HIPC	Highly Indebted Poor Countries
IARCSC	Independent Administrative Reform and Civil Service Commission
ICD	Inland Clearance Depot
IDA	International Development Assistance
IDP	Internally Displaced Person
IMF	International Monetary Fund
IRC	International Rescue Committee
ISAF	International Security Assistance Force
LOTFA	Law and Order Trust Fund
MAAH	Ministry of Agriculture and Animal Husbandry
MAPA	Mine Action Plan for Afghanistan
MDG	Millennium Development Goals
MISFA	Micro-Finance Support Facility of Afghanistan
MIWRE	Ministry of Irrigation, Water Resources and Environment
MoC	Ministry of Commerce
MoF	Ministry of Finance
MRRD	Ministry of Rural Rehabilitation and Development
MSTQ	Metrology, Standards, Testing and Quality
NATO	North Atlantic Treaty Organisation
NDB	National Development Budget

NDCS	National Drugs Control Strategy
NDF	National Development Framework
NEEP	National Emergency Employment Program
NSC	National Security Council
NSP	National Solidarity Program
O&M	Operation and Maintenance
PAREM	Public Administration and Economic Management
PIP	Public Investment Program
PMU	Program Management Unit
PPA	Performance-based Partnership Agreement
PPP	Purchasing Power Parity
PRR	Priority Reform and Restructuring
PRT	Provincial Reconstruction Team
PSP	Provincial Stabilisation Plan
SSR	Security Sector Reform
UNAMA	United Nations Assistance Mission to Afghanistan
UNDP	United Nations Development Program
UNEP	United Nations Environment Programme
UNICEF	United Nations Children's Fund
UNIFEM	United Nations Development Fund for Women
UNODC	United Nations Office on Drugs and Crime
WFP	UN World Food Programme
WSS	Water Supply and Sanitation
WUG	Water User Group

CURRENCY EQUIVALENT

Currency Unit = Afghani

US$1 = 49 AFN (2003/04 Average)

$ refers to US dollars unless otherwise noted

GOVERNMENT FISCAL YEAR

March 21–March 20

2001/02 = 1380

2002/03 = 1381

2003/04 = 1382

2004/05 = 1383

Executive Summary

Afghanistan is emerging from more than two decades of conflict, capped by a severe nationwide drought in 1999–2001, and faces a complex, interrelated set of political, administrative, economic, and social challenges. The energy and resilience of the Afghan people, which served them well during the conflict, is now being channeled into securing their livelihoods, rebuilding a credible state, and restoring the country's economy. Their efforts, with Government leadership and political, financial, and military support from the international community, have already borne fruit in the form of rapid economic growth, rising incomes, initial revival of public administration, and other improvements. There is near-universal popular sentiment for peace, security, and prosperity, manifested recently in the high voter turn-out for the Presidential election despite security threats. Despite the gains made, Afghanistan remains among the poorest countries in the world (average per capita GDP of around US$300 including opium), and it is a highly fragmented society where the authority of the Government is contested. Continuation of recent positive developments is subject to serious risks—political, security, drug-related, macroeconomic, institutional, and climatic.

The Government has set forth a compelling development vision in its *National Development Framework* (NDF), articulated into a detailed strategy and expenditure program in its recent report *Securing Afghanistan's Future: Accomplishments and the Strategic Path Forward* (SAF). The vision and strategy encompass state building, security, private sector-led growth, human development, and political and social progress, with the key national objectives of sustained broad-based economic growth and poverty reduction.

This is the first Economic Report on Afghanistan by the World Bank in a quarter century. It is intended to contribute to a better understanding of the core challenges that lie ahead for the country and key strategic priorities for national reconstruction. It does not repeat the analysis and investment requirements set forth in the SAF document, but instead focuses on the conceptual frameworks, policies, and institutions that will be needed to achieve core national objectives of state building, sustained rapid, broad-based economic growth, and poverty reduction. Analysis of the Afghan economy is hindered by severe data limitations (discussed in the Statistical Appendix) and is challenged by the conflict-related economic structure and dynamics that have emerged during the past two decades. Nevertheless much has been learned about how the Afghan economy functions, at least in qualitative and institutional terms. The report also draws on the great volume of work done on individual sectors and topics by the Government and partners.

This report starts with a description and analysis of the Afghan economy and its recent performance (Chapter 1), and the poverty situation (Chapter 2). Chapter 3 outlines a strategy for growth and poverty reduction, based on the NDF/SAF, and puts forward key strategic priorities and directions for implementation. State building, discussed in Chapter 4, lies at the core of Afghanistan's reconstruction agenda and is essential for progress on political, security, and other fronts. Chapter 5 addresses the development of the private sector, which will have to be the engine of growth and poverty reduction in Afghanistan. Agriculture, covered in Chapter 6, comprises half of the economy and will play a crucial role. Chapter 7 examines Afghanistan's opium economy, which has some short-term economic benefits but very serious adverse effects on state building and security.

Chapter 8 looks at delivery of social services, a key component of the poverty reduction strategy, including the gender dimension. Social protection—strategies and programs to assist the poorest and most vulnerable members of Afghan society—is discussed in Chapter 9. Chapter 10 concludes with a summary of priorities for action, implementation constraints, prospects, and risks.

The Afghan Economy and Recent Performance

The starting point—in late 2001 at the fall of the Taliban—for recent developments in Afghanistan was dire. The Afghan economy was reeling from protracted conflict and severe drought, with cereal grain production down by half, livestock herds decimated, orchards and vineyards destroyed by war and drought, more than five million people displaced as refugees in neighboring countries, and remaining economic activities steered in an informal or illicit direction by insecurity and lack of support services. The Afghan state had become virtually non-functional in terms of policymaking and service delivery, although the structures and many staff remained.

Numerous people were suffering (and still are) from low food consumption, loss of assets, lack of social services, disabilities (for example, from land-mine accidents), and disempowerment and insecurity. The effective Taliban ban on opium poppy cultivation, imposed in 2000, did not much affect trade in opium (apparently based on accumulated inventories) but was devastating to the livelihoods of many poor farmers and rural wage laborers, including through opium-related indebtedness. The collapse of the state virtually excluded the poor from access to services, and moreover the poor tended to be disproportionately affected by insecurity, one of whose important impacts has been a very large number of female-headed households. Even though the fabric of families, kinship groups, and other traditional clusters has held together rather well (demonstrated concretely by the large volume of inward remittances), the penetration of the "warlord" and "commander" culture at the local level has had deleterious effects. In sum, Afghanistan was essentially left out of the last 25 years of global development, with virtually no increase in per capita income during this period and average life expectancy of only 43 years.

Afghanistan's economy has performed very strongly in the past two years, with non-drug GDP increasing cumulatively by almost 50 percent (29 percent in 2002 and 16 percent in 2003), albeit starting from a very low base. This mainly reflects the recovery of agriculture from the drought, revival of economic activity after major conflict ended, and the initiation of reconstruction. With the improved political and economic situation, an estimated 2.4 million refugees have returned to Afghanistan, and 600,000 internally displaced people have returned to their homes. The last two years have also seen a rebound in opium production to near-record levels; the opium economy in 2003 comprised about a third of total drug-inclusive GDP and accounted for three-quarters of global illicit opium production, even more in 2004.

Recent good growth performance has been supported by the Government's sound macroeconomic policies—a highly successful currency reform in late 2002, a prudent "no-overdraft" policy prohibiting domestic financing of the budget deficit, conservative monetary policy which has brought inflation down to around 10 percent per year, and good management of the exchange rate. Progress has also been made in mobilizing domestic revenue, which rose from negligible levels in 2001 to over 4 percent of GDP in 2003; in trade reform—import duties have been rationalized and customs administration reforms are underway; and in financial sector reform, where the Central Bank has been made legally autonomous and several foreign banks have started up in Kabul.

Peace and strong economic performance have been accompanied by improvements in some social indicators. Restoration and expansion of social services has been initiated, notably primary education and immunization. The end of major conflict, combined with national programs like the National Solidarity Program (NSP), has enabled communities and other groups to begin building social capital. Despite this progress, Afghanistan remains a very poor country, with extremely low social indicators (for example, infant mortality of 115 and under-five mortality of 172 per 1,000 live births) and very low access to most public services (such as safe drinking water).

The drivers of recent growth are to a considerable extent temporary and recovery-related (such as the boost in grain output) and are running their course. In order to achieve sustained rapid growth—necessary for poverty reduction, phasing out dependence on opium, and maintaining political buy-in for reforms—other, sustainable growth drivers will be needed. Afghanistan has areas of good potential for growth, ranging from agricultural production and processing to mining, construction, trade, and other services. Exploiting Afghanistan's geographical position as a "land-bridge" between Central and South Asia also can be a source of growth—through trade, transit, and sharing and joint development of resources. Enhancing the role of women in economic life will help ensure that growth is broad-based.

For these and other growth potentials to be realized, the Afghan economy will need to move beyond its present, largely "informal" character. The informal economy, which includes a range of activities in terms of legality and market orientation and accounts for some 80–90 percent of the total economy (including drugs), has been a coping mechanism for Afghans' survival during conflict and has shown considerable dynamism. It is flexible in responding to shocks and to short-term opportunities. On the other hand, the informal economy is the outcome of conflict-related insecurity, short time horizons, erosion of the rule of law, and lack of public services, which have influenced entrepreneurs' decisions toward staying informal, relatively small, and not making longer-term investments. The dominance of the informal economy is a self-reinforcing equilibrium which not only keeps most economic activity informal but also hinders revenue mobilization, state building, security, and ultimately competitiveness and growth (see Figure A).

Toward Sustained Growth and Poverty Reduction

The Government's SAF report puts forward an ambitious goal of 9 percent annual growth of non-opium GDP over the next 12 years, which is argued to be necessary for sustained progress in political normalization, state building, poverty reduction, and phasing out the drug economy. The SAF report is equally ambitious in targeting sharp improvements in social indicators, in line with the Millennium Development Goals. For example, the gross primary school enrollment rate is targeted to rise from 54 percent (40 for girls) at present to 100 percent for boys and girls by 2015, the under-five mortality rate to decline from 172 to 130 per 1,000 live births, the infant mortality rate from 115 to 55 per 1,000 live births, and the maternal mortality rate from an estimated 1,600 per 100,000 live births to 205.

Figure A. The Informal Equilibrium

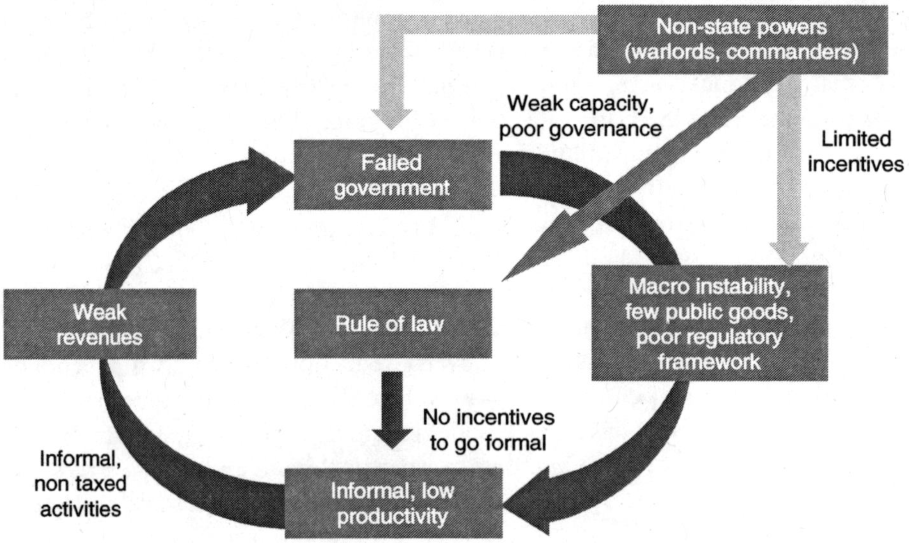

These long-term objectives constitute major challenges for the Afghan Government, the Afghan people, and the international community in support.

Afghanistan faces some major constraints in sustaining recent rapid economic growth, which will have to be led by a strong, competitive private sector: (i) insecurity and lack of rule of law (fueled by the drug industry, which has a strong interest in maintaining an environment of insecurity and lawlessness); (ii) regulatory burden and corruption—although the Government has a pro-private sector policy orientation and has pursued trade and tax reforms, there is still excessive red tape in obtaining permits, land allocations, and the like; (iii) unavailability of key support services for the private sector, ranging from essential infrastructure (power—extremely important for many types of activities, roads, serviced land, water) to finance, insurance, business support services, agricultural extension and marketing, etc.; and (iv) lack of a framework and infrastructure for standards, quality assurance, weights and measures, testing, etc., which will be critical for export development. These constraints all fall within the general rubric of the "investment climate". In addition growth will be constrained by (v) human capital, both extremely scarce managerial and technical professionals—decimated by conflict-related "brain drain" and lack of a credible higher education system in recent years—and literate, skilled labor to work in manufacturing and services; and, related, (vi) weak capacity of the private sector itself, which despite its strong and vibrant entrepreneurship within the informal setting lacks capacity and experience in competitively bidding on international contracts, producing to international export quality standards, and other requirements for longer-term dynamism and competitiveness.

Afghanistan's growth strategy must be multi-faceted to ease these constraints and enable the Afghan private sector to generate broad-based economic activity and robust

Figure B. The Formal Equilibrium

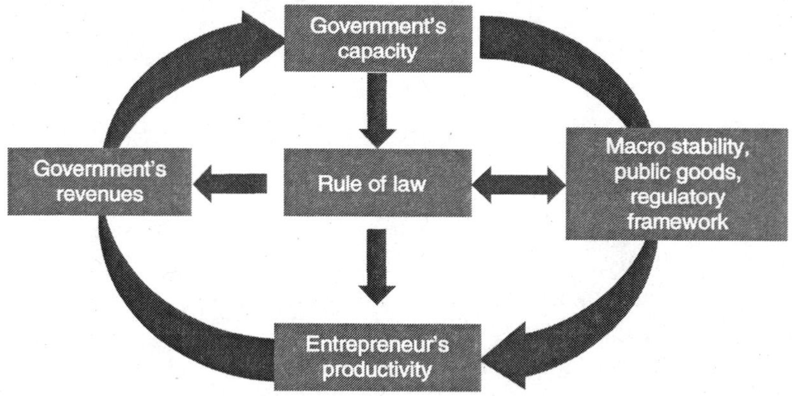

growth on a competitive basis (including competitiveness in exports, whose growth will be essential over the longer term to replace the eventual decline in external assistance). Sustained economic growth will be associated with breaking out of the "informal equilibrium" and moving toward a "formal equilibrium" whereby over time many successful and growing entrepreneurs become part of the formal economy—investing, registering themselves, paying taxes, and benefiting from rule of law and availability of services (see Figure B). This does not mean that the entire economy would become formalized, let alone quickly, but rather that a sizable, dynamic formal sector would come into being. A strategy to shift incentives toward the formal equilibrium, building on the Government's NDF, would have four key elements: (i) improved security through fair and effective enforcement of law and order; (ii) maintaining macroeconomic stability; (iii) effective delivery of support services (such as power, infrastructure, and finance, and essential public goods in support of smallholder agriculture) and building the capacity of the private sector; and (iv) creation of an enabling regulatory environment for business activity through structural reforms. Progress has already been made most notably in trade and financial sector reforms, and macroeconomic stability has been achieved but will need to be maintained. Structural reforms will need to focus on completing those underway, on further deregulation to ease the burden of red tape and reduce vulnerability to corruption, and on new areas such as the privatization agenda. Progress in improving security and public service delivery will be crucial and will depend very much on gains in state building. Over the longer term, human resource development will be essential, requiring adequate investments in education and health, focusing on quality as well as access.

In the short run, rapid economic growth can be supported, and the process of "formalization" jump-started, by:

Importing resources, including (i) aid and technical assistance, and military and police assistance; (ii) imports of goods and services; (iii) foreign direct investment; and (iv) ideas, capital, and skills from Afghans living abroad. To help promote the "formal equilibrium," external assistance going through budget channels should be maximized, contracts awarded through transparent competitive bidding, and good fiduciary practices followed. Domestic capacity building needs to be an integral part of this approach. Regional resources can support this effort, e.g. importing electricity and skilled workforce.

Harnessing the dynamism of the informal sector to generate growth, by (i) facilitating further growth of the informal sector, to the extent that it is legitimate—e.g. through micro-credit, targeting women who account for a large part of the informal sector, stimulating smallholder agriculture, developing cooperation among informal actors; and (ii) gradually shifting informal activities to the formal sector—through expanding linkages between formal and informal sectors, using donor-supported programs as a vehicle for contractors and implementation partners to move into the formal sector, encouraging small concerns to "come into the open" by exempting them from taxes, and putting in place a mining law, NGO regulatory framework, etc.

Starting reforms in specific localities (Industrial Parks, Export Processing Zones, Urban Enterprise Zones, etc.), where land, security, power, and enabling regulations may be easier to provide; the Government has already initiated development of Industrial Parks.

Economic growth will increase opportunities for poor people—by helping them to build their assets, through their investing (and repaying debts) from their own incomes, and accumulating physical capital like livestock. Increasing opportunities for poor people will also require building their human capital, developing community asset-building programs, financing assets through micro-credit, etc. Enhancing the economic role of women will support both broad-based growth and poverty reduction. To empower poor people, these approaches need to be complemented with the development of participatory institutions (for example, the elected Community Development Councils established through the NSP). Finally, poor people should benefit from security improvements. Thus in addition to growth, main elements of a poverty reduction strategy would include:

Asset building on the part of the poor, supported by a range of well-targeted, cost-effective programs, some of which like micro-finance and agricultural development programs would support both growth and poverty reduction. Public works employment programs and other income generation programs can help the poor preserve and over time build physical assets.

Human capital building by the poor, primarily through adequate levels and quality of basic education and health services (see Chapter 8 and, for details of expenditure requirements, the SAF report).

Social protection (see Chapter 9) is another key element of the poverty reduction strategy—in particular, safety net programs for the extreme poor and those unable for various reasons (remoteness, disability, female-headed households, and so forth) to fully take advantage of opportunities created by economic growth.

A final key element of a poverty reduction strategy is *consultation.* A good poverty reduction strategy needs to be "owned" by the poor as well as by other stakeholders. The Government is appropriately planning to engage in extensive consultations with different segments of the society as it develops its Poverty Reduction Strategy, a process that is targeted to reach a first stage of completion with the preparation of an Interim Poverty Reduction Strategy (I-PRSP) early in 2005.

Enhancing trade, both within the region and globally, will be vital to the expansion of market opportunities, and therefore for growth and poverty reduction. Capitalizing on Afghanistan's position as a "land bridge" for trading within the region, and promoting its wider integration in the formal global economy, will require continuing policy and institutional reforms, with emphasis on trade facilitation. Afghanistan has already made significant progress in reforming its trade and investment regime. Nevertheless, official regional trade flows between Afghanistan and its neighbors remain relatively small, comprising only 11 percent of all exports in 2002, the rest being traded globally (World Bank 2004d). Informal trade flows with Pakistan and other countries are quite considerable however. Currently, trade logistics remain very difficult and costly, in a difficult security environment that encourages informal and illicit trading patterns. Hence streamlining Afghanistan's transit links with both regional and non-regional trading partners would reduce transport-related trade costs and would facilitate the growth of economic activity and incomes in Afghanistan and its neighbors. Problems of market access depend not only on formal trade barriers but also on barriers to efficient trade logistics and weaknesses in the operation of market institutions. The implementation of the newly approved tariff schedule as well as enhancing the capacity of the customs service, harmonizing customs procedures, and improving customs valuation, are all vital aspects of enhanced trade facilitation. Given its potential significance, regional trade deserves special attention in bilateral discussions and multilateral forums, such as the Economic Cooperation Organization (ECO), which along with Afghanistan and its neighbors includes Azerbaijan, Kazakhstan, Kyrgyz Republic, and Turkey. The March 2004 ECO Conference held in Kabul demonstrated a closer relationship between Afghanistan and other ECO members.

Building an Effective, Accountable Afghan State

State building forms the centerpiece of Afghanistan's reconstruction. The Government's development vision requires an effective central government that re-establishes the national unity of the country on the basis of government monopoly over the legitimate use of force, strong institutions, and rule of law. The SAF report laid out several specific goals in this regard: (i) *a well functioning and well-structured security sector,* based on institutions that facilitate a return to normalcy in the political, economic, and social spheres; (ii) *an effective public administration* that is small and focused on core functions, more diverse and decentralized, better skilled, equipped and managed, more accountable, and more representative in terms of gender and ethnicity; and (iii) *a budget that is affordable and sustainable* on a multi-year basis and enables delegation of authority based on strong accountability mechanisms.

When the post-Taliban government came into power, it found a public administration (inherited from the pre-war period) that was highly centralized in terms of its structure on paper, but which was denuded of infrastructure, human capacity, and financial resources, and had non-existent or very weak ties with the provinces. The bulk of revenues had been "captured" by illegitimate regional authorities, and service delivery for the most part had ceased or was handled outside government channels by NGOs. Much progress has been made since then: (i) macro control over the size of the civil service has been maintained; (ii) the national budget process has been reinstated, with the budget as the central instrument of policy and aid management; (iii) improvements in fiduciary management (procurement, financial management, audit) are increasing the Government's effectiveness and accountability in using public resources; (iv) civil service reforms are moving forward through the Priority Restructuring and Reform (PRR) process, under which core departments can reorganize themselves, build capacity, and pay qualified staff higher salaries; (v) a cabinet rationalization is being considered to reduce the number of Ministries; and (vi) a start has been made with security sector reform, although security has deteriorated in many areas.

Government faces a twin challenge: it must be fully in charge of running the state—capable of both making policy and implementing it throughout the country, but on the other hand it must not overstate its ability, and should limit its policy ambitions to its limited though growing capacity. Success will depend to a large degree on whether the Government can regain control over national policies and implementation across the country. This is made more difficult by the financial and military strength of regional warlords and local commanders. In this regard, security sector reforms have lagged far behind what is required, and the extremely limited international security assistance outside Kabul has not been helpful. Greater attention to improving security is key to progress in state building and reconstruction. The massive amounts of donor aid largely provided off-budget, which dwarf Government budgetary resources, and the associated existence of a large and well-paid "second civil service" consisting of consultants, advisors, and employees of the United Nations and other international agencies and NGOs, comprise a second major hindrance to state building.

The way forward in state building involves continuing and deepening reforms that are underway, notably public administration reforms, fiscal management improvements, and revenue mobilization; and developing momentum in other areas, including security sector reform and reducing vulnerability to corruption. The ongoing political normalization process will be crucial. Donors' support for state building needs to include reducing reliance on the "second civil service" and maximizing direct budget support relative to other financing modalities.

Encouraging and Supporting Private Sector Development

As seen above, the Afghan private sector is at the heart of the country's growth prospects and strategy but faces some difficult constraints. The Government has been pursuing pro-private sector policies in recognition that a sound investment climate is essential for private sector development. Nevertheless there is still much to be done to improve security, ease the regulatory burden, curb corruption, and make available necessary inputs (land, finance, infrastructure, skills). The legal framework for the private sector (revised investment law, company law, etc.) will be critical. Initiatives are underway for investment promotion through "one-stop shop" and Industrial Parks. Of particular importance will be Government financing of "public goods" in support of private sector growth and competitiveness, for example a metrology, standards, testing, and quality (MSTQ) system, and international market information and other export promotion services. Risk mitigation (for example through MIGA) and development of the insurance industry are important ingredients of a sound investment climate as well. The private sector also very much needs capacity building and business support services, which can be provided by the private sector itself but with active Government support and, where necessary, financing.

Infrastructure and finance will be key inputs for private sector development. While the legal framework for the financial sector has been liberalized and entry of foreign private banks has occurred, the provision of formal financial services in Afghanistan (such as credit) is still at a nascent phase and needs to be developed. At the small-scale end of the enterprise spectrum, micro-finance is being developed through the Micro-Finance Support Facility of Afghanistan (MISFA), and this could lead over time to commercially-oriented financial services to small businesses. In the case of infrastructure (notably roads, irrigation, power, water, and airports), massive investments will be required as detailed in the SAF report. It is of critical importance that appropriate institutional frameworks, accountability mechanisms, incentives, and financing for these services be put in place to ensure further expansion and sustainability as donor assistance eventually phases out. This means, in the case of public utilities, separation of the service provider from the Government and operation of the facilities concerned on an autonomous, commercially-oriented basis. In this regard, cost recovery (either direct or through indirect mechanisms like a road fund) will be necessary, not only for fiscal sustainability but also to improve incentives and enhance accountability (lifeline tariffs for the most poor should be utilized where appropriate).

Agricultural Development Priorities and Prospects

Agriculture, half the Afghan economy, is critical for future growth, poverty reduction, and export development. Maintaining robust agricultural growth requires adequate investments and a sound enabling environment. Key priority areas include the following:

Irrigation: The Government's emphasis on rehabilitation of surface irrigation facilities and subsequently major new investments is appropriate, but early attention is needed to ensure that water user groups (WUGs) fully participate in O&M and financing of O&M. This will require: (i) an appropriate legal framework; (ii) involving WUGs early in rehabilitation/development works, ideally from the design stage; and (iii) developing cost estimates of annual O&M requirements and discussing them with WUGs.

Agricultural Research and Extension: Dissemination of improved agricultural techniques and management practices will be essential to realize the full benefits of irrigation and other investments. Afghanistan needs to focus on adaptive research which must be demand-driven. Public and private sector roles in extension need to be clearly defined, extension services contracted out wherever possible, participatory and community-based approaches adopted, and extension focused on marketing not just production.

Marketing: Investments in both "hardware" (market facilities, cold storages—requiring electric power, roads, etc.) and "software" (grades and quality standards, market research, standards for wholesale markets, market management by market players) will be very important.

Rural Credit: Micro-finance supported by MISFA is an important initiative underway. However, over the medium term additional forms of private, deposit-taking, and commercially-oriented rural credit will need to develop (e.g. through contract farming and similar arrangements).

Land tenure issues are widely considered to be a source of insecurity and problems for agriculture. Such issues are part of the larger governance agenda and can be complex and controversial to resolve, so it would be prudent for the Government to proceed by learning by doing through pilots and involving local communities, before scaling up.

Understanding and Responding to the Opium Economy

Starting from a tiny base in the late 1970s, opium has become Afghanistan's leading economic activity. Opium production (measured at farm-gate prices) generated around one-seventh of estimated total national income in 2003, and downstream trading and processing of opium into opiates generated an even greater amount of income in-country. Overall, the opium economy comprised more than a third of total national income. By 2004 opium spread to all of Afghanistan's provinces and accounted for an estimated 87 percent of global illicit opium production. The impact of the drug industry on Afghanistan's economy, polity, and society is profound, including some short-run economic benefits for the rural population and macro-economy but major adverse effects on security, political normalization, regional relations, and state building. Responding effectively to the drug economy will therefore be essential for Afghanistan's future development.

The opium economy is the lynchpin of a "vicious circle" of insecurity, weak government, powerful warlords, and drug money (see Figure C)—part of the "informal equilibrium"—which will become increasingly entrenched over time if nothing is done. The drug

Figure C. A Vicious Circle

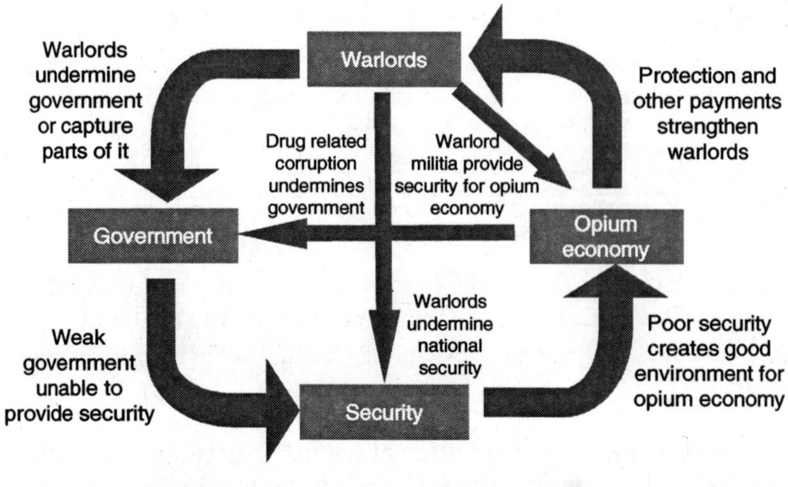

industry has a strong interest in preventing the emergence of an effective, accountable state and thus is highly inimical to the state building agenda. It has enormous financial resources to bring to bear against state building, allies or "sponsors" in the form of warlords with military assets, increasingly entrenched ties with the rural economy, and significant penetration at all levels of government. There is also some anecdotal evidence of linkages between drug money and terrorist networks.

There are no easy answers to this problem, since international experience and Afghanistan's own experience in fighting drugs have been largely unsuccessful, and moreover there is no precedent of such a large drug industry in relation to national GDP, thriving in an environment of poor security, weak government, and deep poverty. To have any hope of success, a multi-pronged approach is essential, addressing each of the key elements of the vicious circle associated with the opium economy warlords (stopping payments to them, disarmament, demobilization, and reintegration of militias—DDR, etc.), insecurity (security sector reform), and weak government (state building, public administration reforms, revenue mobilization), as well as measures related to the drug industry itself (see Figure D).

Experience also suggests that no single instrument of drug control alone will work well. It is the combination, timing, and sequencing of different instruments (interdiction of drug trafficking and processing, alternative livelihoods for poppy farmers and wage laborers, eradication of poppy fields) that will have better prospects of being effective. Phasing out opium production in Afghanistan will be a long-term effort requiring sustained commitment from the Government and international partners. While this report does not make

Figure D. Strategic Framework for Breaking the Vicious Circle

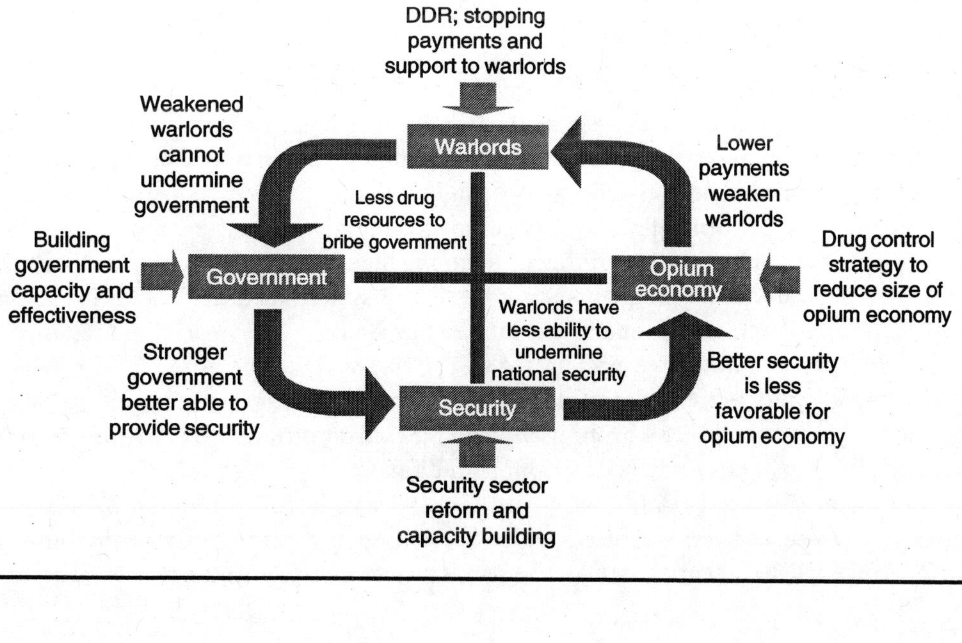

hard-and-fast recommendations with respect to this extremely difficult area, some key considerations include:

Balancing Economic Measures and Law Enforcement. Both are essential—and coordinated international involvement will most likely be required for effective law enforcement. Careful balancing with development programs is needed, taking account of incentives and sequencing issues. The Government may want to initially give priority to interdiction over eradication, as trying to do both equally would disperse scant political capital, energy, and law enforcement capacity. Alternative livelihoods programs, and more generally measures to promote broad-based economic growth and employment generation, could be put in place, with the threat of law enforcement measures to follow. Eradication could then occur once there are credible alternatives and implementation capacity and political support are mobilized.

Prioritization, Monitoring, and Evaluation. Capacity and budget constraints make prioritization essential. Giving priority to action against larger participants in the drug industry would seem to be the most cost-effective approach. A focus on new areas with little or no history of poppy cultivation could make sense. Good monitoring will be needed of implementation, based on understanding the socio-economic situation of stakeholders.

Law Enforcement Capability. Clarifying institutional responsibilities and enhancing capacities with respect to law enforcement remain a priority.

Legal Framework and Judicial and Penal Process. The justice system needs strengthening.

Need for International and Regional Support. The Government is seeking sustained support and cooperation in its efforts against drugs, and in controlling the trade in both transit and consuming countries, both internationally and regionally.

Delivering Basic Social Services and Promoting Gender Equity

Delivery of basic social services—elementary education, basic health services, and water supply and sanitation—to the poor, especially to women and girls, will be a major determinant of Afghanistan's longer-term growth and success in poverty reduction. The country inherited a highly centralized system of government social service provision, which reached only a small proportion of the population (mainly the urban elite) and was devastated during the war. Key issues associated with this system include, in addition to narrow coverage and problematic quality: (i) limited human resource capacity in Afghanistan; (ii) lack of financial resources especially for O&M; (iii) *de jure* centralized service delivery structures and mind-sets; (iv) *de facto* local political autonomy; (v) lack of information and monitoring; (vi) disconnect with households and communities; and (vii) sustainability issues related to the heavy reliance on donor funding.

Getting institutional relationships and incentives right for different actors (service providers, government, and service recipients), so there is meaningful accountability for performance, will be essential for effective social service delivery. In the case of education, schools (the units directly responsible for service delivery) need to be given a greater role in day-to-day management of their activities while enhancing their accountability to beneficiaries through community monitoring (perhaps through the elected Community Development Councils under the NSP). In the case of health, competitive, performance-based contracting of non-government providers is being implemented in a third of Afghanistan's provinces, strengthening accountability of providers to the Government. In both education and health, oversight of service providers needs to be de-concentrated from the center to the provincial level, and in the case of urban water supply to the municipal level. However, central oversight particularly of contracting would need to be maintained in the case of provinces that have been "captured" by regional powerbrokers.

Assisting the Poor and Vulnerable

An affordable, well-targeted social protection strategy is needed for poor and vulnerable Afghans who are unable to fully benefit from economic growth. Income generation and skill development are the Government's preferred vehicles for support, with pure transfers reserved for a minimal safety net for those unable to benefit from other programs. Existing social protection programs, notably the National Emergency Employment Program (NEEP) and other employment programs, while successful in many respects, appear not to be very well-targeted toward the poorest and most vulnerable members of the rural population. While there was a need to inject incomes into the rural economy during the drought, as there may be in the future, and targeting is understandably difficult given low levels of income in most rural households and local social pressures, NEEP and other similar programs need to clarify their objectives and explore ways of improving targeting of the poor.

More generally, the Government is developing a holistic social policy including a National Vulnerability Program. Many of the elements of good policy are already in place. In the near term the key is to ensure that the main national programs are effectively implemented, with monitoring and evaluation providing insights for improved design. It will be necessary to increasingly move beyond a fragmented project-driven approach to a systematic national program.

Conclusions

The challenge that Afghanistan, with support from international partners, faces—to rebuild the state, improve security, sustain rapid, broad-based economic growth, and reduce poverty—is both complex and risk laden. In the short term, the priority is to implement policy and institutional reforms already under way, focusing on the most inclusive measures that contribute to building the nation. Among the areas for action set forth in the table below, a number of key priorities stand out:

Enhance Security and Rule of Law, Respond to Drugs in a Coordinated Manner: The continued existence of warlords and forces disloyal to the national government, funded in large part by drug money, undermines state building and other reconstruction agendas. Security sector reforms need to be given top priority, and administrative reforms in the

Ministries of Defense, Interior, and Justice need to be accelerated. The Afghanistan Stabilization Program (ASP) will need to support improved governance of security in provinces and districts. There are no easy answers on drugs, but it is clear that actions against the opium economy must be integrated within broader national objectives and particularly the security and state building agenda in order to have any hope of success. The recent establishment of a Counter Narcotics Steering Group, chaired by the Government and including the main domestic and external agencies, is encouraging.

Pursue Political Normalization: The successful Presidential election and upcoming Parliamentary elections mark the completion of the political process mandated by the Bonn Agreement, but there is still a long way to go in political normalization. The key priority will be making Afghanistan's nascent political institutions—ranging from the new Cabinet to the new elected legislative bodies and the judiciary—fully functional and effective so they can handle their Constitutionally-mandated roles. Full implementation of the security-related provisions of the Bonn Agreement, including demilitarization of Kabul and more generally the DDR program, will facilitate political normalization.

Maintain Growth with Macroeconomic Stability: This is essential but will face risks—drought, political instability, "poppy shock", "Dutch disease", etc.—as well as other challenges (e.g. fiscal pressures, limited private sector supply response). The Government will need to monitor economic performance closely, making adjustments in response to shocks, while enhancing analytical capacity and macroeconomic policy instruments.

Intensify Public Administration Reforms with Extension to the Provinces: As a critical part of the state building agenda, the Government will need to continue and accelerate current administrative and civil service reforms, including implementation of the PRR process, increasing revenue mobilization, and reducing vulnerability to corruption. It will be especially important to enable provinces to better interface with the public and deliver services, by ensuring timely payments of their employees and access to their non-salary budgets, strengthening their capacity through the ASP, and other similar initiatives.

Accelerate Private Sector Development, Including Agriculture: Priority should be given to implementation of ongoing reforms: adoption of key laws (Investment, Mining, Petroleum), acceleration of micro-credit schemes, and development of Industrial Parks. Irrigation, marketing, credit, and extension services need to be efficiently provided to Afghan farmers, relying on the private sector as much as possible to provide these services.

Poverty Reduction, Gender, and Social Protection: The effectiveness of a poverty reduction strategy will largely depend on national ownership—requiring more extensive consultations with different stakeholders than has occurred hitherto. Enhancing the role of women requires addressing some of their main concerns, such as poor access to education, basic health services, and credit. Building on experience, existing programs need to be improved to effectively target them to the poorest.

Main areas	Priority actions
	For the government
Security and Rule of Law *(Chapters 3 and 4)*	(i) Implement security sector reform and build up well-trained, disciplined security forces (national police, national army) under the control of the national government; (ii) vigorously pursue DDR to meaningfully disarm warlords' militias; (iii) strengthen legal and judicial system; and (iv) improve security of property rights, building on existing informal arrangements.
Macroeconomic Policies *(Chapters 1 and 3)*	(i) Maintain conservative macro-policy mix with light exchange rate management; (ii) monitor sources of macro risk and stand ready to intervene in face of major shocks to maintain robust, broad-based economic growth.
Budget Management *(Chapter 4)*	(i) Increase domestic revenues (customs, simplify income tax code); (ii) prepare, approve, and execute budget in timely manner; (iii) strengthen integration of ordinary and development budgets, linkages between policies and budget; and (iv) adopt and implement Procurement, Public Expenditure and Finance Management, and Audit Laws to enhance accountability and reduce vulnerability to corruption.
Public Administration *(Chapter 4)*	(i) Implement PRR program and avoid pay increases outside PRR; (ii) inject capacity on short-term contracts for key positions; (iii) rationalize number of ministries, with clear portfolios; (iv) implement Afghanistan Stabilization Program; (v) strengthen financial management in municipal governments; and (vi) enhance accountability and reduce vulnerability to corruption (e.g. through civil service law).
Public Service Delivery *(Chapters 4, 5, 8)*	(i) Expand access to elementary education (and improve quality), and to basic health services; (ii) give service facilities (schools, clinics) greater role in day-to-day management, with government oversight deconcentrated to provincial level; (iii) promote client monitoring and greater accountability of service providers to clients; (iv) separate public utilities (power, water) from government, with management and operations on commercial, financially sustainable basis; and (v) use cost recovery to enhance both accountability and fiscal sustainability.
Regulatory Framework *(Chapters 3 and 5)*	(i) Develop and implement reform of state-owned enterprises; (ii) adopt revised Investment Law and reform legal framework, finalize mining, petroleum, and other sector-specific laws; and (iii) continue to pursue structural reforms in trade/customs, financial sector, and taxation.
Support Services *(Chapters 3, 5, 8)*	(i) Develop Industrial Parks with adequate regulatory framework and private sector participation; (ii) accelerate implementation of micro-credit schemes (MISFA), with particular focus on women; (iii) implement infrastructure investment program, especially power, roads, and irrigation; (iv) develop a metrology, standards, testing, and quality (MSTQ) system; (v) implement political risk guarantee facility and liberalize insuance sector; and (vi) strengthen and reform the Export Promotion Department of the Ministry of Commerce and build its capacity with high-quality staff.
Agriculture *(Chapter 6)*	(i) Put in place appropriate legal framework and financing mechanisms, in partnership with water user groups, to guarantee proper O&M of irrigation schemes; (ii) develop public-private partnership-based research and extension systems to disseminate improved agricultural techniques and management practices; and (iii) develop grades and standards, market research, minimum standards for wholesale markets, market management by market players.

Main areas	Priority actions
	For the government
Opium economy *(Chapter 7)*	(i) Take fully into account macroeconomic and poverty impacts of actions against drugs; (ii) mainstream drug policy within broader strategic framework for state building, security, political normalization, reconstruction, and growth; and (iii) avoid premature, single-dimension measures that will encourage a shift of production to other parts of the country or will not be sustainable.
Social Protection *(Chapter 9)*	(i) Adjust existing programs for greater effectiveness toward clarified objectives (targeting poorest, injecting income in face of shocks, or asset-building); (ii) develop well-targeted National Vulnerability Program to provide minimal safety net to those unable to benefit from growth or other programs.
Gender	(i) Develop monitoring mechanisms for public sector employment of women; (ii) favor female employment in social services to increase service delivery to girls/women.
	For the international / donor community
Financial Assistance *(Chapters 3 and 4)*	(i) Maximize assistance through Budget and Treasury and move toward programmatic support; (ii) commit assistance at beginning of or early in fiscal year to facilitate Government budget management; and (iii) be prepared to respond to macroeconomic shocks (e.g. by accelerating and adjusting assistance) to help maintain aggregate demand and growth.
Technical Assistance *(Chapter 4)*	(i) Ensure that all TA responds to national priorities and is under Government leadership and control (consultants reporting to Government with approved TORs); (ii) maximize use of coordinated TA mechanisms; and (iii) coordinate with Government on pay policies for consultants.
Other *(Chapters 4 and 7)*	(i) Work with Government to support effective and timely implementation of reconstruction program; (ii) support security sector reform, including through international security assistance outside Kabul; (iii) ensure that actions against drugs occur within the framework of the Government's strategy and leadership, and mindful of the broader economic and poverty context; (iv) enhance alignment of donor priorities to the national budget; and (v) improve donor coordination within and across sectors.

CHAPTER 1

The Afghan Economy

Afghanistan's economy has been devastated and distorted by more than two decades of protracted conflict, capped by a severe nationwide drought in 1999–2001, but has bounced back in the last two years. The strong economic recovery is attributable to the end of drought and major conflict and initiation of reconstruction, and has been supported by sound, conservative Government macroeconomic policies, a highly successful currency reform, and structural reforms most notably in trade and the financial sector. Nevertheless Afghanistan remains one of the poorest countries in the world, and numerous people suffer from low food consumption, loss of assets, lack of social services, disabilities (for example, from land-mine accidents), disempowerment, and insecurity. Moreover, daily life is still shaped by the consequences of almost a quarter century of conflict. One of these is "informality"—most economic activities do not follow, and are not protected by, official and legal rules and some of them, such as cultivating opium poppy and the arms trade, are criminal. This has important implications for economic structure, policies, and reforms.

This report, the first Economic Report on Afghanistan by the World Bank in a quarter century (the most recent previous report was World Bank 1978), is intended to contribute to a better understanding of the core challenges that lie ahead for the country and key strategic priorities for national reconstruction. The report reflects the development vision set forth in the Government's *National Development Framework* (NDF) and its recent report *Securing Afghanistan's Future: Accomplishments and the Strategic Path Forward* (SAF). The Economic Report does not, however, repeat the analysis and investment requirements set forth in the SAF document, but instead focuses on the conceptual frameworks, policies, and institutions that will be needed to achieve core national objectives of state building; sustained rapid, broad-based economic growth; and poverty reduction.

Analysis of the Afghan economy is hindered by severe data limitations and is challenged by the conflict-related economic structure and dynamics that have emerged and become entrenched. Nevertheless much has been learned about how the Afghan economy functions, at least in qualitative and institutional terms, and there are numerous reports prepared by the Government and partners on specific sectors and topics, which have been drawn upon. This chapter provides a description and analysis of the Afghan economy and recent performance, based on available quantitative data and qualitative information. The first section reviews the state of the economy at the end of the conflict, Afghanistan's strong growth performance since then, and the drivers behind it (including supportive Government actions). The second section outlines the structure of the Afghan economy, with an emphasis on the informal economy and its linkages with conflict and insecurity. The final section summarizes the prospects for growth and areas of growth potential.

Chapter 2 of this report analyzes the characteristics and determinants of poverty in Afghanistan, focusing in rural poverty based on newly available rural household survey data. Chapter 3 outlines the strategy for achieving sustained economic growth and poverty reduction, based on the NDF/SAF, and puts forward key strategic priorities and directions for implementation. State building, discussed in Chapter 4, lies at the core of Afghanistan's reconstruction agenda and is essential for progress on political, security, and other fronts. Chapter 5 addresses the development of the private sector, which will have to be the engine of growth and poverty reduction in Afghanistan. Agriculture, covered in Chapter 6, comprises half of the economy and will play a crucial role. Chapter 7 examines Afghanistan's opium economy, which has some short-term economic benefits but serious adverse effects on state building and security. Chapter 8 looks at delivery of social services, a key component of the poverty reduction strategy, including the gender dimension. Social protection—strategies and programs to assist the poorest and most vulnerable members of Afghan society—is discussed in Chapter 9. Chapter 10 concludes with a summary of priorities for action, implementation constraints, prospects, and risks.

Recent Economic Performance

The Starting Point

The starting point—in late 2001 at the fall of the Taliban—for recent developments in Afghanistan was dire. Protracted conflict in the 1980s and 1990s, as well as drought and other natural disasters, severely damaged the Afghan economy. Resources were diverted to conflict, and payment systems, transport, and trade were disrupted, reducing available inputs as well as potential sales. Second, the conflict depleted and degraded factors of production: (i) less manpower (people joining the conflict or fleeing the country—more than 30 percent of the population has been displaced, see Box 3.2); (ii) lower quality of human capital due to lack of education and a "brain drain" as well-educated people left; (iii) destroyed or useless physical capital, such as damage to the irrigation system and road network, loss of assets of displaced persons, capital flight, and loss of livestock; and (iv) contraction of available land due to landmines. Finally, conflict also had a negative effect on "social capital," weakening governance and the rule of law,

Figure 1.1. Afghanistan's Level of Development in International Perspective (1975–2002)

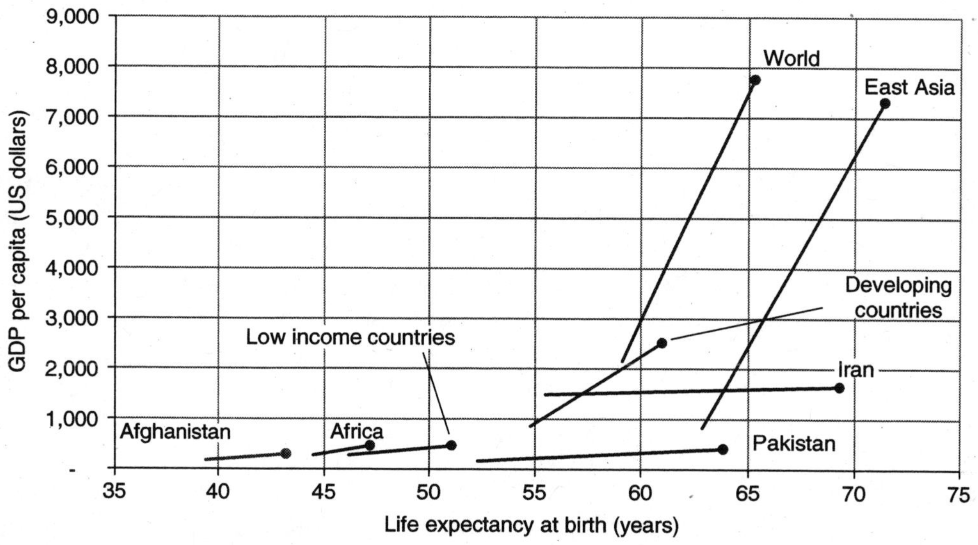

Non-weighted average of country statistics. The non-dotted beginning of each line represents 1975, the dotted end 2002.
Source: World Bank (2004f).

shortening time horizons, through displacement weakening family and community links, increasing the scope for opportunistic and criminal behavior, and so forth. Women faced special difficulties and their role became increasingly restricted during the years of conflict, culminating with the Taliban regime. On the other hand, local family and community "social capital" has been central to many Afghans' coping strategies, and kinship and community networks have continued to function even at long distance through remittances.

As important as the outright damage caused by the long conflict was the loss of opportunity for Afghanistan to participate in the last 25 years of global development and to catch up, or at least maintain pace, with other countries. As shown in Figure 1.1, Afghanistan lagged far behind nearly all of the rest of the world in the 1970s, in terms of both per capita income and life expectancy (as well as other social indicators). Understandably very little progress was made on either front subsequently during the conflict, leaving the country even farther behind the rest of the world. Promising pre-war economic potentials—for example in horticultural exports (Afghanistan accounted for 60 percent of international trade in raisins) and in tourism—atrophied, and the peak level of grain production achieved in the 1970s was not equaled until 2003. In essence, more than a generation's worth of economic development was lost due to the conflict.

Afghanistan is one of the poorest countries in the world. GDP in 2003, after two years of strong economic growth (see below), is estimated at around $7 billion (including $2.3 billion of illicit opiate receipts).[1] With an estimated population of around 22 million, Afghanistan has a per capita GDP of $310 (including the opium economy)—one of the lowest in the world. Moreover, as detailed in Chapter 2 social indicators are among the worst in the world, with large gender gaps: gross primary school enrollment rate 54 percent (40 for girls), under-five mortality rate 172 per 1,000 live births, infant mortality rate 115 per 1,000 live births, and estimated maternal mortality rate 1,600 per 100,000 live births.

The Economic Recovery

Official (non-opium) GDP, starting from a very low base, has grown dramatically by 29 percent in 2002 and by 16 percent in 2003 (Table 1.1). Two-thirds of this growth came from agriculture, thanks mainly to better precipitation and better availability of seeds and fertilizers. Cereal output has strongly recovered, but opium production also has rebounded. Services are booming, mainly in major cities, in construction, and in the public sector, linked to the reconstruction effort. A strong sign of improved confidence, 2.4 million refugees have come back to Afghanistan, and 600,000 internally displaced people have returned to their homes.

The end of major conflict, with associated revival of economic activity, and the end of the drought in many parts of the country, which brought sharp increases in agricultural production, are two key drivers of this dramatic economic recovery. Sound Government policies, as well as structural reforms in certain areas, have supported the recovery.

Political Process. The political normalization process mandated by the Bonn Agreement of December 2001 has been scrupulously implemented, with important milestones like the Emergency Loya Jirga (June 2001), Constitutional Loya Jirga (December 2003–January 2004), and Constitution achieved, and the Presidential election successfully held in October 2004 and Parliamentary elections expected in the spring of 2005 (Chapter 4). Moreover, resurgence of major conflict has been avoided, which together with the political progress has sent favorable signals to the countless Afghans setting about rebuilding their lives and livelihoods. The gains in improved security in Afghanistan have significance for the whole region (see Map at back).

Macroeconomic Policies (fiscal, monetary, and exchange rate management). Another important cornerstone for the economic recovery has been macroeconomic stability—a remarkable achievement by the Government after more than a decade of high inflation. A currency reform was completed successfully between October 2002 and January 2003. Since then, monetary policy has sought to keep inflation under control (it was 10.5 percent in the year ending March 2004), and smooth volatility in the exchange rate. Strong fiscal

1. Macroeconomic data on Afghanistan are very limited and of low reliability—both standard national accounts and even more estimates of the opium economy. Data on opium poppy cultivation from the United Nations Office on Drugs and Crime (UNODC) is based on satellite imagery as well as surveys, but estimates of yields and particularly of border prices of opiates have substantial margins of error. Population data also comprise rough estimates in the absence of a Census or other reliable sources of information. Thus, the macroeconomic data in this report should be treated with caution as the best available but inevitably still rough estimates (see the Statistical Appendix for a more detailed discussion, and UNODC 2003b on opium estimates).

Table 1.1. Macroeconomic Indicators

	1975	2002	2003
Official GDP (US$ billion)	2.4	4.0	4.6
Opium GDP (US$ billion)	—	2.5	2.3
Total GDP (US$ billion)	2.4	6.5	6.9
Official annual growth (%)	3.0	29	16
Total annual growth (%)	3.0	102	5
Population (million)	14.0	21.8	22.2
Official GDP per capita ($)	169	186	207
Total GDP per capita ($)	**169**	**300**	**310**
Inflation (%) (+)	6.6	52.3	10.5
Exchange rate (% increase) (+)	..	52.2	(3.6)
Domestic currency in circulation (growth %)	..	20.1	40.9
Gross foreign exchange reserves (US$ million)	..	426	730.6
Current account (% GDP) (*)	(2.7)	(2.1)	(0.9)
Domestic revenues (% official GDP)	11.4	3.3	4.3
Ordinary expenditures (% official GDP)	9.1	8.6	9.7
Development exp. (% official GDP) (-)	6.1	13.4	31.6

(+) March to March
(*) Excludes opiate exports; 1978 instead of 1975
(–) Estimate for 2003/04
2002 refers to Afghanistan's solar year 1381, from March 02 to March 03.
Source: Statistical Appendix, Table A1.

discipline underpins macroeconomic stability. Under the no-overdraft policy, the Government has been refraining from printing currency to finance its deficit. Considerable success has been achieved in mobilizing domestic revenues, which from negligible levels in 2001 reached more than 4 percent of official GDP in 2003. The Government is following a prudent debt policy, under which most external assistance is sought in the form of grants, and credits are taken only at highly concessional rates.[2]

Budget and Public Administration. Significant reforms are underway in these areas (see Chapter 4). Budget preparation and execution have markedly improved, and the budget is becoming an increasingly effective tool to implement policies and coordinate aid. Public administration reforms have been initiated, in particular the Priority Reform and Restructuring (PRR) scheme to reform the most critical functions of Government by allowing administrative departments to engage in organizational restructuring and place staff selected on merit basis on an elevated pay scale.

2. Currently the Government has verified close to US$200 million of debt incurred by previous administrations. The main uncertainty relates to claims from Russia. Since 2001, the Government has taken credits in the order of US$600 million (13 percent of GDP), all on concessional terms typically involving zero interest and a long grace period.

Finance and Private Sector Development. The Government has also made progress in reviving the financial system and supporting private sector development (Chapter 5). New financial sector legislation (the Central Bank Law and Banking Law) was adopted in the summer of 2003 to grant the Central Bank independence and establish a modern legal framework for the banking system. Several banks have since been licensed under the new legal framework. A new Law on Domestic and Foreign Investment was enacted in September 2002, and the Afghanistan Investment Support Agency (AISA), a single-window clearance and advice center for domestic and foreign investors, was established in August 2003. Significant foreign private investment has been attracted into the telecommunications sector, with very good results in terms of expansion of private mobile telephone services across a number of cities on a competitive, cost-efficient basis.

Trade Reform. The Government has implemented a number of reforms to foster trade. Customs tariffs have been rationalized (elimination of export duties; use of market exchange rate for import valuation; streamlined tariff structure—moving from 25 tariff rates of 0–150 percent to six rates between 2.5 percent and 16 percent; new, more effective broker processes). Existing trade agreements have been renewed and new agreements signed with neighboring countries. At the recent Cancun trade meeting, Government representatives pledged to build a foreign trade regime that will allow Afghanistan to easily pass the standards for World Trade Organization accession over the next few years. Quantitative restrictions are extremely few and not imposed for reasons of protection. Customs administration reforms are underway.

Reconstruction Process. Finally, the Government and donors have started the reconstruction process. Some $1.1 billion of external assistance was disbursed in late 2001 and 2002, mainly for humanitarian purposes and not through Government channels. The Government presented its *National Development Framework* (NDF) in April 2002, which formed the basis of the National Development Budget. Subsequently the *Securing Afghanistan's Future* (SAF) report detailed medium-term investment and recurrent expenditure requirements and external financing needs and was presented at a major donor conference in Berlin in March 2004. The composition of external assistance, which increased to $2.5 billion in the 2003/04 financial year, has shifted in favor of reconstruction, with increasing Government leadership.

Structure of the Economy

The Afghan economy is dominated by agriculture (32 percent of estimated total GDP in 2003), mainly cereal crops (27 percent), and by the opium economy (an estimated 35 percent of GDP). Other sectors are relatively small (Figure 1.2), including manufacturing (9 percent)—most of it small-scale agricultural processing and other small-scale activities, construction (3 percent), and public administration (3 percent). The striking feature of Afghanistan's economic structure is the dominance of the informal sector—not only in agriculture (not surprising) and in the drug industry (outright illegal), but also in most other sectors. A large portion of electricity supply, for example, is provided by small-scale generators in the informal sector. It is inherently difficult to estimate the size of the informal economy, except in sectors where it is dominant like agriculture and narcotics. Nevertheless, it is clear that some 80-90 percent of economic activity in Afghanistan occurs in the informal sector, which has been largely responsible for the recent economic recovery and dynamism.

Figure 1.2. The Informal Economy in Different Sectors

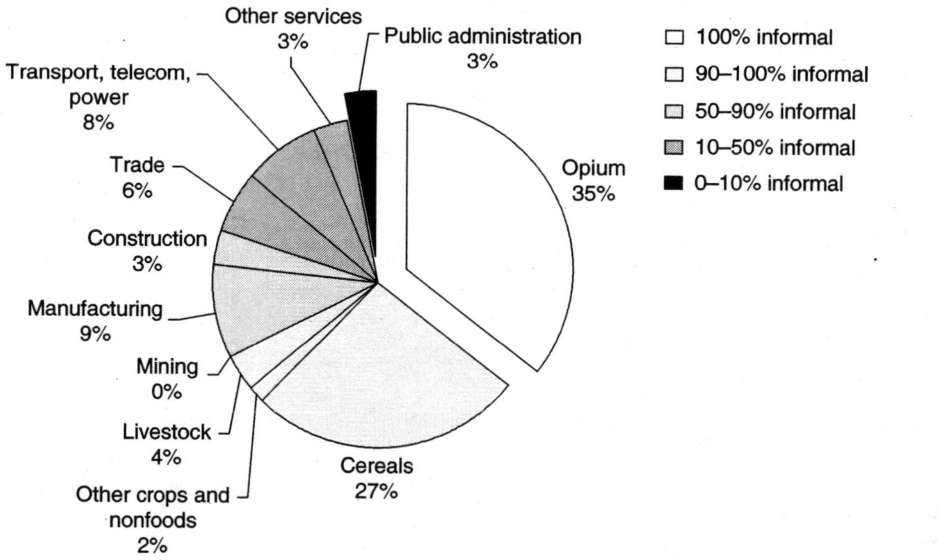

Note: % figures refer to share of sector in total GDP, shadings to very rough estimates of the percentage of the informal economy in the sector.
Source: CSO (2004); UNODC (2003a); staff estimates.

Range of Informal Activities

While the formal sector is relatively easy to delineate, the informal sector covers a range of economic activities. Being registered or paying taxes is usually viewed as a sign of "formality" (Box 1.1). The recorded activities of the Government, 3 percent of GDP and around 350,000 employees, are by definition mainly "formal." The formal private sector includes businesses that are registered,[3] even though they may also have informal activities. The formal sector also includes activities that are registered but by law are exempted from taxation, such as NGOs.

"In-kind" Activities. Outside the formal world, there is a continuum of activities that are more or less legal. Many activities, labeled "in-kind," do not lead to any market transaction or are on a barter basis. A large part of agricultural output is for household subsistence. In addition, sharecropping is an informal arrangement between a landowner and a farmer by which the latter receives a share of the output in kind. A range of services (for example, blacksmith, carpenter, threshers) are being paid in kind, especially in the eastern regions, in the form of a pre-defined share of the crop at harvest time. Exchange of services and products between rural households is widespread, and women perform a major part

3. Three thousand taxpayers have received a Tax Identification Number; AISA registered 84 projects between November 2003 and February 2004 (but they would involve only 4,000 jobs); 80,000 trucks are registered.

Box 1.1. Analyzing the Informal Economy

As suggested by the variety of names used (underground, shadow, black, etc.), the notion of the informal economy is vague. A simple definition of the formal economy is that it includes activities that are measured and subject to regulations (including taxation, even if they are legally exempt). Within the many activities that fall outside this category, a distinction can be made between four groups, depending on (a) the use of market transactions; (b) the legality of the goods and services produced; and (c) the legality of the process to produce and distribute them. While the informal economy should be viewed as a continuum of activities, this classification helps clarify the analysis.

Typology of Economic Activities

Activities	Market transactions	Output	Production / distribution	Registered / taxable	Example
Formal	Yes	Legal	Legal	Yes	Large private firms
In-kind	No	Legal	Legal	No	Subsistence agriculture
Extra-legal	Yes	Legal	Legal	No	Construction; hawalas
Irregular	Yes	Legal	Illegal	No	Smuggling; gemstones
Illegal	Yes	Illegal	Illegal	No	Poppy trafficking

Source: Based on Thomas (1992).

The informal economy is inherently difficult to measure. Direct methods include surveying activities or employment. Indirect methods focus on discrepancies between measured macroeconomic indicators.

Using an indirect approach, one study estimates the size of the informal economy for 69 countries, mainly by comparing data on total electricity consumption and official GDP. There is a significant, negative link with GDP per capita. After correcting for GDP per capita, low revenues, weak networks (roads, telephones), and political instability tend to be more frequent in countries with a large informal sector. Finally, although the link is more ambiguous, the informal economy seems countercyclical (its growth can dampen a fall in official GDP, while it usually decreases when the official economy grows).

Informal Economy and GDP Per Capital

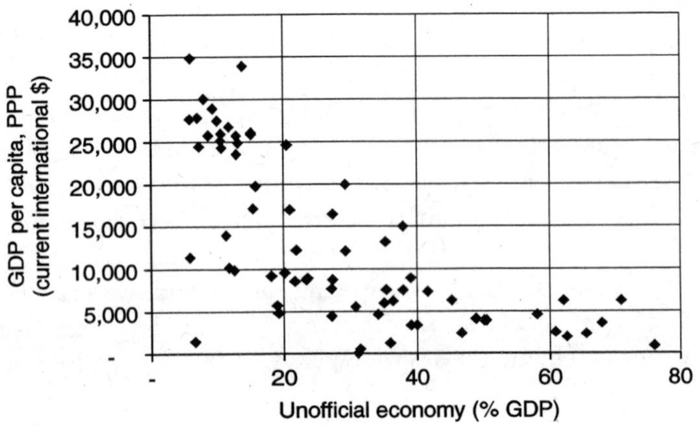

Source: Friedman and others (2000); World Bank (2004f).

of this non-monetized work.[4] Household survey data indicate that 5 percent of the rural labor force is paid in kind or is not paid (see Chapter 2).

"Extra-legal" Activities. Among activities that involve market transactions, some are almost completely legal (the output is legal and the production could be legal if it was registered). These "extra-legal" activities are usually small-scale, and labor is often provided casually. They include money exchange dealers, small shops, small traders, small manufacturing, agriculture, and much construction. Many entities registered as NGOs belong to this category because they perform for-profit activities but, being registered as NGOs, they do not pay taxes. Economic activities of the nomadic Kuchis (an estimated 1.5 million people), mainly selling the products of their livestock, belong to this category. Eighty five percent of the rural labor force is either self-employed or paid casual daily wages; 81 percent work in businesses with less than five employees. Most businesses are owned by a family and employ only one or two workers (or owners).

"Irregular" Activities. Moving further away from legality, production and transactions for legal output can be illegal if they do not follow the rules. Trade in illegally exploited natural resources falls in this category (underground mineral resources belong to the State). Examples include: trafficking of illegally harvested timber; trafficking of emeralds from the Panjsher Valley (estimated at around $3 million per year); illegal exploitation of gravels and construction materials (up to $56 million per year); and most notably smuggling (possibly as much as $1 billion per year or more). Traders have strong incentives to "go informal" and thereby pay less fees and taxes. For example, because import duties are much higher in Pakistan than in Afghanistan, there is an incentive to bring goods in from other countries (including Pakistan) and then smuggle them to Pakistan.

Illegal Activities. Finally, the output itself can be illegal, the main example being opium production, with as many as two million people involved (Chapter 7). Illegal activities also include usurping the privilege of the state (for example, appropriation of customs duties and illegal taxation). According to the International Organization for Migration, there are several forms of human trafficking practiced in Afghanistan including exploitation of prostitutes, forced labor, practices similar to slavery, servitude, and removal of body organs. Illegal excavation or theft and export of valuable archeological artifacts falls in this category. The criminal economy also includes arms trafficking, land seizures, and real estate speculation based on armed force or corruptly obtained contracts. The criminal economy encompasses both a "war economy" (activities pursued to finance a war effort) and a "black economy" (activities pursued for profit).

Implications of the Informal Economy

Overall, most jobs in Afghanistan are in the informal economy, with most people in rural areas relying on several jobs, diversified beyond agriculture, as a coping mechanism. Informal activities increase access to goods (such as food) and services (such as credit associated with opium cultivation). They also finance assets, including in the formal economy. The

4. People who do not own a house often live as so-called hamsaya ("neighbors") in return for supplying domestic services to the house-owner. These labor services are mainly provided by the female members of the tenant household.

Figure 1.3. The Informal Equilibrium

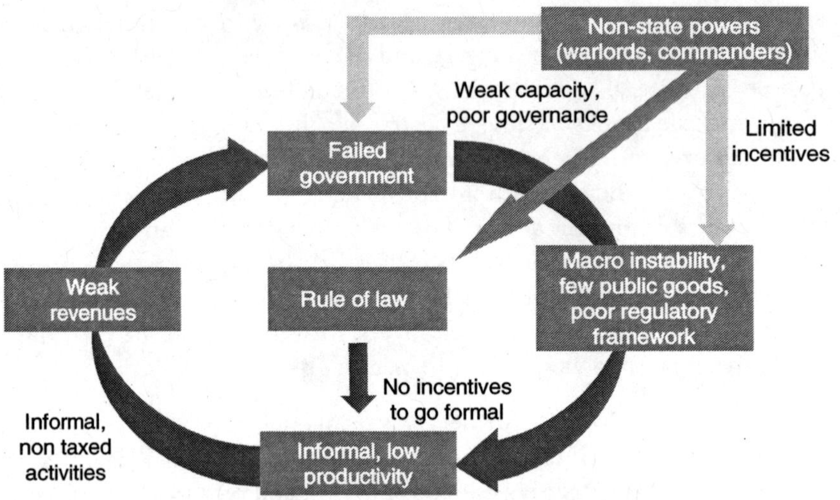

opium economy is a major source of investment in durable goods, housing, and, less frequently, working capital.

The predominance of the informal economy in Afghanistan represents a self-reinforcing equilibrium, involving failed government; other, competing power bases; insecurity; lack of rule of law; and a very poor investment climate for formal-sector activities (Figure 1.3). As the government cannot ensure security around the country, local powers (warlords) take over this role, which leads to lower government revenues and thereby even lower capacity to ensure security. Local powers have limited capacity and incentives to develop infrastructure and create a strong investment climate, which in turn reduces opportunities for trade and financial services. Local powers have incentives to promote illegal, profitable activities to finance their armed forces. They may try to control markets through a monopoly of their protégés. Rule of law suffers, and entrepreneurs have no interest in going formal as doing so would not provide any security or other public goods but on the contrary would make them easy targets for predation. Most fundamentally, this "vicious circle" creates a strong constituency—whose leading element is the drug industry—that is hostile to the strengthening of the central government.

The entrenchment of the "informal equilibrium" came about through Afghanistan's historical experience. The pre-1978 Afghan economy was dualistic, with a small yet developing urban economy in contrast to a large rural economy which was informal but linked to world markets through exports. The Government relied mainly on external resources to fund its development budget, obviating the need for major domestic taxation. The Soviet occupation reinforced this duality between an externally-supported State and formal economy and an informal economy in non-Government controlled areas. The civil war in the early 1990s, with generalized insecurity, strengthening of local powers, no government provision of public goods, and macroeconomic instability (due to the monetization of the government deficit) greatly diminished the role of the State and formal economy, while the informal economy became the main source of livelihoods for Afghans. Incentives to develop the informal or "war economy" were at their highest since warlords had to pay for their military spending with reduced external support. The greater security brought by the Taliban in the mid-1990s generated some growth in trade and agriculture (cereals before the drought and opium poppy before the 2000 ban), from which the Taliban took substantial revenues. However, they did not generate public goods, try to record and monitor economic activities, or refrain from looting, so their actions did not break the "informal circle."

While the informal economy has been dynamic, it probably cannot be the "engine" of sustained long-term growth. International experience suggests that development, beyond a certain point, is accompanied by a decrease in the share of the informal sector (Box 1.1). In the case of Afghanistan, the adverse impact on institutions of the illegal component most probably outweighs the positive impact of the informal economy as a source of livelihoods and coping mechanism. Informal activities generate hardly any resources for the State but may support forces opposed to the State and provide scope for opportunism and rent seeking. Informality does not protect property rights and reduces the possibility to formalize and enforce contracts, weakening incentives to invest and opportunities for division of labor and trade. Savings tend to be channeled toward investments with lower risks (e.g. in real estate and trade) or transferred outside Afghanistan. Entrepreneurs in an informal setting have an incentive to remain relatively small and to diversify their activities to manage risk, which prevents them from exploiting economies of scale and in many cases from adopting more modern technologies.

Economic Prospects

Some of the drivers behind the economic recovery will diminish in coming years. For example, after two years of sharp increases, Afghan cereal yields in 2003 approached those in neighboring countries (Figure 1.4). There is scope for substantial further yield increases

Figure 1.4. Cereal Yields

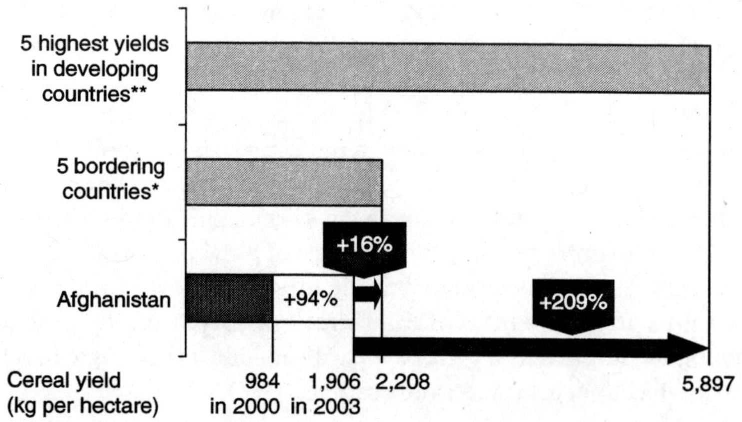

Afghanistan: 2000 and 2003;
other countries: 2000–02 average
* Iran, Pakistan, Tajikistan, Turkmenistan, Uzbekistan;
** Mauritius, Egypt, Croatia, Chile, China.
Source: World Bank (2004f).

by moving toward best-practice levels, but this will require good agricultural policies, institutions, and investments (see Chapter 6). Although significant increases in opium poppy cultivation are continuing, yields have fallen, and the large decline in farm-gate prices in 2004 (Chapter 7) suggests that income generation and the stimulus for the rest of the economy from this activity may not further increase sharply. In any case, long-term dependence on opium is undesirable and is contrary to national objectives. While construction and other activities associated with the reconstruction program are likely to continue to boom, there is a need for other leading sectors to emerge in support of sustained rapid economic growth over the medium term.

Afghanistan has areas of good potential for sustained long-term economic growth, ranging from agricultural production and processing to mining, construction, trade, and other services (Box 1.2). There is no certainty regarding the specific sectors where Afghanistan will grow and export: with appropriate institutions and policies, the economy itself will "discover" areas of growth potential. However, two broad areas, trade and construction, stand out for their growth potential.

Trade. Exploiting Afghanistan's position as a land bridge between Central and South Asia as well as other economies can be a significant source of growth (see Map). Although as a land-locked country Afghanistan faces certain disadvantages (such countries have average transport costs 50 percent higher and trade volumes 60 percent lower than similar coastal economies), the experience of land-locked countries like Uganda and Laos demonstrates that improving trade logistics, diversifying transit routes, heavier reliance on air transport, and supporting corridor agreements can overcome this geographical disadvantage. Regional cooperation, moreover, can turn Afghanistan's geographical position into a positive advantage, by expanding markets, lowering costs of long-distance trade, and sharing on an efficient basis regional resources like electricity and, over the longer term, water. Processed agricultural products have export potential (Chapter 6), which would have strong synergies with the strategy to respond to drugs, since such exports could provide livelihoods to offset, at least in part, a drop in opium production (Chapter 7). Afghanistan could also export some natural resources (for example, copper). Achieving robust long-term growth of trade will require sustained effort in terms of structural reforms as well as immediate actions to foster a strong enabling environment. The latter include: (i) implementing a functioning payments system for international and domestic transfers though the formal banking system; (ii) defining and implementing regulatory conditions and terms on which foreign banks or joint venture banks will be permitted to operate in Afghanistan; (iii) making transit bonds and transport insurance available with entry of companies capable of providing coverage; (iv) developing the role of Government as a promoter and facilitator of trade and investment; (v) supporting a larger role for a private chamber of commerce to assist in export promotion activities; and (vi) designing and implementing major capacity building programs to develop skills and professionalism in banking, insurance, and customs.

Construction. The reconstruction process will sustain growth in demand for construction activities, from the extraction of sand and gravel to building of roads and houses. The sector is currently a good example of the costs of informality (high security costs, barriers at entry and lack of competition, corruption). Sustained growth in this sector requires improvements in the security and rule of law environment, as well as a regulatory framework that enables private sector development (Chapters 4 and 5).

Box 1.2. Discovering Afghanistan's Growth Potential

Today the economy of Afghanistan is still largely agriculture-based. Industries and services are mainly small businesses—upstream and downstream activities with ties to agriculture, construction reflecting the housing boom and reconstruction program, and other small-scale activities. Growth potentials exist in a number of sectors.

- **The agricultural sector** (73 percent of GDP, including poppy) is largely subsistence-oriented, and cereal crops (mainly wheat) are predominant. Other crops and vegetables, such as grapes, apricots, and almonds, generate higher income yields and potentially exports. The livestock sector produces milk, meat, and wool. The main cash crop is poppy, which in 2002/03 generated gross revenues of some $1 billion for farmers and $1.3 billion for traffickers (one-third of total GDP). Expansion of irrigation should raise land productivity and bring previously non-arable land under cultivation; improved techniques will also increase yields; diversification will increase average income per hectare, particularly when improved transport linkages open up new markets; and restoration of livestock herds and better husbandry will contribute to steady growth of livestock production. This growth potentially would be somewhat offset the gradual reduction of opium cultivation.
- Although under-exploited, Afghanistan has rich **underground resources** (accounting for only 1 percent of GDP in 2003/04). These include copper, coal, construction materials, gemstones, etc. There are also deposits of iron and gold, not currently exploited. There are some reserves of natural gas, which were exploited in the 1970s and 1980s, generating significant activities and public revenues. These sectors provide a good illustration of the need for the Government to create an adequate regulatory framework and security conditions, and the complementary need for sizable private sector investments.
- Large-scale **industry** is not much developed, and what little there was in the late 1970s—most of it in the public sector—has become defunct, or is poorly performing. Most industrial production (9 percent of GDP) consists of upstream (fertilizers) or downstream (mostly handicrafts) activities related to agriculture. The electric power sector has only limited capacity to import electricity and even more limited capacity to generate and distribute electricity domestically. Construction is very important at present (4 percent of GDP), and reconstruction activities are expected to continue to support its growth. The industrial sector will benefit from better infrastructure and greater supply of skilled labor due to education and training. Also, development of the financial sector—micro-credit and commercial lending—will create a climate conducive to greater investment.
- Among **services** (13 percent of GDP), trade has been very important, stimulated in large part by restrictive trade regimes in neighboring countries, which encourage unofficial trade (in particular smuggling). The financial sector is almost completely in the unofficial economy, financial services being provided by the hawalas. The recovery of the economy is expected to generate considerable additional demand for financial services.

Out of the many products and processes that do or could exist in Afghanistan, the economy will have to discover those that are most valuable. The carpet industry is an important export that survived the conflict. Organized traders, providing advice on demand and sometimes raw material and capital, have managed to continue their business throughout the last quarter-century. However past experience, while useful, cannot give investors or the Government any certainty about potential successes. For instance, dried fruits from California have taken a major part of the market in India, which Afghan products used to occupy. California has now established a technological advantage for this market (adding variety to suit Indian tastes with new treatments for dried fruit).

CHAPTER 2

Poverty in Afghanistan: A Preliminary Analysis

By any measure—average per capita income (see Chapter 1), life expectancy, other social indicators, or broader indexes like the U.N. Human Development Index (HDI)—Afghanistan is one of the poorest countries in the world. In 1996, the country ranked 169th out of 174 countries in the HDI. Afghanistan was a very poor country before the war and fell further behind the rest of the world during the past quarter-century. Recent rapid economic growth and improvements in some social indicators have not yet changed this situation. In order to take on the challenge of poverty reduction and underpin the development of the Government's poverty reduction strategy, it is essential to understand poverty—its dimensions, characteristics, and determinants. New household survey data, while far from perfect, represents a major advance from what was available earlier and does permit a preliminary analysis of rural poverty in Afghanistan.[1] This chapter first (in the first section) provides some general background and discusses Afghanistan's social indicators, based on survey data for both urban and rural areas. The second section presents a profile of rural poverty in Afghanistan, based on rural household survey data, which identifies some of the main correlates of poverty. The third section outlines the determinants of rural poverty based on multivariate analysis.

1. The main databases are the Multi-Indicator Cluster Survey (MICS), conducted by UNICEF in 2003 and covering urban and rural areas (UNICEF and CSO, 2003), and the National Rural Vulnerability Assessment (NRVA) conducted by the Ministry of Rural Rehabilitation and Development with support from the World Food Program and the World Bank (Afghanistan Government 2003). *See also* World Bank (2004b).

Historical Background and Social Indicators

More than two decades of conflict, interspersed with a number of serious earthquakes, and culminating in a severe nationwide drought in 1999–2001, had dramatic impacts on the Afghan population and particularly its poorest segments, as noted in Chapter 1.

- First, *conflict generated insecurity*, with numerous adverse effects on the poor. The collapse of the state and rule of law resulted in local power-holders taking control in regions and localities, often with no check on their authority. An estimated 5.9 million Afghans left the country and one million Internally Displaced Persons (IDPs) were displaced within Afghanistan, making one in every three Afghans a refugee or an IDP.
- Second, *the conflict destroyed physical capital*, including the small-scale traditional infrastructure which the rural poor relied on for livelihoods as well as personal assets.
- Third, *the lack of an effective state led to collapse of public service delivery* (see Chapter 8) and took a heavy toll on human capital. Under the Taliban, school attendance was low and girls were almost completely barred from attending schools. Infant and under-five mortality as well as maternal mortality were estimated to be among the highest in the world, and malnutrition affected about 50 percent of children under age five. The average life expectancy was little more than 40 years, similar to the pre-conflict level.

Since the fall of the Taliban regime and end of major combat, economic growth has been rapid. There has been a strong recovery, albeit from very low levels of activity (Chapter 1), accompanied by an improvement in some social indicators. In the past two years 2.5 million Afghan refugees have returned to their home country, while an additional 600,000 IDPs have moved back to their place of origin. About 40 percent of refugees have returned to Kabul and many others to urban centers across the country. School enrollment has continuously increased: more than three million students were enrolled in Grades 1–12 in 2002 and 4.3 million in 2003, of which 3.9 million were in primary schools. Progress has also been made in health. A massive vaccination program led to a marked reduction in confirmed polio cases. A measles mortality reduction campaign was conducted and reached more than 90 percent of children six months to 12 years of age, and iodized salt has been provided to 300,000 malnourished women and children.

Despite the impressive economic recovery and initiation of a development strategy based on sound principles (outlined in the Government's *National Development Framework*), Afghanistan still ranks very poorly on all social indicators (Table 2.1). Based on a 2003 sample survey, infant mortality at 115 per thousand live births and under-five mortality at 172 per thousand live births are among the highest in the world. The situation is particularly grim in rural areas where one out of five children dies before reaching five years of age. The estimated rate of maternal mortality (1,600 per 100,000 live births) is among the highest in the world. Nine out of ten births are not taking place in health facilities, and the corresponding figure is even higher in rural areas. Family planning is largely non-existent.

Morbidity rates are extremely high: 30 percent of children under five years of age were reported to have diarrhea during the two-week period that preceded the survey and 19 percent to have suffered from severe respiratory diseases over the same period. Malnutrition is also a critical issue. Seventy percent of children do not receive timely complementary feeding (which could damage their physical and learning capacity

Table 2.1. Social Indicators 2003

Indicator	Rural	Urban	National
Survival			
Infant mortality (# of deaths per 1,000 infants under 1 year)	121	97	115
Under five mortality (# of deaths per 1,000 children under 5 years)	183	142	172
Morbidity (%)			
Diarrhea (children under 5 reporting incidence in past 15 days)	30	30	30
Increased fluid and continued feeding given during diarrhea	54	51	53
Acute Respiratory Infection (children under 5 reporting incidence in past 15 days)	19	19	19
Advice or treatment sought from hospital/HC during ARI	27	32	28
Malnutrition (%)			
Children that have not received timely complimentary feeding (6–9 months)	73	66	71
Households consuming non-iodized salt	90	74	85
Pregnancy (%)			
Births not taking place in health facility	96	68	89
Married women (<49 years) who have not heard of a method to delay pregnancy	78	55	72
Married women (<49 years) not currently using a method to delay pregnancy	94	79	90
Disability and Orphanage (%)			
Children 1–4 years that are disabled	2	3	3
Children 7–17 years that are disabled	3	4	3
Children with both parents dead	6	6	6
Preventive Health (%)			
Children 12–23 months that have received DPT 3 immunization	23	48	30
Children 12–23 months that have received Polio 3+ immunization	43	71	51
Children 9–59 months that have received Measles immunization	73	84	76
Children under 5 that have received BCG immunization	55	73	60
Access to Sanitation and Water (%)			
Households with drinking water from pump/protected spring	31	61	40
Households having a flush or pit toilet	59	87	67
Households with water source and latrine within 15 meters	77	60	67
Education			
Illiteracy rate: Male (% of pop. aged 15 and over)	64	40	57
Illiteracy rate: Female (% of pop. aged 15 and over)	92	72	86
Primary school net enrolment rate (% of 7 to 13 year olds) Male	61	81	67
Primary school net enrolment rate (% of 7 to 13 year olds) Female	30	63	40

Note: The nomad population known as "kuchi" are not included and are estimated at 1.3–1.5 million. According to CSO (2003) 22 percent of the estimated population is urban.

Source: UNICEF and CSO (2003).

irreversibly), and 85 percent of households consume non-iodized salt. Three percent of children are disabled and 6 percent are orphans.

Preventive health is lacking as demonstrated by low vaccination rates especially in rural areas, and poor access to potable water. Routine immunization coverage (Diphtheria, Tetanus, Pertussis—DTP3) is estimated at 30 percent (23 in rural areas). Inaccessibility to health centers, hospitals, or doctors that could provide preventive and curative services, as well as lack of medicines including essential drugs, are major contributing factors to the poor state of public health. Forty percent of health facilities do not have female staff, which implies that women are very unlikely to use those facilities. Forty percent of the population report having access to safe drinking water, but this is likely to be a substantial overestimate of actual access to safe drinking water.

Illiteracy is extremely high, with stark provincial and gender disparities. Fifty-seven percent of men and 86 percent of women above 15 years of age are illiterate. Illiteracy is particularly high in rural areas. Despite progress, education is still limited. While the net enrollment ratio in major cities is as high as 80 percent, it is only 47 in rural areas. Nationally, the female net enrollment ratio is 40 percent while that of boys is 67. However, the net enrollment ratio for girls is as low as 1 percent in some provinces. Missing out on primary education generally has irreversible negative effects on well-being, as there are few "catch-up" and adult-literacy services available.

The serious gender disparities in Afghanistan's social indicators reflect not only the protracted conflict and its impact on women and girls but longstanding historical patterns. A number of efforts to improve gender equity over the past century have been reversed, and the gender issue has been highly politicized, detracting from a focus on the large human and social costs resulting from poor and gender-biased social indicators. The historical context (discussed in Box 2.1), as well as the current political and legal situation for women, need to be fully factored into strategies to improve female social indicators.

Box 2.1. Gender in Afghanistan—A Politicized Issue

Throughout the 20th century, the debate on women's rights and their role in Afghan society has been closely interlinked with the national destiny. Women not only carry the burden of symbolizing the honor of the family, but they often are seen as embodying the national honor and aspirations as well. Gender has thus been one of the most politicized issues in Afghanistan over the past 100 years, and attempts at reform have been denounced by opponents as un-Islamic and a challenge to the sanctity of the faith and family. In 1929, the reformist King Amanullah's government was overthrown soon after he tried to impose social reforms, including the abolition of *purdah* (separation and veiling of women) and establishment of coeducation. It took another 30 years before then-Prime Minister Mohammad Daoud in 1959 officially abolished *purdah*. Starting in the late 1970s, leaders of the Communist government pushed new reforms including abolition of the "bride-price" and forced adult education for women, fuelling the opposition to the Communist regime and Soviet occupation. When the regime finally collapsed in 1992 and a loose coalition of Mujahedin parties was installed in Kabul, decrees instructed women to observe *hijab*—covering of the head, arms, and legs. During the years of conflict, legitimate concerns about women's security led to the imposition of ever stricter interpretations of socially acceptable female behavior, supported by the most conservative reading of the holy scriptures. Despite the rhetoric, women suffered from very serious human rights violations throughout the conflict. While it justified itself on the basis of protecting women, the Taliban regime's retrogressive views on gender resulted in the opposite, as women were not allowed to work or receive even basic education or medical care.

(*continued*)

Box 2.1. Gender in Afghanistan—A Politicized Issue (*Continued*)

While Afghan women have enjoyed Constitutional gender equality since 1964, the legal system granted differential rights to men and women, although the 1977 Civil Code introduced significant reforms. During the years of conflict and break-down of state functions, the 1977 Civil Law withered away and a largely unreformed Hanafi family law and customary law ruled in practice. The 2003 Constitution states with regard to the functioning of the Judiciary that "whenever no provision exists in the Constitution or the laws for a case under consideration, the court shall follow the provisions of the Hanafi jurisprudence within the provisions set forth in this Constitution." The legal framework guiding Afghan women's lives thus consists of a mixture of civil law, customary law, Islamic (Hanafi and Shia) Law, and traditions all of which stress the complementarities of male and female roles more than their equality. Religious traditions are characterized by ideals of mutual respect and dignity between female and male roles, but these normative complementarities have often been accompanied by more heavy-handed and oppressive practice, with customary law in many cases discriminating against women considerably more than Islamic law.

Afghanistan has signed a number of international human rights treaties and in March 2003 ratified the United Nations Convention on the Elimination of all forms of Discrimination Against Women (signed in 1980), which will require new legislative and administrative measures. In the meantime, there appears to be a large degree of confusion over the exact rights of women and their legal status, and widespread violations of the most basic rights of women and girls, including physical abuse, under-age marriage, and exchange of girls to settle feuds.

There is growing awareness at all levels of Afghan society that economic and social progress require contributions by all of the country's active and able human resources, including women. Yet, there are serious impediments to "gender mainstreaming" in national reconstruction and development, including limited awareness of what it means, how to apply it, and who to draw upon for support. With gender issues having been highly politicized during the past 100 years, soliciting or addressing the interests of women runs the risk, once again, of being seen as an imposed "Western" agenda running counter to local traditions. In order to garner significant public support for policies promoting gender equity, the discourse needs to be shifted from the religious to the social domain—and such policies must be seen as not running counter to Islam. This challenge can only be met through close collaboration with religious and legal experts, with professionals in line ministries and civil society organizations across the various sectors of society.

The voice and initiative for making improvements needs to come from women (and men) within Afghan society. In this context it is encouraging that the Government has provided significant leadership roles for women, including the appointment of three women ministers, 14 percent women representatives in the first Loya Jirga, and women's participation in the constitutional drafting commission, the Judicial Commission, and the Electoral Body. A further important step was taken by the Constitutional Loya Jirga in December 2003, which provided for equality between women and men before the law, and allocated to women a minimum of two seats per province in the Lower House and half of the one-third membership of the Upper House selected by the President. In total this will secure for women at least a 25 percent share in the National Assembly. Women are already exercising their right to participate in local and national level politics, including through the National Solidarity Program where women at par with men elect (and can be elected to) Community Development Councils. As far as national politics is concerned, although voter registration was hampered by lack of security and resources (disproportionately affecting women), women nevertheless comprised more than 40 percent of the total number of voters registered for the Presidential election and voted in large numbers, but with great regional variation.

Although the size of Afghanistan's population is not known with any degree of certainty, and population growth is hard to predict, it is clearly a major concern for Afghanistan's future. By all indications the current population growth rate is well above two percent per year, which will lower the benefits to people (in terms of average per capita income) from any given level of overall economic growth, and increase the burden on social services like education and health. Population growth is likely to be accompanied by accelerated urbanization and associated needs and costs. One key driver of population growth in international experience is low female social indicators.

Rural Poverty Profile

The 2003 National Risk and Vulnerability Assessment (NRVA) included 1,850 rural villages and some 11,200 households surveyed between July and September 2003. Besides detailed food consumption data, the survey also collected demographic and socio-economic data such as age, education, employment, access to public goods, detailed information on agricultural activities, prevalence of shocks over the previous year, debt, remittances, and participation in social programs. Information on "essential" non-food expenditures (medicine, clothing, taxes, fuel, oil, and education) was collected for three wealth groups in each community (better-off, average, poorer), generating some 5,600 data points for non-food expenditure. While this data set has some important limitations—most notably it covers rural areas only, and is based on a single survey done shortly after the harvest time when rural people were likely to be consuming more food than at other times of the year—nevertheless it marks a major advance in our knowledge and provides important insights into rural poverty in Afghanistan.

A standard approach to identifying characteristics associated with poverty is to divide the sample of households surveyed into "quintiles"—five groups each comprising 20 percent of the sample—based on a selected indicator of welfare. Here we use total food and essential non-food expenditure per capita as the welfare indicator. Some of the most salient characteristics by quintile are shown in Figure 2.1 and are discussed below, while a more complete set of characteristics is listed in Table A3 in the Statistical Appendix.

Expenditure. As seen in Figure 2.1, average per capita (food and basic non-food) expenditures rise from $66 per year in the first (poorest) quintile to $301 in the fifth (least poor) quintile, with an average of $165 for the sample as a whole. The biggest gap—more than 50 percent—is between the fifth and fourth quintiles. About 21 percent of households did not consume 2,100 calories per person per day—a commonly-used indicator of caloric sufficiency in food consumption. Because the survey was carried out in the summer right after a bumper harvest, it would be expected that the year-round average percentage of households in this situation would be higher. As expected, poorer families more often report difficulties in satisfying their food needs. Dietary diversity is also strongly correlated with poverty, with the households in the poorest quintile consuming a small number of food items and getting most of their calories from wheat.

Welfare. On average, households do not perceive their welfare to have improved by very much over the last 12 months. This is somewhat surprising as the economy and particularly agricultural production grew considerably during this period with the return of normal rainfall (Chapter 1). Households' perception of welfare improvement is positively correlated with per capita expenditures, however (see Table A3). Family size declines slightly as average per capita expenditure rises, reflecting primarily that better-off households have relatively fewer young children or elderly people in the household. Households in the highest quintile tend to own their home more than those in the bottom quintile (93 percent versus 76). Also, the number of persons per room decreases as per capita expenditure rises.

Land and Opium Poppy. The proportion of households who own some land is high and increases with per capita expenditure—from 78 percent in the lowest quintile to 92 percent in the highest quintile (Figure 2.1). The relationship between per capita expenditures and amount of land owned, and whether it is irrigated or rain-fed, is not very clear, however (Table A3). A significant proportion of households (4.8 percent) report cultivating opium poppy, and the ratio tends to rise with per capita expenditure (Figure 2.1). However, households appear to under-report cultivating poppy. Scaled up to cover the whole population, the survey would suggest that around 103,000 households cultivate poppy on a total area of 24,000 hectares, which is below the 264,000 households reported by UNODC to cultivate poppy on 80,000 ha (see Chapter 7). Moreover, the survey does not provide data on the large number of wage laborers who work on poppy cultivation and harvesting.

Figure 2.1. Selected Correlates of Rural Poverty (by quintiles)

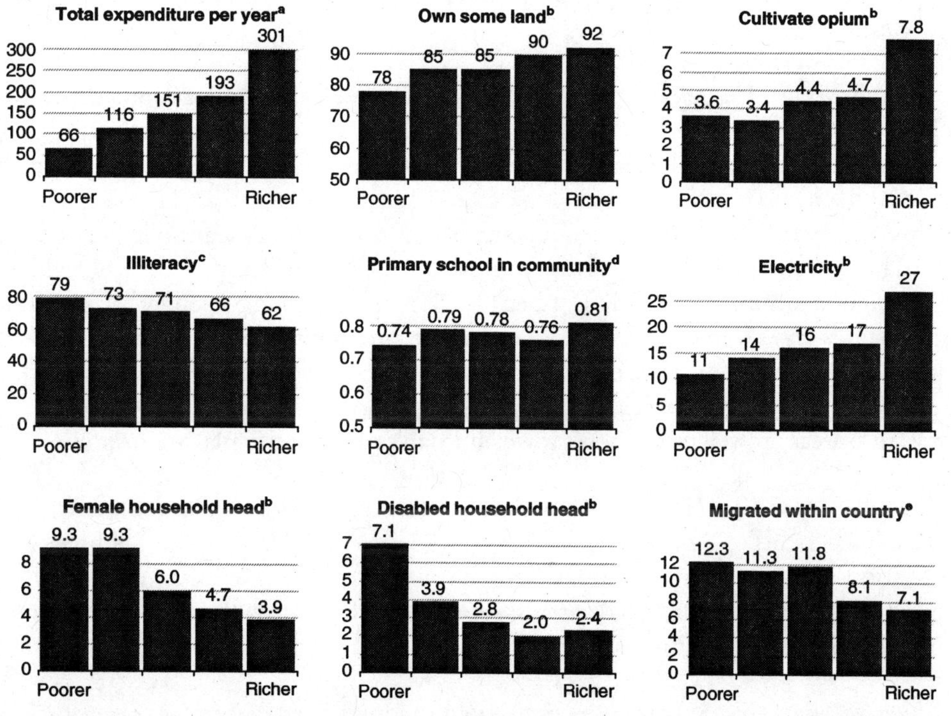

Note: Each chart shows the concerned characteristic for each quintile (20 percent) of the sample in terms of average per capita expenditure (food plus basic non-food), starting with the poorest 20 percent at left and moving up to the richest 20 percent at right.

a. US$ per year;

b. Percent of households;

c. Percent of household heads;

d. Average (0 = school more than 1 day travel away; 1 = school in village);

e. Percent of household heads that have migrated within country over the past five years.

Source: Statistical Appendix, Table A3.

Education and Literacy. Although illiteracy is high throughout the sample (on average 70 percent of household heads are illiterate), as shown in Figure 2.1 the proportion is considerably higher for the poorest quintile (79 percent) than for the highest quintile (62). While underscoring the magnitude of the task ahead, this pattern is fully consistent with the universal lesson from international experience that basic education is extremely important for development. Most households (78 percent) lived in villages with a primary school, but there is not a clear relationship between this and per capita expenditure (Figure 2.1). The same is also broadly true of health facilities (Table A3).

Basic Services. A relatively small proportion of rural households report having access to electricity (17 percent), but having electricity is strongly correlated with per capita expenditures; only 11 percent of lowest-quintile households have electricity compared to 27 percent of highest-quintile households (Figure 2.1). This pattern most likely reflects that better-off households do have the option of purchasing a small generator to provide their own power. Most other basic services do not show such a clear relationship (Table A3), because access does not tend to be within the discretion of households even if they have financial resources, and may be related to other factors also correlated with income, such as proximity to an urban area.

Female-headed Households. The relationship between average per capita expenditure and whether a household is female-headed is striking (Figure 2.1). The relatively high percentage of female-headed households in the sample as a whole (6.6 percent)—which is likely to understate the real level for various reasons—reflects the direct and indirect toll of more than two decades of conflict. It is striking, however, that the proportion of female-headed households in the two poorest quintiles (9.3 percent) is more than double the level in the highest quintile (3.9). This phenomenon highlights the gender dimension of Afghanistan's development challenge and most probably reflects that female-headed households in many cases have lost or do not have a very important human asset (working-age male) and the severe restrictions against women working outside the household in many rural areas, as well as women's lower human capital (particularly education).

Disabled Household Heads. Although the percentage of households reported to be led by disabled persons (3.6 percent) is lower than in the case of female-headed households, the relationship with per capita expenditure is just as striking (Figure 2.1). In the poorest quintile 7.1 percent of households are disabled-headed, whereas the figures are 2 and 2.4 for the fourth and fifth quintiles, respectively.

Internal Migration. Whether the household head migrated within the country over the past five years is negatively correlated with per capita expenditure. The average for the sample as a whole is 10.1 percent, but for the poorest quintile it is 12.3 and for the richest quintile only 7.1 (Figure 2.1). Internal migration may be capturing two phenomena, both associated in different ways with poverty: (i) displacement due to conflict—Internally Displaced Persons (IDPs)—which entails a wholesale loss of assets, livelihoods, and social networks; and (ii) internal migration in search of opportunities to earn incomes elsewhere in Afghanistan. Phenomenon (i) reflects a "shock" associated with conflict that makes people poorer than they were before, whereas phenomenon (ii) may be associated with being poor in the first place—poorer households have a strong incentive to migrate in search of labor and livelihood opportunities, as a coping mechanism. The available data do not allow us to disentangle these two possible explanatory factors. In the case of Afghan refugees who have returned from other countries over the past five years (10.5 percent of the sample), refugees from conflict have similarly been mixed together with economic migrants. However, there is no systematic relationship between this characteristic and per capita expenditure (Table A3).

Remittances. The proportion of households who receive remittances increases with per capita expenditures (Table A3). Lower quintile households tend to receive remittances from neighboring Pakistan and Iran while households in the higher quintiles tend to receive them from farther away. The absolute level of remittances increases with household expenditures while the ratio to expenditure decreases with household expenditures, indicating that remittances are more important in relative terms for the livelihood of worse-off households.

Determinants of Rural Poverty

The profile of poverty in rural Afghanistan sketched out above has potentially important implications for policies and programs to reduce poverty. However, it is necessary to take the analysis further in order to derive more robust and reliable policy implications. The analysis based on quintiles is "bivariate"—whereby the relationship between each of a number of different household characteristics and the poverty indicator (per capita expenditure) is looked at individually. However, it is likely that some of these characteristics are reflecting the influence of other characteristics, thereby clouding the underlying relationship (or lack thereof) between the characteristic concerned and poverty. For example, poorer households tend to be disproportionately headed by females and by illiterates, as compared with the sample as a whole. However, because education and literacy levels among women in Afghanistan are much lower than for men, it is possible that the reason female-headed households tend to be poorer is not primarily because they are female-headed *per se*, but rather because being female is associated with a higher degree of illiteracy. Thus a "multivariate" analysis is necessary—whereby different characteristics are simultaneously compared with the poverty indicator in an effort to distill their separate effects.

Based on a multivariate regression analysis,[2] rural poverty in Afghanistan is clearly associated with lower levels or constrained use of key variables, including education, occupational activity, physical assets, basic services, and remittances, as well as with certain household characteristics (female-headed, larger households, etc.). The full results of the technical analysis are presented in the Statistical Appendix (Table A4). The main findings are summarized below:

i. *The data appear to show significant geographical differences in rural poverty.* Other things equal, per capita expenditure in the Western region is 29 percent lower, in

2. Log of per capita expenditure is regressed on a number of key variables considered to be at least somewhat exogenous to households' decisions. It is important to note the limitations of this analysis. It is restricted to rural areas. Second, it does not capture the dynamic impact of certain causes of poverty over time. Third, the analysis is limited by the variables available at the household level from the survey. Finally, any interpretation of the included variables as having a causal effect on poverty should be treated with some caution.

the Central region 16 percent lower, and in the Eastern region 12 percent lower, as compared to the Southern region. These findings need to be investigated further, as some of them (such as the relative wealth of the Northeast—indicated as the best-off region in the analysis by a slight margin over the South—and the apparent poverty in the West) do not appear to coincide with traditional patterns. It is possible that regional patterns are reflecting the location of opium poppy cultivation, which is concentrated in the South and Northeast. Further work is required before deriving significant policy implications, however.

ii. *Large households and those with more young children and elderly tend to be poorer.* Keeping all other factors constant, the presence of one additional member decreases per capita expenditure in the household by 3 percent. Each additional child under five also decreases per capita expenditure by 3 percent, while each member over 65 years decreases per capita expenditures by 4 percent. This is similar to the bivariate patterns in the poverty profile.

iii. *Female-headed households tend to be poorer (but not households with a higher share of women).* Per capita expenditures for female-headed households tend to be 14 percent lower than for households headed by a male (and this is separate from the impact of household head's illiteracy which is a separate variable in the analysis—see Table A4). Thus female-headed households could be used as a proxy for targeting poverty interventions. However, households with a larger presence of women do not tend to be poorer, which may suggest that with a male household head, women can provide important complementary skills for income generation (e.g. handicrafts which can be sold on the market by the household head) and therefore do not pay a penalty as compared to other households.

iv. *Domestic migration (including internal displacement) is associated with greater poverty, but not return from abroad.* Per capita expenditures for households whose heads have migrated within the country over the last five years tend to be 7 percent lower than for households who have not migrated. This suggests that poverty interventions could be designed to target this group. Households that have returned from abroad do not seem to be significantly poorer. However, a quintile regression analysis reveals that grouping all returnees from abroad together misses some important differences among them. For high-performers (those whose per capita expenditures are higher than expected given their characteristics), returning from abroad generates a higher level of expenditure, while low-performers (whose per capita expenditures are lower than expected given their other characteristics) seem negatively affected by their return. Thus programs for returnees need to be carefully designed to reach the low-performing group.

v. *Education levels are closely linked with poverty.* When the household head is literate, per capita expenditure is 7 percent higher than when he/she is illiterate, other things equal. The education level of the household head is one of the most critical factors in determining poverty status, although two-way causation may be at work (richer households may be better able to educate their children).

vi. *Differences in access to basic service facilities are not a strong determinant of poverty.* Access to electricity is correlated with higher levels of per capita expenditure, although the direction of causality is probably reversed since most electricity in rural areas is provided by personal generators. The presence of a secondary school is also correlated with higher expenditures, but a secondary school may serve as a proxy for closeness to urban centers. Access to other services (water, market, transport, primary school, and health facilities) is not significantly related to poverty. However, a quintile regression analysis reveals that access to clean water and a permanent food market has a positive effect on better performing households and a negative effect on worse performing households. This suggests that only better performing households translate access to these basic services into higher levels of expenditure and well-being.

vii. *Farming characteristics are significant determinants of rural poverty.* Land ownership has a positive impact on per capita expenditure, whereas sharecropping or agricultural wage labor tends to be associated with greater poverty. Land ownership and rural contractual arrangements often reflect imperfections in other markets (credit, labor, etc.).

viii. *Except for disease, shocks over the last 12 months have little impact on poverty.* However, lumping all households together hides some important differences among them. A quintile regression analysis reveals that insecurity and violence, return of refugees, and the occurrence of a drought have significant negative effects on low performing households. This suggests that actions to mitigate these shocks could be effective components of a poverty reduction strategy.

ix. *Poppy cultivation is correlated with higher expenditures.* The possible implications of this result need to be treated with caution however. Opium poppy eradication may affect negatively the livelihoods of many rural poor engaged in opium production, including the large numbers of wage laborers involved (see Chapter 7).

x. *Sickness of a household member has a negative impact on per capita expenditures.* This suggests the need to design and implement an adequate safety net to provide affordable basic health services to the population and to the poor in particular. The counter-intuitive significant positive effect of livestock disease on per capita expenditure probably is reflecting that those who were severely affected by livestock disease had large herds and were therefore richer families.

xi. *External remittances help alleviate poverty.* Remittances ease households' budget constraints and are associated with higher per capita expenditures. About 15 percent of the rural population receive remittances, which represent about 20 percent of their expenditures on average. The percentage of recipients is lower in the lowest quintile (10 percent) but remittances represent a larger proportion of their expenditures (about 30 percent).

Although these findings are preliminary and will be further developed and refined, they have policy and budgetary implications for the poverty reduction strategy that the Government will be developing (Chapter 3), and for social protection in particular (Chapter 9). Basic education and health are clearly very important for poverty reduction and (especially health) for social protection. Targeting of female-headed households, households headed by disabled persons, and IDP households in poverty reduction programs appears to make good sense, whereas many (though not necessarily all) returning refugees tend to be better-off than the rest of the rural population. Further work is required to assess regional patterns of poverty and their implications for poverty reduction strategy, which could be important. The role of opium in rural households' welfare needs to be better understood, including wage labor on poppy cultivation and harvesting which micro-level studies indicate is an important source of income for the rural poor. And the importance of remittances in the coping strategies of many rural households is confirmed.

CHAPTER 3

Toward Sustained Growth and Poverty Reduction

The Government has set ambitious targets for growth and human development, reflecting the country's need to make up for a quarter of a century of conflict. *Securing Afghanistan's Future* (SAF; Afghanistan Government 2004b) outlines a scenario with average annual growth of 9 percent for non-drug GDP during the medium term, with income per capita rising to $500 in 2015.[1] This scenario is underpinned by an investment program of $25.6 billion over seven years (with external assistance requirements, including for recurrent expenditures, of $27.6 billion). The SAF report is equally ambitious in targeting large improvements in social indicators, in line with the Millennium Development Goals. The gross primary school enrollment rate is targeted to rise from 54 percent (40 for girls) at present to 100 percent for boys and girls by 2015. The under-five mortality rate is targeted to decline from 172 to 130 per 1,000 live births, the infant mortality rate from 115 to 55 per 1,000 live births, and the maternal mortality rate from an estimated 1,600 per 100,000 live births to 205.

Indeed, robust, sustained economic growth is essential for Afghanistan to secure peace and improve human development. First, it is a necessary condition to get out of deep poverty—and therefore the central element of a poverty reduction strategy. Second, growth is crucial for state building and political stabilization (Chapter 4). Economic growth impacts positively on security, by creating revenues for the Government to build police and army forces and by providing people with more of a stake in society. Economic growth

1. The scenario is based on a natural population growth rate of 1.9 percent per annum, to which was added the estimated impact of return of refugees. This may be an underestimate, and moreover the population growth rate could further increase if health interventions are successful and begin to reduce mortality rates. Higher population growth and a rapid pace of urbanization would increase overall growth and investment requirements.

will also generate viable alternatives to opium production (Chapter 7). Finally, economic growth creates revenue potential, which if tapped in a transparent and non-distortionary way through effective taxation, will generate the domestic fiscal resources that will enable Afghanistan over time to become financially self-sufficient and to provide effective services to its people—another key factor in poverty reduction (see Chapter 8 on social service delivery). Thus the key development challenge for Afghanistan is to put in place the institutions, policies, and services that will generate sustained, broad-based economic growth.

As noted in the SAF report (Afghanistan Government 2004b), in addition to the level, the quality of economic growth will be critical:

> The quality of growth is very important. What is needed is growth with improving social indicators (reflecting investments in human capital) and without a significant deterioration in income distribution. This ensures continuing broad consensus around the policies and decisions needed to create the enabling environment for economic growth. In the Afghan context, growth needs to be labor-intensive, sustainable macro-economically and financially, and environment-friendly and conducive to social development. Growth also needs to be reasonably well-balanced ethnically and regionally in order to avoid exacerbating political tensions among different groups and regions.

On this basis, growth will enable and fully support poverty reduction.

This chapter outlines a strategy for growth and poverty reduction, based on the NDF and SAF. The first section summarizes the Government's growth and poverty reduction strategy, provides a conceptual framework, and discusses the four key elements of growth strategy and further elements of a poverty reduction strategy. The second section summarizes implementation priorities and risks.

Growth and Poverty Reduction Strategy

The Government's development strategy is presented as a development vision in the NDF, further articulated in the SAF report (Afghanistan Government 2004b), and embodied in the twelve national development programs of the NDF (Table 3.1). The NDF and SAF are anchored in three "Pillars" of development: (i) human capital and social protection; (ii) physical infrastructure and natural resources; and (iii) private sector development, including security and rule of law and public administration reform and economic management. The NDF also emphasizes three cross-cutting themes: (a) governance, financial management, and administrative reform; (b) human rights, security, and rule of law; and (c) gender. The Government's holistic vision and broad development strategy provide a solid foundation for specific strategic directions and programs discussed later in this chapter, which can be organized around conceptual frameworks for poverty reduction and for growth strategy.

To underpin the implementation of the NDF, the Government put forward six National Priority Programs (NPPs) in late 2002 as the "vehicle for promoting its development vision to mobilize national capacity to manage its own policies and programs in a manner accountable to the public, and in partnership with the international community." The goals of the NPPs are: (i) to unite Government, donors, the private sector, NGOs, and civil society around national policies; (ii) to create efficiency, accountability, and transparency in public spending; (iii) to enable resources to be allocated for large national programs, as opposed to smaller and less efficient projects; (iv) to enhance the leadership and

Table 3.1. National Priority Programs

Priority national program	Lead ministry
Six initial NPPs	
National Transport Program	Ministry of Public Works
Afghanistan Stabilisation Program	Ministry of Interior
National Emergency Employment Program	Ministry of Rural Rehabilitation and Development
National Solidarity Program	Ministry of Rural Rehabilitation and Development
National Irrigation and Power Program	Ministry of Water and Power
Feasibility Studies Unit	Ministry of Finance
Seven new NPPs	
National Agriculture Program	Ministry of Agriculture and Animal Husbandry
National Skills Development and Market Linkages Program	Ministry of Education
National Urban Program	Ministry of Urban Development and Housing
Private Sector Development Program	Ministry of Commerce
National Vulnerability Program	Ministry of Martyrs and Disabled
National Water Supply Program	Ministry of Rural Rehabilitation and Development
National Justice and Rule of Law Program	Ministry of Justice

ownership of Government and Ministries in the reconstruction process; and (v) to enhance provincial equity in national program execution. Progress in implementing some of the programs, notably the National Emergency Employment Program and National Solidarity Program, has been impressive. At the Berlin Conference, the Government announced an additional seven NPPs (Table 3.1). However, the current experience with implementation highlights some risks. For example, the capacity to oversee implementation of the ASP is substantially overstretched. The National Transport Program has not been implemented by the Ministry of Public Works as originally planned, but rather through an *ad hoc* Government and donor committee. Thus while the NPP approach has merits particularly if fully incorporated in the national budget, there are a number of concerns that need to be addressed. These include the risks related to the creation of Program Management Units (PMUs) as executive bodies reporting the relevant National Steering Committee. PMUs could become part of a second, far better-paid, and more highly-skilled civil service (see Chapter 4), which would be unsustainable, siphon away part of the limited pool of professional Afghans, work in parallel with (and thereby weaken) line ministries, and inadvertently undermine administrative and civil service reform efforts.

Conceptual Framework

Opportunity, Empowerment, and Security. Poverty in Afghanistan is, as much as or even more than in other countries, multi-dimensional. As discussed in the *World Development Report 2000/2001: Attacking Poverty,* poverty can be broadly defined to encompass issues

Box 3.1. National Program Structure

Pillar 1: Human and Social Capital
1.1 Refugee and IDP Return
1.2 Education and Vocational Training
1.3 Health and Nutrition
1.4 Livelihoods and Social Protection
1.5 Cultural Heritage, Media, and Sport
Pillar 2: Physical Infrastructure and Natural Resources
2.1 Transport
2.2 Energy, Mining, and Telecommunications
2.3 Natural Resource Management
2.4 Urban Management
Pillar 3: Security and the Private Sector
3.1 Trade and Investment
3.2 Public Administration Reform and Economic Management
3.3 Justice
3.4 National Police, Law Enforcement, and Stabilisation
3.5 Afghan National Army (ANA)
3.6 Mine Action Program for Afghanistan (MAPA)

related to opportunity, empowerment, and security (World Bank, 2001b). Insecurity in Afghanistan has a very real, physical meaning for Afghans, especially the poor—their persons and property are often at risk from illegitimate local power-holders. Insecurity also encompasses vulnerability to shocks ranging from natural disasters to serious health problems to the ravages of conflict. Lack of empowerment has meant that the poor in Afghanistan have not only been unable to exercise political power in general (ideally in a democratic political structure) but more specifically have not been able to ensure delivery of adequate basic services to them. This is somewhat different from the situation in many other developing countries, where an existing and reasonably functional state may be unresponsive to, or even misused against, the poor. Thus security and empowerment for the poor are intimately linked with the state-building agenda (Chapter 4) and service delivery (Chapter 8). The third component of poverty, lack of opportunity, is at the heart of the growth agenda and also encompasses building human capital, physical assets, and livelihoods.

Breaking Out of the Informal Equilibrium. Many of the most important constraints to sustained, broad-based economic growth in Afghanistan are part of the confluence of factors that have generated the "informal equilibrium" described in Chapter 1 (Figure 1.3). These include: (i) insecurity and lack of rule of law, one of the most serious deterrents to business growth and longer-term investments; (ii) regulatory burden and corruption—although the Government has a pro-private sector policy orientation and has pursued trade and tax reforms, there is still excessive red tape in obtaining permits of various kinds, land allocations, and the like; (iii) unavailability of key support services for the private sector, ranging from essential infrastructure (power, roads, serviced land, water) to finance, insurance, business support services, agricultural extension and marketing, and so forth; and (iv) the lack of a framework and infrastructure for standards, quality assurance, measures, testing, and so forth, which will be critical for export development. All of these constraints shift incentives toward the informal sector, inhibiting the emergence of larger, efficient, and potentially internationally competitive businesses. They especially hinder export growth, international competitiveness, and productivity growth based on use of increasingly advanced technology—which require activities to be in the formal sector for at least part of the value chain. These constraints are compounded by the lack of skills and capacity, managerial as well as technical, available in Afghanistan. And in the informal equilibrium, businesses tend not to gain the experience or build the capacity needed to operate effectively in the formal economy—one of the many self-reinforcing aspects of the informal equilibrium.

The "formal equilibrium" (Figure 3.1) is a convenient conceptual framework to illustrate the changes needed to increase entrepreneurs' productivity and support sustained growth and export development. It emphasizes the importance of security and rule of law, effective state functioning in providing macroeconomic stability and essential public services, and an enabling environment for the private sector achieved through regulatory and structural reforms. Stronger capacity in the government will enable it to improve security, enforce the rule of law, and provide macroeconomic stability and public services. This in turn will provide more incentives for businesses to "go formal" and, among other things, pay taxes, enabling further strengthening of government capacity, and so on. The formal equilibrium concept does not mean that the entire economy would become formalized, let alone quickly—there would always be a sizable informal component. Yet, unlike at present, there would also be a sizable, dynamic formal sector. Going formal does not necessarily imply large scale—although some of the most successful enterprises would become large, Afghanistan's business landscape will continue to be dominated by small and medium-sized enterprises which need to be supported as an integral part of the private sector development strategy (see Chapter 5).

Figure 3.1. The Formal Equilibrium

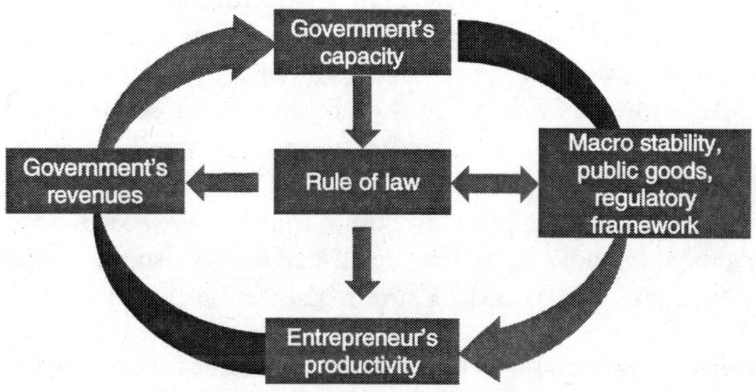

Main Elements of Growth Strategy

In essence, the Government's strategy for rapid, sustained, broad-based economic growth centers around the development of a dynamic private sector and is anchored in four key elements: (i) improving security through fair and effective enforcement of law and order and building an effective, accountable State, (ii) maintaining macroeconomic stability, (iii) delivering support services (especially infrastructure), and (iv) creating an enabling environment for business activity through regulatory and structural reforms. This strategy appropriately addresses the main constraints discussed above.

The Government has already made a very good start by maintaining macroeconomic stability and initiating some important structural reforms (see Chapter 1), as well as capacity building in the administration (Chapter 4). These very successful and important initiatives need to be complemented by capacity building and delivery of key infrastructural services, by easing the regulatory burden on the private sector (Chapter 5) and reducing vulnerability to corruption (Chapter 4), and most urgently by improving security and strengthening the rule of law (Chapter 4).

Security, Rule of Law, and State Building. The first and most fundamental requirement to break out of the "informal equilibrium" is to build security, an appropriate legal framework and functioning judicial system, effective law enforcement mechanisms, and a capable and effective state (Chapter 4). In the medium term, the stability, security, and prosperity of Afghanistan will depend on the ability of the state to raise the resources needed to fund the provision of necessary public services (Chapter 4 and 8). In the SAF report, the Government stated its intention to cover its wage bill in five to six years time, and its entire recurrent budget in nine to eleven years time. Over the last two years, it has already achieved a significant increase in revenues. Additional progress in mobilizing resources will depend on (i) the security situation and administrative capacity of the Government, and (ii) the structure of the economy. Security sector reform is critical, and this component will also need to include reintegration of disarmed combatants. Government capacity building is underway and needs to be accelerated, on a sustainable basis. Progress in strengthening and reform of the judiciary, which has lagged, will be crucial.

Building on informal institutions to create formal institutions is a promising option for moving toward a functioning legal system. Adequate property rights, for instance land titles, enhance the value of assets because, with appropriate institutions for property disputes, they can be used as collateral for credit and facilitate a longer time horizon on the part of their owners. As shown by the work of Hernando De Soto in *The Mystery of Capital* (De Soto 2000), existing practices can guide the formal definition of property rights. In Peru, 276,000 small entrepreneurs voluntarily recorded their business because formal regulations were adapted to informal practices. In Africa, on the contrary, attempts to impose a system of formal land titles failed by running into conflict with traditional arrangements: since lenders knew the new system would be opposed by communities, the expected benefits in terms of financial development did not materialize. Rural land tenure issues in Afghanistan are discussed extensively in Wily (2003) and are summarized in Box 6.3 of Chapter 6.

Macroeconomic Policy Framework. A stable macroeconomic framework is very important to sustain growth and shift incentives toward the formal sector. The Government intends to sustain recent achievements in fiscal, monetary, and exchange rate management (conservative monetary policy, light management of the exchange rate, no-overdraft rule, prudent debt management) and deepen budget and public administration reforms (Chapter 4). The Government is committed to develop a multi-year fiscal framework to manage effectively its fiscal policy. More generally, the policy framework will need to be responsive to potential shocks affecting the economy (see the discussion of macroeconomic risks at the end of this chapter). Also, in the short run a key challenge for macroeconomic management is the size of the informal economy itself. Monetary policy is weakened because the informal economy does not rely on the banking system, which suggests the need for some monitoring of the hawala system. Moreover, the policy mix can be inadequate if based on incorrect information from national accounts or employment data that poorly reflect the informal economy, which suggests that the policy mix should be very neutral.

Provision of Support Services. The third element of the strategy, effective delivery of services required by the private sector, improves productivity and provides incentives for parts of the informal economy to "come out into the open." Infrastructure, business services, and research and development have significant externalities in terms of increasing entrepreneurs' productivity:

i. *Infrastructure* services augment inputs available to entrepreneurs (more water through irrigation, more and cheaper seeds, more inputs available through roads, more power) and thus improve production efficiency. They also enlarge markets (through roads, airports, telecommunications) and therefore have a similar effect to a reduction in trade barriers. While some of these services can be used by informal activities (telecom services for instance have quickly developed), others require investments or registration (for example, with the power company) that tend to self-select formal activities. A program of public investment is outlined in the Government's development budget based on the SAF report. Issues related to selected infrastructure sectors are discussed in Chapter 5.

ii. A second important category of support services is *business services* (see Chapter 5). These are delivered by the private sector, but public policies should facilitate their development. Development of the financial sector provides important incentives for the formal sector to develop, as do mechanisms to reduce investment risks, like risk guarantees provided by MIGA.

iii. A third category of public goods is *research and development.* For Afghanistan the priority is to adapt and adopt existing technologies (see Chapter 6 on agriculture). The rate of global technological progress is very rapid, and Afghanistan should exploit the opportunity to make use of the most efficient modern technologies suitable for the country.

Enabling Regulatory Framework and Structural Reforms. A fourth element of the growth strategy seeks to improve the enabling environment to set clear rules for entrepreneurs and not require them to go through endless steps in the bureaucracy to comply with these rules. Regulatory and structural reforms can be classified in five groups (Table 3.2). Two key issues affecting all of these areas are the excessive complexity and non-transparency

Table 3.2. Structural Reforms

Reform area	Recent reforms	Issues	Government's plan
Labor market	None	Labor Code from the 1970s; no enforcement capacity	Labor Code being drafted
Product markets (Chapters 5 and 6)	No price restrictions Revision of the Investment Law (including amendments in 2004 to eliminate tax holidays)	Large but mainly defunct state-owned enterprise sector Significant, disparate set of laws and regulations	Mining and Petroleum Laws being drafted Commercial Code, Trademark Law under revision Reform of state-owned enterprises
Financial market (Chapter 5)	No restrictions on exchange rate and financial flows Banking Law and Central Bank Law passed in 2003	Bank licensing process started and resolution for state-owned banks ongoing	Dissolve or merge state-owned banks without licenses Strengthen Central Bank's supervision function
Tax (Chapter 4)	Tax package approved	Need to increase revenues in an efficient manner	Tax policy and administration reforms
Trade	Reform of import tariffs New or adjusted trade agreements with Pakistan, Iran, Tajikistan, India, US, and the EU Joined the World Customs Organization	Customs Code obsolete	Customs Code under revision Work towards WTO accession

Source: Based on information provided by the Center for International Management Education (CIME); IMF (2004); World Bank (2004c).

of regulations and the limited administrative capacity to provide fair and effective enforcement (see Chapter 4).

i. The *labor market* is regulated by a Labor Code drafted in the 1970s, whose provisions covering hiring and firing, applicable only to firms with more than 20 employees, are rather light. Moreover, in the absence of Government capacity these provisions are not enforced.

ii. Reforms in the *product and financial markets* are discussed in Chapter 5 (and in Chapter 6 for agriculture). State direct interventions in the economy are very limited—there are almost no price restrictions, virtually no controls applying to foreign exchange transactions, payments, and capital movements, and state-owned enterprises are mainly defunct—but regulations remain numerous and potentially costly, discouraging formalization.

iii. Although the Government initially focused on customs, the main source of revenue, broader *tax reforms* also have been initiated (see Chapter 4). New tax policy reforms have been enacted in 2004 (a final wage withholding tax on higher income employees, an improved income tax regime, a streamlined business establishment tax, a tax on a limited range of services consumed by high income earners, a rent tax, a land tax, and an airport departure tax). Tax administration is being modernized, which will give more clarity to taxpayers. The Ministry of Finance is creating a "Large Taxpayer Office" in Kabul to focus on revenue collection from the top 100 tax-paying entities. In addition, there are plans to create units in the provinces, reporting directly to the Ministry in Kabul, for medium-sized taxpayers. The Government intends to modernize the tax code in 2004/05.

iv. *Customs reforms* have been initiated with the adoption of a reform package in 2003 (see Chapter 1). Implementation of customs administration improvements is underway. The Government is now reviewing the customs code.

Structural reforms, as well as other elements of the strategy outlined above, are in particular necessary to encourage growth of trade, both within the region and globally, which will be vital to the expansion of market opportunities, and therefore for growth and poverty reduction. Capitalizing on Afghanistan's position as a "land bridge" for trading within the region, and promoting its wider integration in the formal global economy, will require continuing policy and institutional reforms as well as investments, with emphasis on trade facilitation. Afghanistan has already made significant progress in reforming its trade and investment regime. Nevertheless, official regional trade flows between Afghanistan and its neighbors remain relatively small, comprising only 11 percent of all exports in 2002, the rest being traded globally (World Bank 2004d). Informal trade flows with Pakistan and other countries are very large however. Currently, trade logistics remain difficult and costly, combined with a problematic security environment which encourages informal and illicit trading patterns. Hence streamlining Afghanistan's transit links with both regional and non-regional trading partners would reduce transport-related trade costs and facilitate the growth of economic activity and incomes in Afghanistan and its neighbors. Problems of market access depend not only on formal trade barriers but also on barriers to efficient trade logistics and weaknesses in the operation of market institutions. The implementation of the newly approved import tariff schedule as well as improving the capacity of the customs service, harmonizing customs procedures, and improving customs valuation, are all vital aspects of enhanced trade facilitation. Given its potential significance, regional trade deserves special attention in bilateral discussions and multilateral forums, such as the Economic Cooperation Organization (ECO), which along with Afghanistan and its neighbors includes Azerbaijan, Kazakhstan, Kyrgyz Republic, and Turkey. The March 2004 ECO Conference held in Kabul demonstrated a closer relationship between Afghanistan and other ECO members.

Some Additional Elements For A Poverty Reduction Strategy

Economic growth is expected to increase opportunities for poor people. Its impact in this regard will depend on whether and to what extent growth helps the poor to build their assets, through investing (and repaying debts) from their own incomes, and accumulating physical capital like livestock. Improvements in opportunities for poor people will also require building their human capital (education, health, training), developing community asset-building programs (notably NSP), financing assets through micro-credit (the Microfinance Support Facility of Afghanistan—MISFA), and so forth. The economic role of women should be enhanced in the interest of both broad-based growth and poverty reduction.

To empower poor people, these elements need to be complemented with the development of participatory institutions (as started with the elected Community Development Councils, part of the NSP). Finally, poor people should benefit from security improvements, which in any case are key to economic growth.

Asset building on the part of the poor is expected to be a very important outcome of economic growth and needs to be supported by a range of well-targeted, cost-effective programs, some of which like micro-finance support both growth and poverty reduction. Public works employment programs and other income generation programs can help the poor preserve and over time build physical assets, enhancing their opportunities for progress (see Chapter 9). Sector development programs, for example in agriculture, can play a significant role in this regard, both directly (for poor farmers) and indirectly (through stimulating demand for wage labor in agriculture and other rural activities).

Human capital building by the poor, primarily through adequate levels and quality of basic education and health services, is critical for poverty reduction, as emphasized in the NDF. While the financial resource requirements for social services are detailed in the SAF report, Chapter 8 focuses on service delivery issues and ways forward to ensure adequate accountability for performance in service delivery.

Social protection (Chapter 9) is another key element of a poverty reduction strategy—in particular safety net programs for the extreme poor and those unable for various reasons (remoteness, disability, female-headed households) to fully take advantage of opportunities created by economic growth.

A final important element is consultation. A good poverty reduction strategy is not only technically and economically sound—it needs to be fully "owned" by the poor as well as by other stakeholders in the society. In this regard, the role of civil society groups, including the private sector, to identify key policy, institutional, and infrastructure constraints, as well as to suggest ways forward, will be vital to establishing a poverty reduction strategy that clearly identifies the problems that it seeks to address and builds ownership across the society. The role of both national and international NGOs in this process will be very important for enhancing ownership. The Government is planning to engage in extensive consultations with different segments of society as it develops its Poverty Reduction Strategy, a process targeted to reach a first stage of completion with the preparation of an Interim Poverty Reduction Strategy Paper (I-PRSP) early in 2005.

Implementation Priorities and Risks

Near-Term Options for Moving Forward

The Government's national priority programs, presented in April 2004, include a number which will promote sustained economic growth via the formal equilibrium, directly or indirectly. For example, the Afghanistan Stabilization Program will enhance the Government's presence and capacity on the ground in provinces and districts, and the National Accountability and Rule of Law Program will encourage compliance with transparent competitive procedures, enhance fiduciary safeguards, and promote rule of law. In addition, three complementary opportunities can be seized to move forward the growth agenda: (i) importing resources, (ii) harnessing the dynamism of the informal sector to generate continuing growth, and (iii) instituting reforms first in specific localities.

First, *importing resources* is a way to overcome the lack of human, technical, and financial capacity in the country in the short run. This includes: (i) aid and technical assistance, as well as military and police assistance, from bilateral donors and multilateral agencies; (ii) imports of goods and services; (iii) foreign direct investment by the private sector; and (iv) ideas, capital, and skills from Afghans living abroad. From Bonn in December 2001 to Berlin in March 2004, the international community has been responsive to this challenge. The impact of external assistance will be sustainable if it supports the Government budget (Chapter 4) and the development of formal sector activities. This entails maximizing the amount of assistance through budget channels, awarding contracts through transparent competitive bidding, and the like.

In particular, the regional economy can be an important resource. Fostering regional trade is vital for Afghanistan. Importing electricity from Turkmenistan is an example of the benefits of trade in the context of low domestic generating capacity. Reconstruction activities will benefit from imports from regional countries (for example, of construction materials) and regional contracting of services. Regional investors have also expressed interest in investing in Afghanistan. If corridor agreements are developed, exports to neighboring countries can be expanded. Informal networks (especially those built by refugees) will support this development, even though there will be incentives for this trade to stay informal initially. Neighboring countries can also provide skilled workforce. The role of refugee return is more complex: Afghanistan would benefit from the return of more skilled refugees, but there would be an associated reduction in remittances (Box 3.2).[2] There is

Box 3.2. Refugee Return and Remittances

During the past 25 years, more than 30 percent of the Afghan population has been externally or internally displaced. While this has taken a heavy toll in terms of human suffering and disruption, displacement has fostered a highly integrated regional labor market with remittances a substantial source of income for families that remain in Afghanistan. Remittances from Pakistan, Iran, North America, Europe and parts of Australasia remain a central element of Afghan households' coping strategies (Chapter 2). In 2003, 17 percent of a sample of rural Afghan households reported having a household member who had emigrated in the previous year.

Although 2.4 million Afghans have now been repatriated (1.8 million from Pakistan and 600,000 from Iran) and 600,000 IDPs have returned home, an estimated 3.4 million Afghans still remain outside the country (largely in Pakistan and Iran), and approximately 200,000 IDPs remain uprooted within Afghanistan. In many provinces, security conditions are not yet sufficiently stable to expedite the return of large numbers of refugees. Many families who left Afghanistan years ago tend to seek reintegration in an urban setting, as they have become cut-off from their land and social relations.

Finding solutions for the remaining refugee populations represents a complex and continuing challenge. From a socio-economic point of view, there is still considerable uncertainty about the volume of remittances, the economic opportunities for refugees in their host country, and economic growth in Afghanistan. From a political economy point of view, there is also uncertainty regarding stability in Afghanistan, while neighboring Pakistan and Iran are looking for near-term solutions to stabilize their own political economy.

During 2005, the trilateral agreements with Pakistan and Iran will lapse, and the longer-term status of remaining refugees (probably to be given the status of economic migrants) will need to be clarified.

2. The use to which remittances are put (e.g. for investment versus consumption) also is a very important consideration.

already considerable degree of integration of informal labor markets with Pakistan and Iran, which is expected to continue.

Second, the *existing dynamism of the informal sector* can be harnessed to generate growth. Women can play an important role in this strategy (Box 3.3).

- *Further Facilitating Growth in the Legitimate Informal Sector.* A potentially important element is micro-credit. The Microfinance Investment Support Facility for Afghanistan (MISFA) has already provided assistance to nearly 20,000 clients, of which more then 90 percent are women. Greater cooperation among informal

Box 3.3. The Role of Women in Afghanistan's Reconstruction

The participation of women is regarded as critical in all countries. But in Afghanistan their participation will bear particular fruits. First, their participation will increase the available labor supply. Second, their participation will bring additional knowledge, techniques, and ideas, which will enhance the economy's productivity. For instance, having female staff in health facilities is necessary to increase women's use of these facilities, and the same is true of female teachers with respect to increasing girls' enrollment.

Current Role. Women's involvement in agricultural production is considerable—in certain regions women's time input equals men's but in other regions traditions restrict their work to the household where they are involved in crop processing (threshing, cleaning, drying, preserving) and also are in charge of most of the household activities (water and fuel collection, cooking, cleaning, sewing, tailoring, weaving, and child rearing). Women play an increasingly important role in poppy production (Chapter 7). Women also play a major role in livestock production and processing of dairy products. Most women's labor is non-monetized, but they make major labor contributions to a number of marketed products such as dried fruits, poppies, fuelwood, dairy products, and handicrafts. Women's contribution to pastoral livestock production both for domestic consumption and for domestic and international markets is high, reflected in a range of key export products (carpets, hides, qarakul skins, wool). Even when women's domestic production such as carpet weaving forms the main income of the household, they rarely control the marketing of these products, which is most often managed by male relatives or middlemen. Women's involvement in the formal sector has mainly been as civil servants working on health and education, where they had a sizeable presence before the conflict, which was severely disrupted by the strong restrictions on female employment during the Taliban. Currently less than 1/3 of all teachers are female while an estimated 40 percent of all basic health facilities lack female staff, which constitutes a major hindrance to delivery of basic services (health in particular) to women (see Chapter 8).

Constraints. The traditional role of women in Afghanistan is a constraint to their participation in economic activities. In particular, female wage labor is still viewed as a solution of last resort for households in desperate straits, and their wage rates are normally only half the level of men's. Women have fewer marketable skills and generally poor education, with an estimated female literacy rate of 21 percent. But other constraints should not be underestimated. With a fertility rate of 6.9 and an estimated maternal mortality rate of 1,600 per 100,000 live births, reproduction and related health issues occupy much of women's time. A recent study by the International Rescue Committee (IRC) found that 40 percent of women mentioned lack of childcare as the first constraint to their participation in the labor market. The absence of many services and the need to produce agricultural products for subsistence also impose an opportunity cost for women who want to join the labor market. Women often lack ownership, control, and access to productive assets such as land, equipment, and materials, and their legal right to inheritance is usually bypassed. The lack of working capital and absence of credit reduce opportunities to start activities that require an initial investment. In the carpet industry, financial constraints have been somewhat alleviated since traders often supply equipment and raw materials, but this has reduced households' control over production and marketing. These various constraints are even more acute for female-headed households (IRC estimated that 13 percent of surveyed women were widows).

activities also can facilitate growth in the informal sector. In the case of horticulture, growers' associations could help farmers to negotiate prices, package their products in a way that preserves quality during transport, and increase market information.[3]

- *Gradually Shifting Informal Activities to the Formal Sector.* Surveys in Brazil and Peru show that developing direct links with formal firms provided the needed incentives for informal suppliers to become formal themselves. Donor-supported programs, such as the National Solidarity Program, which have formal procedures in line with international guidelines, can help build the capacity of informal actors to prepare and execute contracts. By explicitly exempting them from regulations and taxation, small activities (those with few employees and small revenues) could be given access to the formal economy (public services, judicial system, trade network, financial services). Such a regime of "micro-enterprise" does not immediately generate additional revenues, but as some of these firms grow they will naturally join the tax base. The law on NGOs will also clarify the status of these organizations and how they can access tax exempt status.

Third, *reforms can be started in specific localities.* Within geographically narrow "Industrial Parks" or "Export Processing Zones," security, other key services, and enabling regulations may be easier to provide. The Government has already initiated development of Industrial Parks, a welcome development which should be pursued (Chapter 5).

Managing Risks

The implementation of the growth and poverty reduction strategy faces five major risks with economy-wide implications, which will need to be carefully managed in order to sustain rapid economic growth.

Political and Security Risks Remain. The cost of resumption of civil war, or of delays in political normalization, would be very large. International experience suggests that a typical country at the end of a civil war faces a 44 percent risk of returning to conflict within five years. Generating sustained rapid growth and robust employment generation is the main mitigation strategy for this risk (see Chapter 1 of the SAF report).

Second, there is *climatic risk.* While the recent four-year nationwide drought was unusually severe, droughts covering large areas of Afghanistan are estimated to happen every 9–11 years and more localized droughts every 3–5 years. The drought at the end of the 1990s reduced cereal production by 50 percent (a loss of about $700 million in foregone output). Regional droughts—such as the continuing drought affecting the South and parts of northern Afghanistan—would adversely affect growth and would increase demand for public expenditures (such as cash-for-work programs). External assistance would thus be critical in the face of a significant drought.

3. For example, in India dairy cooperatives in Bihar State have proved successful in federating producers and providing them with entry to markets. In Ahmedabad, also in India, the Self-Employed Women's Association provides cooperative financial, health, and childcare services to 550,000 women and helps provide a women's voice in policy circles.

Table 3.3. Prices, Wages, and Exchange Rates

Annual growth rate (March to March)	2001/02	2002/03	2003/04
Consumer Price Index	(43.4)	52.3	10.5
Exchange rate (Afg. Per US$)[a]	(56.9)	52.2	(3.6)
Real Exchange rate[ab]	(23.8)	(0.0)	(12.7)
Daily wage of unskilled casual labour (US$)	86.1	9.0	70.0

a. An increase represents a depreciation of the Afghani.
b. Exchange rate depreciation divided by inflation (against US$, deflated only by Afghan prices)
Source: CSO (2004); IMF (2003, 2004); wage data provided by WFP.

Third, the combined impact of large exports of opium, inflows of foreign assistance, and remittances from abroad could have an adverse impact on growth through an exchange rate appreciation (the so-called "*Dutch disease*"). Aid and opium exports totaled around $4 billion in 2003/04, and remittances are hundreds of millions of dollars per year. If partly spent on non-tradable goods, these inflows would put upward pressure on domestic prices leading to real exchange rate appreciation. This in turn would result in a shift of labor to the non-tradable sector and opium sector, putting upward pressure on wages in terms of tradable goods (other than opium). The negative impact on competitiveness (in both exports and import substitution activities) could be harmful to growth. There is some evidence of an increase in wages, and appreciation of the real exchange rate may be occurring (Table 3.3).

However, the overall net impact of the "Dutch disease" depends on the associated supply response. If aid flows (and, in the Afghan case, opium export receipts) lead to productive investments, the resulting increased capacity of the economy will ease bottlenecks and moderate inflationary pressures, and associated rising productivity will offset loss of price competitiveness. Over the longer run, aid flows would be expected to decline, and it is planned to eliminate opium production over time. This requires Afghanistan to develop a dynamic export sector to provide increasing amounts of foreign exchange. Careful exchange rate management also is called for.

Fourth, *a reduction in opium production* would have very significant macroeconomic implications, and a reduction of poppy prices to their pre-2000 level would represent something like a $1 billion shock for the economy. Based on recent information, farm-gate prices have sharply declined since late 2003 (see Chapter 7), undoubtedly with an adverse effect on rural incomes. In addition, a fall in opium exports will: (i) adversely affect the Government's revenues through a reduction in imports currently funded by poppy income; (ii) reduce foreign exchange inflows; and (iii) dry up credit provided by the opium economy, further depressing economic activity through the equivalent of a credit crunch. This will lead to a real depreciation (with a nominal depreciation, due to lower demand for the Afghani, and deflation, due to lower demand for goods). While the depreciation will have a positive impact on price competitiveness, somewhat offsetting the depressing impact of the "poppy shock" on income, the overall impact on growth will largely depend on the response from external assistance to finance public expenditures and offset the decrease in foreign exchange inflows.

Fifth, Afghanistan's heavy reliance on *external assistance* is potentially an additional risk. Reliance on donor funding for services could risk building in higher costs of service delivery and entrench parallel delivery mechanisms, which would be unsustainable in the long term (Chapter 8). And volatility of external assistance would constitute a significant risk for the growth and poverty reduction strategy. The Government intends to develop an adequate multi-year fiscal framework to manage this risk. Donors are encouraged to use Government systems and policies to implement their programs. The critical risk mitigation strategy is in this regard is to further strengthen domestic resource mobilization.

As the above discussion illustrates, the challenge for the Afghan Government, with support from the international community, is to plan for and manage these risks with sound macroeconomic policies, building fiscal and balance of payments sustainability over time, and relying on international assistance when necessary to respond effectively to shocks. In this way, and based on the structural reforms and other measures outlined earlier in this chapter, Afghanistan will be able to sustain its recent good growth performance and reduce poverty.

CHAPTER 4

Building an Effective, Accountable Afghan State

The state-building agenda is at the heart of Afghanistan's economic, political, and social reconstruction—with strong linkages to economic growth and private sector development (Chapters 3, 5, and 6), poverty reduction (Chapters 2 and 9), phasing out dependence on the drug economy (Chapter 7), and delivering public services to the Afghan people (Chapter 8), as well as to the all-important dimensions of security (discussed in this chapter) and political normalization. The centrality of state building has been emphasized by the Government in its *National Development Framework* (NDF), in *Securing Afghanistan's Future* (SAF), and in other public pronouncements. Considerable progress has been made during the past two years, as elaborated below, but there is a long way to go in building an effective, accountable state that meets the needs of the Afghan people. This chapter, building on analysis by the World Bank and partners,[1] focuses on selected critical aspects of state building. The first section lays out the state-building agenda and strategy and accomplishments to date. The second section reviews ongoing reforms—"work in progress"—focusing on interim public administration reforms and improvements in fiscal management. The third section discusses the two key tasks of addressing corruption and improving security. The final section outlines the way forward in state building and public sector reform.

1. This chapter draws heavily on research by the World Bank and AREU on public administration in Afghanistan, including Evans and others (2004a and 2004b). It also draws on World Bank (2004c).

The State-Building Agenda

The Starting Point

More than 20 years of conflict in Afghanistan resulted in the collapse of the national state as a legitimate political entity with monopoly over the legitimate use of force. Thus, the state-building agenda, including political normalization, improvements in security, administrative capacity-building, and other key components, is paramount for Afghanistan's reconstruction. State building is defined and discussed in more detail in Box 4.1.

In the face of political collapse the administrative structures of the state have somewhat surprisingly survived, providing a possible entry-point for state building, which would complement and facilitate the fundamental political and security agenda. Afghanistan's administrative arrangements are highly centralized yet provide a coherent management and accountability framework for government. The administrative practices are basically sound and understood—even if not always adhered to. Nevertheless, the government administration is far from effective, and suffers from a number of systemic problems, including:

i. Fragmented administrative structures, with many overlapping and unnecessary functions.
ii. Lack of skilled professionals with management and administrative experience, and the Taliban's dismissal of women staff resulted in a very serious gender imbalance.[2]
iii. Pay and grading structures are unable to attract, retain, and motivate skilled civil servants.
iv. Merit-based recruitment procedures are absent, resulting in patronage appointments.
v. Mechanisms for performance management are inadequate.
vi. Administrative systems are slow and cumbersome, with virtually no delegation of authority to lower ranks or to provincial departments.

While progress has been made on a number of these fronts in the last two years, it will take time for meaningful capacity improvements to reach broadly across the civil service and down to the rank and file. Success will depend to a large degree on the ability of the central government to regain control over national policies and implementation across the entire country. This is made more difficult by the financial and military strength of the regional warlords (or "power-brokers") and local factional commanders, and by the massive amounts of donor aid that dwarf the Government's own budget, largely provided through off-budget mechanisms.

De jure *and* de facto *State Structure.* Afghanistan is a unitary state with a highly centralized government structure (Figure 4.1). *Politically,* all formal authority is vested in the center. Leaders at sub-national level—provincial Governors and municipal mayors, for instance—are appointed by the center. Most government services are delivered at provincial

2. Limited data are available on women in the civil service. CSO and UNIFEM estimate that in 2002 approximately 27,742 women held karmand (regular) positions within government. A further 5,753 were employed as agirs (contract employees). Women civil servants appear to be significantly less educated than their male counterparts. UNICEF surveys indicate that 27 percent of teachers are female (more than 50 percent in Kabul).

Box 4.1. State-Building

The state is the basic unit of political control and legitimacy in the modern world. The international system is primarily composed of states that recognize each other's sovereignty—that is, ultimate legal authority—over a demarcated territory. According to international law and norms, the exercise of this sovereignty imposes obligations to respect the rights of citizens, other people, and other states, according to the law of nations. Yet, no state can carry out these obligations unless it has certain capacities.

The basic capacity that defines a state and enables it to carry out the obligations of sovereignty is a monopoly, or near monopoly, of the legitimate use of force within the territory over which it is sovereign. To merit recognition, a state is expected to use force legitimately, in accordance with law. The monopoly of the use of force is a pre-requisite for carrying out other obligations of a state, such as protecting the rights of and providing services to its citizens and other inhabitants, as well as participating in international organizations and institutions to promote and protect international security according to international law.

During the past quarter-century in Afghanistan, several governments used the state to exercise violence lawlessly. In addition, the growth of numerous armed groups deprived any of them, including governments in Kabul (whether or not they received international recognition) of a monopoly of the use of force. All of these entities violated the rights of Afghans, and the ability of any of them to provide even a low level of services declined. Rather than participating in efforts to provide international security, Afghanistan became a source of international insecurity.

Building a state that can protect rights, provide services, and promote security requires a number of interdependent processes. At a minimum, these include:

i. Demobilizing and dissolving all armed forces not controlled by the state.

ii. Forming and training armed forces and police to protect international and domestic security in accordance with law.

iii. Forming and training all components of a legal system, from legislators to judges and prosecutors, to provide a legal framework for the functioning of the state and other social relations.

iv. Raising revenue in accordance with law to pay for the functioning of the state.

v. Creating and training an administration capable of raising revenue and providing services to citizens and other inhabitants.

In a state long torn by conflict, all of these processes have to be started over, sometimes from a very low level.

It is useful to make a conceptual distinction between *de jure* and *de facto* states. *De jure* states exist by fiat of the international community, which recognizes them as sovereign entities whether or not they have a government that can effectively control or administer their territory. *De facto* states actually administer a territory. States that enjoy international recognition and exercise control through adequate institutions are both *de jure* and *de facto*.

States may provide better services and otherwise perform better when they are democratic, but building a state is not the same as building democracy. A functioning state is the foundation on which democracy must be built. Without a state apparatus capable of providing security and rule of law, the election of office holders does not enable people to govern themselves, for those elected have no tools to govern, and the people have no instrument to hold them accountable. Hence building a state is the primary task of building sustainable peace.

and district levels, but powers and responsibilities of sub-national administration are determined by the center.

Fiscally, Afghanistan is highly centralized. Expenditures at provincial and local levels are made through national programs carried out by provincial arms of central ministries.

Figure 4.1. Afghanistan's Administrative Structure

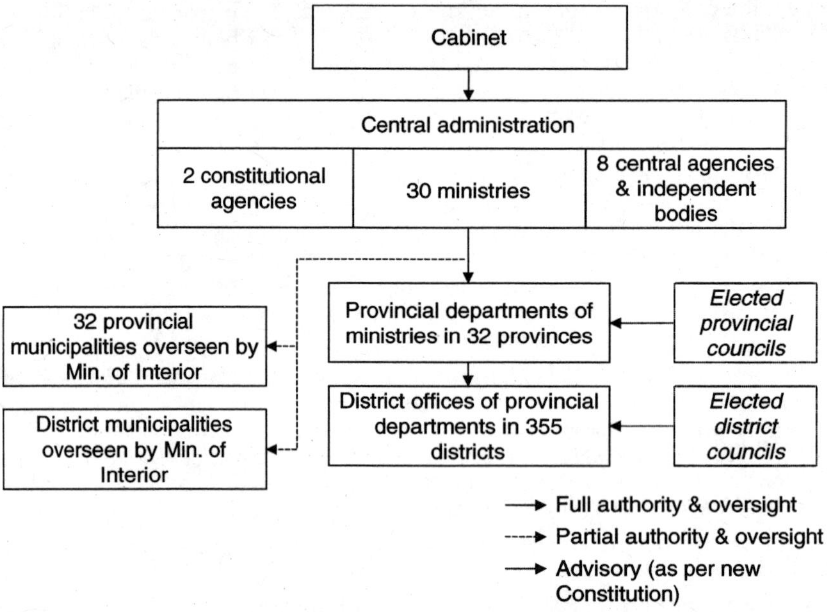

No fiscal transfers as such go to sub-national levels. With almost 40 percent of the civil service workforce in Kabul, funds are concentrated at the center. Budgets of provincial departments are set in Kabul, and approval from Kabul is required for even minor changes. On the revenue side, Afghan districts and provinces have no independent authority to impose taxes. The only expenditure autonomy is at municipal level. Although all tax and fee rates are set in Kabul, revenues collected by municipalities remain there and fund municipal spending.

Administratively, government in Afghanistan is also highly centralized. Provincial and local governments have only a very modest formal role in decisions concerning their own structure, recruitment of senior staff, size of establishment, composition of workforce, and so forth. Such decisions are made by each ministry in Kabul, in conjunction with the Office of Administrative Affairs, and signed off by the head of the Independent Administrative Reform and Civil Service Commission (IARCSC). The ministry in Kabul or the President makes staff appointments at middle to senior grades, while the provincial Governor appoints junior staff down to district level.

Despite this very high degree of *de jure* centralization, the *de facto* reality is that central control is very weak, given the strength of regional and local warlords who command substantial revenues and military power, and have captured the government administration in the localities they control. Certainly in the revenue-rich provinces, Governors make resource allocation decisions except on basic salaries. Staff appointments from Kabul are often rejected in favor of those loyal to regional factions, and even Kabul-based appointments often reflect loyalties and ethnic ties rather than merit. In these areas, where the warlords (and in some cases Governors) have "captured" both strategic decision-making and overall fiscal resources, the

Figure 4.2. *De Jure* and *De Facto* Centralization

	de Jure	*de Facto*
Administrative central/provincial relationships	Strong *de jure* administrative centralization, with virtually all administrative decisions made at the center.	• Most provinces accept that Kabul has a role to play in approving senior level appointments, but there are significant departures from this for some provinces, particularly with regards to police. • All provinces accept the basic rules of the administrative game concerning grades and tashkeels.
Fiscal central/provincial relationships	Strong *de jure* fiscal centralization, with no own - source revenues or authority over expenditures at the subnational level.	• Provinces do report and transfer locally raised revenues to the Ministry of Finance; however, there are significant amounts of unreported (and locally withheld) revenues. • All provinces accept the basic rules of the fiscal game concerning budget preparation and execution.
Political central/provincial relationships	Strong *de jure* political centralization, with all subnational political positions appointed by the national government, and no mandatory regional representation in the national government.	• Self-evidently, politically there is major *de facto* decentralization, with regional warlords or local commanders setting policy.

public sector is essentially autonomous from the central government. As shown in Figure 4.2, the degree of centralization in practice varies across administrative, fiscal, and political spheres.

Factional loyalties are strengthened by a general lack of financial support from the center. Pay levels are very low, especially for the middle-level and senior staff, and payment of salaries is often delayed. Financial support in the form of non-salary budgets has been low to non-existent for provinces and districts (see Table 4.3), and physical infrastructure (offices, desks) is lacking. Civil servants report a sense of pride in their jobs—"serving in the government is a mark of distinction, and something to be proud of"—but without adequate motivation, resources to do the job, or the "trappings" of their official posts, they lack influence with and respect from the populace.

International Aid and the "Second Civil Service." In fiscal year 2003/04 (1382), total Government expenditures, including ordinary and development budgets, reached \$2.0 billion. The international community funded all but about \$208 million of this, or approximately 89 percent, and most external assistance is not channeled through the Government's Treasury (see Box 4.2). Among other implications, this has resulted in a "second civil service" consisting of NGOs, consultants, advisors, and employees of UN and other international agencies, including expatriate consultants and Afghans attracted by relatively high salaries. Not only has this second civil service taken some of the best talent from the Government, but with the relatively small share of resources at the Government's disposal, it is a constant challenge for the Government to stay "in charge"

Box 4.2. The Berlin Security and Rule of Law Declaration

At the March 2004 International Conference on Afghanistan, security was one of the key themes for international deliberation. The Government committed to finalizing a National Security Reform Strategy prior to the Presidential election. The plans presented were ambitious and included:

- Demobilization of 40 percent of Afghan militia forces (using stated troop strength as the base) by June 2004 (the previous scheduled date for presidential elections), including the decommissioning of military units.
- Agreement that NATO and the Coalition deploy international military forces in support of the national police and Afghan National Army (ANA)—including to other regional cities.
- Extending full cooperation to the Independent Afghan Human Rights Commission (IAHRC).
- Strengthening Afghanistan's institutional capacity to meet its reporting obligations under the international instruments to which Afghanistan is a party.
- Developing human rights monitoring, documenting, and reporting mechanisms with the international community.
- Establishing a Supreme Court according to the Constitution with the necessary capacity to fulfill its mandate.
- Strengthening the administrative and financial management capacity of justice institutions.
- Accelerating the legislative reform process through adoption of key laws that would be compatible with the Constitution, including laws and procedures on the organization of judicial offices, criminal, civil codes and a penitentiary law.
- Establishing a national legal training center.

of the development agenda. There is a tendency for the various agendas of the international aid community to shape broader public policy and influence planning processes—intentionally or not. As public administration reforms move ahead, it will be crucial for longer-term sustainability for donors to work within the existing Government administration and budget, so that they reinforce efforts to strengthen the civil service rather than inadvertently undermine it. Furthermore, as the costs of running this second civil service are significantly higher than current civil service pay levels, the sustainability of such an approach needs to be carefully assessed.

The Strategy

Government in Afghanistan faces a twin challenge. On the one hand, it must be fully in charge of running the state—which means that Government must be capable of both making policy and implementing it throughout the country. On the other hand, it must not overstate its ability—and should limit its policy ambitions to its still limited though growing capacity.

Afghanistan's policy ambitions are laid out in the NDF, which articulates a clear vision of the role of government as limited to creating an enabling environment and providing only the most essential services. The NDF also recognizes that achieving even this focused vision will require an effective national government that re-establishes the unity of the country on the basis of strong institutions and rule of law, and through a sound national budget. In the more recent SAF document, specific goals on the role of government are laid out, including:

i. A well functioning and well structured security sector, based on institutions that facilitate a return to normalcy in the political, economic, and social spheres (Box 4.2).
ii. A public administration that is small and focused on core functions; more diverse and decentralized; better skilled, equipped, and managed; more accountable; and more representative in terms of gender and ethnicity.
iii. A budget that is affordable and sustainable on a multi-year basis, is used as the central policy instrument of the Government, and enables delegation of authority based on strong accountability mechanisms.

National programs have been formulated, within the framework of the national budget, that support the overall state building strategy. The Afghanistan Stabilization Program (ASP), for example, offers an integrated strategy for addressing security, governance, and reconstruction challenges at the provincial and district levels. The ASP recognizes the integrated nature of the political, security, fiscal, and administrative and other reconstruction-related problems facing Afghanistan. It responds to the clear demand from the majority of Afghans for an alternative to the power of regional and local power-holders and for the establishment of a strong central government. While these wishes are often expressed in terms of a desire for a centralized state, this does not necessarily imply a centralization of operations, with all activities based in Kabul. In fact, the strategy requires some modest delegation, although not broad-based decentralization.

Key Accomplishments

A number of important steps have already been taken toward the achievement of these strategic goals, in particular with respect to the Constitution, budget, economic management, and security sector reforms. These core reforms underpin the state building agenda.

The New Constitution. The process to establish democratic political institutions was laid out in the 2001 Bonn Agreement. Two Loya Jirgas have been held, the first to elect a President by secret ballot, the second to ratify a new Constitution. The Constitution establishes a unitary state with a strong central government, providing for a democratically elected President and for separation of powers among the judiciary, executive, and legislative branches. The Government is allowed to delegate certain authorities to local administrative units (provinces) in the areas of economic, social, and cultural affairs, and to increase the participation of the people in development. To this end, it establishes a role for elected provincial, district, and village level councils to work with the sub-national administration. Municipalities are to administer city affairs under the oversight of elected mayors and municipal councils. The Presidential election was successfully held in October 2004, while elections to the National Assembly have been delayed by about six months. A Joint Electoral Management Board ran the Presidential election, including the Afghanistan Interim Electoral Commission and a UN support unit. The process of voter registration was remarkably successful, with some 10.6 million voter registrations occurring in

Afghanistan, more than 40 percent of them women. Despite security concerns, voter turnout in the Presidential election was generally good.

A Stronger Security Sector. To date, progress in security sector reform (SSR) has been limited, and greater efforts are required to extend the rule of law beyond Kabul into major regional cities and the provinces. There have however been some modest achievements. As of early 1383 (mid-2004): (i) DDR had been initiated and over 10,925 former soldiers disarmed and demobilized; (ii) the Counter Narcotics Directorate and Counter-Narcotics Police had been established and a National Drugs Control Strategy adopted; (iii) 7–8,000 police had been fully trained with police academies established in Kabul, Gardez, Kandahar, Kunduz, and Mazar-i-Sharif; (iv) reforms had been initiated with respect to the staffing and structure of the Ministry of Defense; (v) 9,500 soldiers had been recruited to the ANA; and (vi) some early judicial reforms had been initiated. Despite these actions, the security situation across much of the country has deteriorated, interfering with the Government's state-building agenda. Further, the demilitarization of Kabul, mandated by the Bonn Agreement, has not yet been fully implemented. A strong commitment to security sector reform was made at the Berlin International Conference (see Box 4.2 and Afghanistan Government 2004c).

Currency Reform and Monetary Policy. A major early achievement was the introduction of a new currency within the first six months of the Transitional Administration. Since then, monetary policy has been restrained, supported by adherence to strong fiscal discipline and a "no overdraft" rule that prohibits Central Bank financing of the deficit.

Revenue and Customs Collection. Domestic revenues have increased significantly during the past two years, reaching $163 million in 2002/03, a level higher than expected in part because of exceptional revenues such as telecom licenses. As targeted, revenues reached $208 million in 2003/04, largely as a result of the Government's political will to start effectively controlling revenues collected in the provinces.

The Budget as a Policy Instrument and Aid Coordination Tool. Since it came into office, the Government stated its intention to use the budget as a policy instrument and an aid coordination tool. After a first, rudimentary budget in 2002/03 and a much improved budget process in 2003/04, the most recent budget, for 2004/05, has been underpinned by a better analytical base and a more participatory process in the Cabinet. The 2004/05 budget signals, or confirms, that a number of key policy decisions have been taken (see Box 4.3). These include a significant effort to increase revenues, continuing the "no overdraft" commitment (to refrain from domestic deficit financing) as well as a substantial budget increase in education to recruit teachers. Furthermore, a new policy to deliver health services by contracting their provision to NGOs (basic package of health services, funded through the development budget) has been put in place. The ongoing commitment to pay and administrative reforms (with a $34 million provision for PRR departments, discussed below) has been confirmed, and the PRR process is now fully operational and has made considerable progress. On the security side, the Government has sought to increase the size of security forces (police and army) and finance their cost directly through the budget.

Box 4.3. Improvements in the Budget

The national budget has two components (see the figure below). The core budget includes all funds flowing through the Treasury, while donors directly execute the external budget. For the first time in 2004/05, The definition of a core budget unifies the budget flowing through the Treasury, with total expenditures fully funded by domestic revenues and external assistance (fast disbursing loans, project loans and grants, and reimbursements from ARTF and LOTFA). Within the core budget, operating expenditures include the wage bill, most non-salary recurrent costs, and some capital expenditures. Development expenditures include all technical assistance, most capital expenditures, and some recurrent costs (for example, health services contracted out). Operating expenditures are structured around ministries, while development expenditures are composed of projects structured around development programs (from the National Development Framework and the National Priority Programs).

All projects in the core budget have an identified source of financing, while some projects in the external budget are partially funded. The Government expects that it will mobilize more resources than budgeted expenditures: the expected additional funding is set aside for the National Priority Programs and for co-financing existing projects and will be allocated during the fiscal year.

Further progress toward an integrated budget involves securing funding for projects earlier in the year so that more projects are included in the original core budget (which requires projects to be at an advanced stage of design), and channeling a higher share of external assistance through the Treasury so that monitoring and reporting processes are standardized. Further integration of the budget also requires that ordinary expenditures match some of the features of development expenditures, including having a multi-year horizon and program basis.

1382 Expenditure Structure and Financing

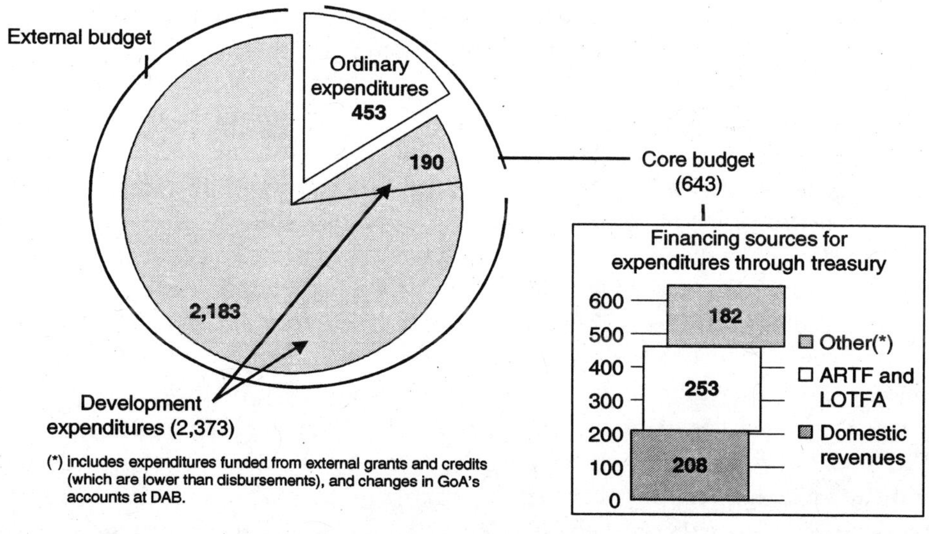

These are estimates as accounts have not yet been finalized.

Source: Ministry of Finance, Staff estimates.

Using the national budget to coordinate aid is sensible but complex. Unified planning, management, and control of expenditures—whether funded from domestic resources or external assistance—makes sense. Yet, the budget thereby includes projects over which the Government has little control with its announced policies. Also, earmarking donor funds for specific projects undermines the scope and possibility for Government prioritizing between programs and projects.

Priority Reform and Restructuring Decree. On July 10, 2003, the Government passed the Priority Reform and Restructuring (PRR) Decree, creating the primary vehicle for reforming and modernizing the most critical functions of government. The PRR process permits ministries and agencies or functions within them to place key staff on an elevated pay scale for a fixed term, and provides funds to obtain technical assistance for restructuring and re-engineering.

Work in Progress

Key Responsibilities

Overall responsibility for public administration reform (PAR) rests with the IARCSC, established in June 2003 with responsibility for appointments and appeals, civil service management, and administrative reform. It is now staffed at one-third of its projected complement. The IARCSC is pivotal to achieving significant improvements throughout the civil service, especially in human resources management, and specifically in embedding the principle and practice of merit-based recruitment and promotion. Therefore, getting the IARCSC fully staffed and effective is an urgent priority.

The Ministerial Advisory Committee (MAC) on Public Administration Reform supports the Chair of the IARCSC. Its role is to provide advice on reform proposals—for example approval of PRR applications—and on dealing with problems and issues that may hamper progress. Members of the MAC include all the core central Ministries and, on a rotating basis, line ministries at the forefront of reform. The Committee therefore provides an important degree of political legitimacy for the difficult choices that must inevitably be made.

The Ministry of Finance (MoF) is central for fiscal and economic management reform. It has adopted the PRR framework on a department-by-department basis, focusing first on the departments responsible for key reforms. Almost all key functions in Kabul have now obtained PRR status. As the next step, the Ministry plans to extend PRR to the provincial Mustoufiats (finance departments). The aim is to bring the whole of the Ministry within the PRR framework soon. This will achieve the following objectives: (i) improved administration and management of all key departments; (ii) significant downsizing with surplus staff redeployed; (iii) strengthened middle and senior management capacity across the departments; and (iv) confirmation of actual employment and resolution of problems with ghost workers, and multiple payments of salaries.

Ongoing Reforms

A number of reform initiatives are well underway, largely under the framework of the PAR program, covering seven major components: civil service legal framework; personnel management, institutional and functional streamlining and development; financial management and machinery of government; administrative efficiency; and improvement of government physical infrastructure. Some of the more significant reforms are discussed below.

PRR Program. This is the Government's central vehicle for reforming key functions. As of October 2004, 66 functions in eleven ministries, one department in Kabul Municipality, Da Afghanistan Bank (the Central Bank), the Central Statistics Office, and the IARCSC had received stage two approvals. A further 37 functions in sixteen ministries and one department in the Office of the President had received stage one approvals. A monitoring tool is being developed which will enable the IARCSC and the MAC to take stock at regular intervals of the impact of PRR. Looking forward, the rollout of the PRR process to the provinces is a critical next step. Some initial forays have begun, in the Offices of the Governors in five provinces, and in provincial departments of the Ministry of Public Health. But this also presents a major challenge. In particular, there is a risk of political capture of the PRR process by regional and local warlords given the lack of presence of the IARCSC at the provincial level and the difficulty in effective monitoring outside of Kabul. Nevertheless, the PRR process will continue to be an important vehicle for building capacity within the Government.

A major issue in civil service reform is the very low public sector salaries, especially at middle and senior levels, exacerbated by competition for local staff from international aid agencies and NGOs. There have been strong arguments to increase salaries at all levels, as well as to decompress the salary scale, all within the context of very limited fiscal resources. During 1382 the Government made a series of decisions to increase pay levels for teachers, police, and other civil servants. The pay increase for general civil servants, shown in Table 4.1, provides for some decompression of the wage scale. In addition, a new "Interim Additional Allowance" has been established as part of the PRR program. By the end of October 2004, 7,900 posts had received PRR approval for the new pay scale. Some 10,000 posts could realistically be approved by the end of 1383 with adequate technical assistance, perhaps as many as 15,000. The IARCSC is introducing merit-based recruitment at the senior levels, and is launching a comprehensive pay and grading review, which will likely lead to a decompressed pay scale patterned on the additional pay awards provided under the PRR. A key challenge for the IARCSC will be to manage comprehensive pay reform within the context of the higher paid "second civil service." To meet critical capacity gaps in the civil service, the Government has approved the Afghan Expatriate Program under the ARTF, which enables the recruitment of professional and technical Afghans from the diaspora to take up advisory positions. The Lateral Entry Program opens a window through which to inject professional and technically qualified Afghans into line government positions for 1–2 years at salary levels that are comparable to those in the NGO and international agency labor market in Afghanistan and the regional labor market, especially Pakistan and Iran. These two windows complement the PRR initiative.

Accountability mechanisms comprise two principal components: enforcing individual compliance to fiduciary standards and ensuring transparency and public access to information (Table 4.2). The Government has begun to put in place elements of a legal framework to ensure that civil servants are accountable for the execution of their duties. The proposed Public Finance and Expenditure Management Law provides specific penalties to be applied by a civil court to any civil servant who uses his or her position for material gain

Table 4.1. General Pay Levels (Afs/Month)

	General civil servants		PRR reformed depts.[1]	
Grade	Total pay before pay rise[2]	Total pay after pay rise	PRR scale	PRR total pay
"beyond"	2,019	3,279	A	13,417
"above"	1,955	2,975	B	11,893
1	1,908	2,688	C	10,486
2	1,888	2,548	D	9,056
3	1,873	2,443	D	9,041
4	1,856	2,324	E	7,614
5	1,848	2,268	E	7,606
6	1,840	2,212	F	6,188
7	1,835	2,177	F	6,183
8	1,829	2,135	F	6,177
9	1,824	2,100	U	1,824
10	1,818	2,058	U	1,818

Notes:
1. The distribution of PRR grades shown is illustrative. There is intentionally no simple mapping of PRR grades onto the existing pay scales as staff should be considered individually as new job descriptions are prepared.
2. A general pay rise was approved in the eighth month of SY1382. Excludes teachers and police.

Source: Evans and other (2004a).

Table 4.2. Examples of Accountability Mechanisms in Proposed Laws

Laws	Individual accountability: Enforce penalties on individuals	Collective accountability: Transparency and public access to information:
Civil service law	Code of conduct to deal with conflict of interest.	IARCSC reports on the quality of recruitment processes.
Public finance and expenditure Management law	Penalties for civil servants who use their position for material gain.	Public release of reports on budget execution; mandatory use of Treasury Single Account; mandatory external audit.
Procurement law	Penalties for civil servants who use their position for material gain. Exclusion of contractors from bidding process after misconduct is proved.	Open, competitive, transparent bidding process (with public notice ex ante and ex post).
Audit law	Code of ethics for external auditor.	Independence of the external auditor; guaranteed access to information for external auditor; mandatory external audit released to public; mandatory response from the Government.

or otherwise abuses the position. The proposed Procurement Law is expected to have similar provisions. The draft Civil Service Law will include a code of conduct with conflict of interest rules and other provisions. Reforms to the Auditor General's Office and Attorney General's Office need greater support. Enforcement will depend on the establishment of effective mechanisms within IARCSC and Ministry of Finance.

Accountability is not just an issue for civil servants; ultimately ministers are accountable for the actions of their departments, and for executing their responsibilities with honesty, integrity, and impartiality. A draft Ministerial Code of Conduct is soon to be adopted. Ensuring that reports of the independent auditor and the Cabinet's responses are available to the National Assembly is an important part of the accountability framework. The Constitution also calls for the wealth of the President, vice presidents, ministers, members of the Supreme Court, and the Attorney General to be registered and monitored. This is not a simple provision to implement, but a review of mechanisms that could be suitable for Afghanistan would be useful.

The Afghanistan Stabilization Program (ASP). This is a major new initiative, intended to bring together both existing and new efforts to improve security and governance throughout the country, targeted first at the most sensitive locations. The ASP is the first major effort to build capacity at the provincial level, and is somewhat reflective of the selective approach adopted by the PRR. It is also a significant departure from more traditional donor-centered project delivery mechanisms. It will use coordinating mechanisms to bring together Government and donors, but implementation of most of the specific components will be done through ministries. While funding will be managed separately from the Government's ordinary budget, the intention is to pool donor funds and work through local administration, such as the Mustoufiats, as much as possible. In fact, an important aspect of the program will be to build financial and administrative capacity at the local level through hands-on involvement. In particular, the Provincial Reconstruction and Development Fund will be managed out of the provincial Governor's office, providing an opportunity to build capacity for managing small projects.

Rationalization of Ministries. The Government is planning to reduce the number of ministries (currently 29) in order to focus on the core functions of government, eliminate the current overlap and duplication between ministries, and optimize the use of scarce skills and resources. Although no decision has been announced at time of writing, the number of ministries could be significantly reduced in the short run, go down to 20 later, and possibly even be reduced to 15 in the longer run. Although the process of implementing a realignment of ministries is not a simple one, it offers an important opportunity to push the PRR process further, and use it to ensure that the new organizations are more effective.

Coordinating Aid. Managing aid flows is a daunting task in a post-conflict context, for at least three reasons. First, their magnitude is very high (about 37 percent of non-drug GDP disbursed in 2003/04, more than 150 percent of GDP pledged in the Berlin Conference for the next three years). Second, they are delivered through various channels (including at least direct bilateral assistance, grants to multilateral trust funds, and grants and concessional lending from development banks). Third, they rely on heterogeneous allocation mechanisms (different budget timing, diverse country priorities and interests). The Government has taken a phased approach to coordinating aid. It started by recording all proposed and on-going projects in its development budget. Then it linked the development budget to its development strategy (initially formulated in the NDF and refined in the SAF report). As an additional step, in 2004/05 the core budget has been defined to include only funds flowing through the Treasury: in the core budget, all development expenditures have adequate financing. Thus the development budget has moved from little more than an aggregation of what donors are planning to do ("project shopping list") to a demand-driven expenditure program ("prioritized project list").

Improving Budget Implementation. The budget can be a useful policy tool only if it is properly implemented. Significant progress has been made developing institutions and systems to raise fiduciary standards, including implementation of the Afghanistan Financial Management Information System in Treasury; creation of the Central Procurement Facility; and initial preparation of procurement, public finance and expenditure management, and audit laws. Moving forward, the proposed reforms to strengthen accountability mechanisms (see above) will develop institutions and systems that give civil servants the incentives and tools to use public resources effectively. These reforms will also reduce corruption, and give comfort to donors to channel their assistance through the Treasury and through budget support.

The quality of expenditures in provinces, in particular, is critical both to deliver public services and to give the state an effective and accountable face. Progress has been made in paying salaries with smaller delays, but much remains to be done to certify the legitimacy of all paid employees. While centralization of payroll processes after the fall of the Taliban was an important step to start payroll payments, the re-decentralization to provinces should address the issues of delays and legitimacy. Progress on non-salary payments has been uneven. In an effort to improve cash management, the Government replaced all provincial accounts with a single revenue and an expenditure account in 2003. Without the right to spend directly the revenues they collected, provinces were fully dependent on Kabul to make non-salary payments. Since then, a system of cash advance has been set up to expedite these payments. However, there are apparently still constraints, and provinces collecting large revenues have been able to spend more on non-salary items than others (Table 4.3). In 2004/05, the Government is committed to ease another constraint—the low level of allotments for non-salary expenditures in provinces. The Afghanistan Stabilization Program will also facilitate expenditures outside Kabul.

Increasing Domestic Revenue Mobilization. If Afghanistan is to have a fiscally sustainable budget, it will need to greatly increase domestic revenue. The SAF target is for domestic revenues to cover the Government wage bill by 2008/09. In the short run, additional revenues will reduce transaction costs from heavy aid dependence: even with better aid coordination and budget systems, external financing will remain fragmented, uncertain, and often inflexible. Domestic revenues have increased from $132 million in 2002/03 to almost $208 million in 2003/04 (Table 4.4), with a stretch target of $300 million for 2004/05. Much remains to be done to augment the revenue base and ensure that all revenues due are collected and remitted to the center. Special efforts are required in provinces collecting most of the revenues, which may have been "captured" by regional powerbrokers.

Table 4.3. SY1382 Budget Execution

	Revenues		Allotment		Expenditures			
	Total	% total	Total	% non salary	Salary	Non salary	Total	% non salary
	US$ million	%	US$ million	%	US$ million	US$ million	US$ million	%
Centre	73	35	280	55	115	124	239	52
Provinces	135	65	185	28	118	72	189	38
Heart	84	40	15	25	12	33	45	74
4 other provinces with large revenues	41	20	55	31	36	19	54	34
Other provinces	10	5	115	28	71	20	90	22
Total	208	100	465	45	233	196	429	46

Source: Information provided by Ministry of Finance, Government of Afghanistan; staff estimates.

Table 4.4. Domestic Revenues

	2003/04 Revenue (est.)	
	(US$ million)	(% total)
Import duties	111	54
Other Tax Revenues	20	9
Tax Revenues	*131*	*63*
Administrative fees	37	18
Sales	31	15
Other Non Tax Revenues	9	4
Non Tax Revenues	*77*	*37*
Total	**208**	**100**

Source: Information provided by Ministry of Finance, Government of Afghanistan; staff estimates.

A key element in the effort to raise revenues is the Customs reforms adopted in 2003 (use of market exchange rates for import valuation and streamlined tariff structure—moving from 25 tariff rates of 0–150 percent to six rates ranging between 2.5 percent and 16 percent). Combined with better compliance at border posts, this reform is expected to generate $26 million in additional revenue in 2004/05. New tax policy reforms enacted in 2004 (a final wage withholding tax on higher income employees, an improved income tax regime, a streamlined business establishment tax, a tax on a limited range of services consumed by high income earners, a rent tax, a land tax, and an airport departure tax) are expected to generate an additional $14 million.

The Ministry of Finance is creating a "Large Taxpayer Office" in Kabul to focus on revenue collection from the top 100 tax-paying entities. In addition, there are plans to create units in the provinces for medium-sized taxpayers, reporting directly to the Ministry in Kabul.

Table 4.5. Revenues (Percent of GDP)

	Afghanistan		Post-conflict countries	
	1975	2003	Y1-3 after conflict	Y3-5 after conflict
Taxes	7.1	2.4	11.2	12.6
Of which direct taxes	1.1	0.1	n/a	n/a
Of which import duties	5.5	2.9	n/a	n/a
Non tax revenues	3.3	1.7	3.8	5.8
Total revenues	**10.4**	**4.6**	**14.9**	**18.4**

Source: Information provided by Ministry of Finance, Government of Afghanistan; World Bank (1978 and 2004f).

Turning to the longer term, based on Afghanistan's history and a comparison with other post-conflict countries, a target of 12.5 percent of GDP, as indicated in the SAF report, is plausible (Table 4.5). The critical question is the pace at which Afghanistan can mobilize additional resources. International evidence suggests that continual significant yearly increases in revenue to GDP ratios are difficult to achieve over a long period of time. In the case of Afghanistan, two factors will be critical.

i. *Security and administrative capacity.* As discussed above, the first priority is for the Government to fully regain control of the existing revenue base. Assessing and collecting taxes throughout the country requires strong administrative capacity, including buildings, enforcement capacity, information systems, and skills. In particular, further growth in Customs revenues will be predicated on greater Government ability to control its borders. Focusing on large taxpayers and on the main provinces in terms of revenue collection should provide quick results, but significantly scaling up resource mobilization will require considerable administrative efforts.

ii. *Nature of economic growth.* The structure of the economy also will be critical (see Chapter 1). The informal sector is difficult to tax, although the existing presumptive taxes (e.g. on shops, mills, buses), while probably too complex, provide a means to tax informal businesses. Agricultural taxation can also be considered (for example, taxing the largest landlords), but its administration costs tend to be very high. The nature of economic growth also matters because promising taxes could vanish (import duties if trade is reduced by trade policy decisions in neighboring countries) or materialize very slowly (mineral taxation) if a sector does not grow rapidly.

Some Key Tasks Ahead

Controlling corruption and enhancing security and the rule of law are among the key tasks ahead. The positive impact of these factors on growth is analyzed in Chapter 1, and they are critical as well for poverty reduction, state building, and building popular loyalty toward the state.

Addressing Corruption

In the short run corruption—defined as the abuse of public position for private gain—undermines the nascent institutions of state, rule of law, and democracy and justice. Over the longer term corruption will also jeopardize the attainment of broad-based and sustainable economic development objectives. Corruption is one of the major constraints to private enterprise, particularly in South Asia where nearly two-thirds of firms report making "irregular payments" to get things done, and for smaller firms. Of notable concern in Afghanistan are the close links between corruption and the drug industry and other criminal activities.

A Typology of Corruption. Building on the classification of economic activities in Chapter 1, Table 4.6 provides an overview of the likely linkages between different types of economic activity and associated corruption. While Afghanistan is a *de jure* unitary state, the national government maintains only marginal control over many provinces. With the adoption of the 2004 Afghan Constitution, any provincial Governor or other

Table 4.6. Economic Activities and Probable Associations with Corruption

	Activities	Market transaction	Output	Production/ distribution	Recognized by law/ regulated/ taxable	Key actors (examples)	Associated corruption
Private sector	Formal	Yes	Legal	Legal	Yes	Small, medium and large private firms	Probably high: officials paid to avoid tax, for licensing and/ planning applications, etc.
	Extra-legal	Yes	Legal	Legal	No	Construction companies; hawalas	Probably low—nothing to bribe to obtain
	Irregular	Yes	Legal	Illegal	No	Smugglers	Probably moderate—e.g. bribes paid to customs staff
	Illegal	Yes	Illegal	Illegal	No	Poppy, arms and human traffickers	Probably high—bribes paid to provincial officials and police.
Public sector	Constitutional	Some	Legal	Legal	Yes	"Official" Government bodies	Probably high in procurement, in ghost employment, and in patronage positions. Extensive theft of public resources in past.
	"Captured"	Some	Legal	Legal	Partly	Autonomized provinces like Herart and Balkh.	Variable, but could be high in some cases.

Source: Based on Thomas (1992); Box 1.1.

power-holder using political or military force to maintain power, status, or wealth must officially be viewed as illegitimate. In the current transitional situation, such parallel (or autonomous) governance structures are perhaps best described as the "captured" public sector. There are differing views as to whether such autonomous structures are likely to be involved in high levels of administrative corruption, but anecdotal evidence suggests that this is likely.

Toward a Strategy. Public sector corruption associated with private sector activities is the product of either unenforceable or weak regulations, so re-regulating activities or deregulation to match weak enforcement capacity is called for. For the public sector, actions required include enforcing penalties on individuals for corruption, improving transparency and public access to information, and simplifying processes to deter collusive relationships. In March 2004 President Karzai, aware that levels of corruption were damaging public perceptions of the Government, ordered the establishment of an anti-corruption department.

Private Sector Regulation. The formal private sector is made up of small, medium, and large companies, which pay bribes to central, provincial, and municipal government officials (see Box 4.4 for some examples) to avoid payment of taxes and get around certain regulations—many of which are archaic. Anecdotal evidence indicates that bribes are paid by larger companies to ministry and municipal staff to gain planning approval, to obtain investment licenses, and to smooth the importation of goods and their smuggling to other countries.

Irregular private sector activities involve illegal mechanisms of production or distribution and so provide great incentives for corruption, as officials must be persuaded to turn a blind eye. The most notable example is smuggling, including re-export of imported goods to Pakistan, import of petroleum products, and export of lumber to Pakistan and northern neighbors of Afghanistan. Bribes to smooth the way in making transactions are probably very common. The most prominent example of corruption associated with the

Box 4.4. "Water is Muddy from the Source"

This Afghan saying refers to corruption, which is endemic and often seen as a normal requirement for business. Bribery is widely considered to be common among the police force, within the judiciary, in public utilities, and in public enterprises. Below are some examples:

- A resident of east Kabul said he had to pay $500 in bribes before he could begin reconstruction of his family's house, $260 to the local police and $240 to city planning officials.
- A Supreme Court deputy acknowledges that bribery exists among the judiciary. By way of justification, he said that judges in other countries are paid high salaries to discourage them from resorting to accepting bribes.
- A senior official of the anti-crime department at the Ministry of Interior all but concedes that corruption is rampant in Afghanistan. "We have information that bribery is common within government and that bribery takes place in all government institutions."
- A petrol station owner says he paid $4,000 dollars in bribes to city and police officials when he was setting up his business.

illegal private sector relates to the opium economy, where systematic bribery, concealment, and money laundering are required among producers, local officials, and drug traffickers (see Chapter 7). The Hawala system is a good example of extra-legal private sector economic activity. Associated public sector corruption is probably low as there are no licenses or permissions that a briber needs to obtain.

The challenge is to regulate private sector activities only to the extent that is strictly necessary for economic or security reasons, and only to the degree that the regulators are able to match with enforcement. Unenforceable regulations will simply redefine extra-legal activities as irregular—and thereby increase corruption.

Public Sector Activities. Administrative corruption is doubtless found across the public sector, and any strategy needs to involve a twin-track approach of re-regulating and de-regulating private sector activities to reduce incentives and opportunities for corruption, while simultaneously increasing public sector staff accountability through enforcing penalties on individuals for corruption and improving transparency and public access to information (see Table 4.2 above). Theft of public resources—both cash and other assets—undoubtedly has been a significant problem. Improving accountability and simplifying and automating business processes will assist in removing opportunities for collusive relationships between officials and members of the public, and between officials responsible for releasing funds.[3] In the "captured" public sector, pending political normalization under the Constitution a primary focus should be on building the legitimacy of municipalities as honest service providers, as a counterbalance to de facto provincial authorities and "captured" provincial administrations.

Enhancing Security and the Rule of Law[4]

Insecurity, in all its forms, is an extremely serious problem in Afghanistan. The almost total absence of well-trained and accountable police and judiciary services has led to a culture of security violations and impunity. The existence of tribal militias, security forces loyal to regional power brokers, drug mafias, and terrorist bands fosters insecurity and leads to tensions between these forces and the modest security forces loyal to the Government. Other aspects of insecurity include uncertainties about land tenure (see Box 6.3 in Chapter 6) and lack of a supportive legal system for enforcing property rights. Improving security is a critical element of the growth strategy (Chapter 1), and the recent mini investment climate survey heard from investors that, in places like Mazar-i-Sharif, security remains the major constraint to expansion of businesses (Chapter 5). In this context, achievements in security sector reform have lagged far behind what is required to consolidate the early gains made in state building. Many provinces remain largely autonomous from the Government, and efforts to disarm militias, in sequence with the creation of a national army and police force, must be substantially stepped up if insecurity is to be substantially reduced. Outside Kabul, different powerbrokers and non-Constitutional authorities have varying degrees of power and loyalty to Kabul, and are in

3. For example, business re-engineering within the Ministry of Finance reportedly has significantly reduced levels of corruption, particularly in the Treasury.
4. This section draws mainly from Afghanistan Government (2004b, Chapter 6; and 2004c).

competition with each other. A broad assessment of the current writ of the national government across the provinces and border areas highlights the lack of formal state control and the continued co-existence of opposing military forces in the south (elements of the former Taliban) and to a lesser extent in the north.

Enhancing security and the rule of law requires two main thrusts. First, and probably most essential, hearts and minds must be won to achieve a reasonable degree of consensus on the authority of the national government. This requires gaining political, civil servant, and citizen loyalty to Kabul. Second, enforcement capacity must be adequate with a workable judiciary and police force (with military back-up). The current co-existence of formal and informal justice arrangements across Afghanistan is a manifestation of the fragmentation of security, and the critical need for reforms to reclaim popular and national ownership of judiciary services, thereby reducing the prevalence of rough justice under the control of warlords and commanders. Reform efforts need to focus on building core capabilities of judiciary services through legal reforms, capacity building, and new recruitment.

Winning Loyalty. Lack of loyalty to Kabul by some provincial Governors and regional powerbrokers, whose militia forces maintain only a semblance of security while being involved at least indirectly in permitting extortion, criminal activities, and drug smuggling, has a significant impact on all segments of society—rich and poor. In the past year alone, thousands of security incidents have taken place across the country, claiming the lives of nearly 1,000 civilians, peace keepers, and aid workers. Human rights abuses, including rape and human trafficking (of women and children), have gone unpunished. Criminal acts do not reach the courts. Moreover, the existence of warlords and militia alongside the national government creates disunity, allows crimes to go unpunished, and encourages illegal activities.

Some of the political interests resisting re-imposition of national authority have deep roots and need to be dealt with accordingly. Yet, weaknesses in fiscal and administrative arrangements contribute to the problematic politics. Delays in payment of civil servants' salaries, under-provision of non-salary budgets, and a high-handed central administration provide provinces with an excuse to not remit revenues to the central Treasury. This contributes to inequalities between provinces, and allows the Governors or local powerholders in resource-rich provinces to claim credit for services with funds diverted from the Government Exchequer. Ill-equipped, poorly paid, and ineffective provincial and district administrations suffer from poor morale and undermine the image of the national government in the eyes of the people. They cannot do their jobs, or are forced to depend on local commanders or other local political elites who provide funds, thereby further entrenching the power of these interests. Getting funds out to the provinces and districts is therefore critical for the national government, not only to improve service delivery but also to shore up weak loyalties to Kabul. Poll research suggests that there is strong public attachment to the idea of central government—even though citizens are aware of its limited capacity. However, lack of evident Government functionality at provincial and local levels and slow visible progress in reconstruction are doubtless eroding this.

Weak government administration thus contributes to a vicious circle, further eroding loyalty to Kabul with adverse effects on the enforcement of rule of law and revenue collection. Not only are senior police officers usually appointed by local commanders, but police forces are being weakened by the accommodation of large numbers of former combatants in them. These demobilized forces are usually untrained, often unqualified, and therefore lack the capacity to function as professional police. The lack of professional security forces loyal to the center increases the reliance of administrators on local commanders for security. Timely expansion of international forces into the major cities, as well as the further expansion of PRTs and the ASP, will also be very important.

Building Enforcement Capacity. The SAF report suggests that building the capacity of the police has, to date, been limited by poor coordination between the main stakeholders in the police reform process. In addition, military support for the police, whether in the form of PRTs or a detachment of the International Security Assistance Force (ISAF), has been inadequate to provide a secure environment for police reform and capacity-building (the expansion of ISAF out of Kabul to other major urban locations has been extremely limited so far). There are reported to be capacity problems in the Ministry of Interior, as well as difficulties in the chain of command and its perceived legitimacy given ethnic imbalances in staffing. Funding shortfalls, affecting both the major security programs and the Interior Ministry's recurrent budget, also have hindered the reform process. For the judiciary, key steps include basic infrastructure in the main provincial capitals and districts, with adequate security for magistrates. Revision of rules and procedures for appointment, promotion, disciplinary action, and transfer of magistrates to ensure their independence, basic databases of caseload and court decisions, and reconstruction and capacity building in correctional facilities are needed.

The Way Forward

Continue and Deepen Ongoing Core Reforms

Public Administration. Considerable progress has been made in public administration reform, including the creation of the IARCSC and the PRR program. Beginning to address pay issues through PRR has had an important incentive effect. The introduction of merit-based recruitment through the IARCSC will be an important next step.

In order to develop a professional civil service, one of the key challenges for the IARCSC is to develop a top management group, working together to lead and manage the implementation of civil service reform. Developing such a top management cadre requires that employees with potential to rise to the top are identified early, and tested in a series of challenging positions during the course of their careers. Major, long-term investments are required to meet these needs, including the establishment of a permanent training institution. In the short run a sizeable injection will be required of competent staff on short-term contracts who can be placed in key positions where they are able to play a pivotal and authoritative role.

It will take time for reforms to have a significant impact at the sub-national level, where services are actually being delivered. In addition, civil service reforms need to go beyond basic capacity building, so that the roles, responsibilities, and accountability structures among central units and local administration better reflect the Government's service delivery model (see Chapter 8). While recognizing that the pace of change has to be realistic, delegation of more administrative decision-making closer to where services are being delivered is needed. The ASP offers a vehicle for this, in a way that responds to needs and readiness.

The rationalization of the Cabinet's structure also provides an opportunity to clarify roles and accountabilities.

National Security. Post-conflict experience suggests that security sector reform—including international security provision—is the key investment in the early post-conflict years (see World Bank 2003a). Progress will need to occur within the following broad framework:

i. *A Unified Security Framework:* Greater international support is needed for a unified security framework, where national and international stakeholders adopt a clear reform plan, based on national consensus and national institutions. Currently, security objectives are not fully shared between domestic stakeholders (internecine conflict) and international partners (fight against terrorism). Efforts to bring all security spending within the national budget framework are also needed to make it more accountable.
ii. *Ownership in Building Center-Periphery Relations:* Enhanced national ownership of the reform process is needed, including a focus on strengthening center-periphery relations.
iii. *DDR:* DDR objectives need to be realigned as there is neither a standing army to disarm, nor an adequate national army in existence to fill the security vacuum created; there needs to be a focus on demobilization of commanders, not just their troops—otherwise DDR may not prove sustainable.
iv. *Priority Reforms and Restructuring:* Administrative reform within the Ministries of Interior, Defense and Justice is of the highest priority, and the PRR program should be stepped up in these institutions.
v. *Justice:* Reforms in the area of Justice are critical for sustained economic growth, private sector development, combating drugs, and resolving land disputes. Progress with strengthening and reform of the justice sector has lagged so far, however. Given the multiplicity of justice arrangements, it is necessary to install new capacities at central and sub-national levels, and more generally to establish a sound formal justice system. The traditional informal justice system, although widely used and having some advantages, becomes highly inequitable and vulnerable to corruption where it is controlled by warlords and factional commanders.
vi. *Army and Police:* Training of the new national army and police needs to proceed on a fast track, but in line with building such capacities, provincial and district government capacities will need to be strengthened around the provincial Governor's office, including through the ASP.

Fiscal Management. Over the medium term, cautious budget management is required to prepare for the eventual decline in external aid. It is necessary to properly cost proposed policies, integrate the ordinary and development budgets, and develop a multi-year fiscal framework:

i. *Health and Education.* In education the multi-year implications of recruiting large numbers of teachers should be costed, taking into account the impact on the wage bill and needs for training and equipment. For health, integrating the ordinary and development budgets in a multi-year framework is required to assess the medium-term affordability of health services (currently mainly financed by donors through the development budget).

ii. *Security Costs.* The affordability of large security forces, currently financed by external assistance, should be assessed against the Government's multi-year framework.

iii. *Operation and Maintenance Costs.* A critical goal of the integration of the ordinary and development budgets is to plan for operating and maintenance costs of the reconstruction program and to give adequate consideration to cost recovery (see Chapter 5).

iv. *Salary and Pensions.* As pressures to increase salaries and pensions continue, pay reforms should be costed and should remain in line with the Government's multi-year fiscal framework.

v. *State-Owned Enterprises (SOEs).* Decisions on SOEs (currently mainly defunct) should be based on a detailed analysis of the fiscal implications of their activities.

vi. *Debt Management.* Uncertainties about the level of debt (related to debates about claims on previous regimes) should be clarified so that the Government builds its multi-year budget framework on a sustainable debt scenario.

Develop Momentum in Priority Areas

Reduce Vulnerability to Corruption. The fight against corruption is best mainstreamed as part of the broader public administration reform program. Anti-corruption bodies established in other countries have often been largely ineffective in curbing corruption. A number of priority corrective measures have been identified (Table 4.7).

Reduce Reliance on the Second Civil Service. The "second civil service" in Afghanistan will continue to exist for some time, along with significant donor assistance and while Government capacity remains weak. The incentives for donors to pay high rates to consultants and staff to maximize the prospects for effective project implementation are well-known, and although these can be moderated by strong expressions of concern by the Government, the problem will remain. As outlined above, the Government is moving in key areas to strengthen the capacity of its civil service, in particular through the PRR program, as well as more comprehensive pay reform. To maximize the benefits of these reforms, donors and aid agencies will need to make every effort to control their use of salary top-ups and not recruit people at pay levels far above what can be reasonably offered by Government, or at a minimum coordinate their pay policies with the Government. Government also needs to maintain tight discipline on compensation levels that it pays to individual consultants and that it approves in firm contracts. There is now a comprehensive menu of options for enhancing capacity within the Government (Table 4.8), which should assist the Government in setting rates for consultants that it contracts, and should also provide a baseline for donor agencies' compensation policies.

Further Integrate External Assistance within the National Budget. External assistance needs to further strengthen rather than undermine the budget processes. The Government's efforts to integrate the development program and the ordinary budget (Box 4.3) need to be supported. Donors should support only projects that are in the budget (that have gone through the decision-making process that leads to inclusion in the budget)

Table 4.7. Priorities for Reducing Administrative Corruption

Sector	Activities	Specific priorities	Overall strategy
Private sector	Formal	Adopt the draft private investment law, draft and approve new laws regulating the establishment and functioning of foreign and domestic companies. Developing the enabling legislative, institutional, and regulatory framework for implementing investment policy (Chapter 5). Strengthen the MoF office of taxation and revenue departments, the Judiciary and Attorney Generals Office. Conduct a review of national NGOs, their activities and accounts, to identify those that are profit seeking. Refine the current NGO code of conduct to include a minimum requirement for independent audit and the annual publication of accounts, including identifying the names of Board Members.	Re-regulating activities where appropriate or deregulating activities to match weak enforcement capacities.
	Irregular	Reform the customs service (as under the Customs Modernization Program). Provide tighter border controls through better trained and motivated border guards.	
	Illegal	Strengthen the counter-narcotics institutional framework and law enforcement capacity (e.g., counter-narcotics police), while ensuring that broader economic and poverty aspects are fully taken into account in counter-narcotics drugs strategy (see Chapter 7).	
	Extra-legal	Regulate hawalas cautiously.	
Public sector	Constitutional	Adopt and implement the draft Procurement, Public Finance and Expenditure Management, Civil Service, and Investment laws. Adopt the draft Ministerial Code of Conduct and introduce asset declarations. Support reforms to the Auditor General's Office and Attorney General's Office. Introduce awareness of the anti-corruption dimension into core civil service training modules for existing and new recruits.	Enforcing penalties on individuals for corruption. Improving transparency and public access to information. Simplifying business processes to deter collusive relationships.
	"Captured"	Support for Municipal governments, with a focus on service delivery not on rent extraction. Prioritize municipal reform programs.	

Table 4.8. Options for Enhancing Capacities within Government

	Interim additional allowances under PRR	PRR super-scale	ARTF expatriate window	TAFSU	Lateral entry program
Parameters	Key officials in PRR agency	Restricted to key officials in PRR agencies	In exceptional circumstances where the case is clearly made and exceptional candidate available	Short term consultants where the need is clearly justified and a terms of reference submitted to TAFSU	Key positions in each ministry through basic capacity assessment
Salary range	Upto $300 per month	Up to $2000 per month	$3000–$5000 per month	$200–$700 per day and DSA at UN rates	$1000–$2000 per month and in exceptional circumstances higher

and should progressively channel more of their assistance through the Government Treasury. Over time external assistance should move toward programmatic support. This requires further building the Government's capacity, raising fiduciary standards (see accountability mechanisms above), and developing sector-wide strategies and programs. The ARTF is already largely programmatic (through its support to the ordinary budget), and its support is conditioned on fiduciary standards monitored by an international firm. Donors should have increasing comfort to move more assistance through Treasury channels as the Government is establishing a track record through compliance with benchmarks in the IMF's staff monitored program and a World Bank budget support operation (World Bank 2004c).

CHAPTER 5

Encouraging and Supporting Private Sector Development

A dynamic private sector will be essential for Afghanistan to achieve the robust, sustained economic growth that is necessary for national poverty reduction, state building, and other reconstruction objectives. Tremendous entrepreneurial talents exist in Afghanistan, but in order to be the "engine of growth" the private sector must be able and encouraged to move beyond the bounds of the informal economy (see Chapter 3). While Afghanistan will continue to have a great many small, household and family-based businesses in agriculture, handicrafts, trade, and other services, some enterprises need to grow into medium or even large firms, thereby becoming a source of competitiveness for Afghanistan. The challenge for the Government in encouraging and supporting private sector development is: (i) to support through macroeconomic policies a strong demand environment for the private sector, by maintaining robust economic growth (Chapter 1); (ii) to create a structural and regulatory enabling environment in which private enterprises can compete and grow; (iii) to ensure that key infrastructure services (power, roads, water, telecommunication) are efficiently provided to the private sector; and (iv) to help the private sector build capacity (including through financial services and business support services) so that it will be able to respond effectively to opportunities.

The SAF report outlines a number of key characteristics of the Afghan investment environment that will need to be taken into account in the private sector support strategy:

i. Afghanistan is a land-locked country, with porous borders and surrounded by neighbors with different trade and investment policies, in many cases quite restrictive.
ii. The Afghan economy is largely informal and undocumented, with the informal economy including most importantly the illegal drug industry (see Chapters 1 and 7).

iii. Insecurity severely constrains the most productive private sector development and channels it into shorter-term activities.
iv. Infrastructure constraints, nationally and in the region, undermine the cost efficiency of trade and transit and thereby adversely affect private sector production and profitability.
v. Afghanistan's rich underground resources are under-exploited, and large-scale industry is still in its infancy.
vi. Afghanistan's labor market is already highly integrated into the regional economy, as a result of the large numbers of refugees and economic migrants.

The first section of this chapter pieces together a picture of Afghanistan's non-agricultural private sector (agriculture is covered in Chapter 6), based on available information. The second section discusses the constraints affecting private sector activities. The third section summarizes the Government's strategy for private sector development and outlines priorities for moving forward.

The Afghan Private Sector

The Enterprise Spectrum

At the core of private sector development are business enterprises. Different types of enterprises have different roles in stimulating economic activity, growth, and poverty reduction. They also differ in the constraints they face. While some policies will have effects across the board, others may affect different enterprises differently. Table 5.1 summarizes the enterprise spectrum—consisting of formal enterprises plus those that have potential to become formal.

At one end of the spectrum are *large enterprises* (generally defined as those with over 250 employees), which are extremely few in Afghanistan at present although a number of

Table 5.1. The Enterprise Spectrum

Enterprise size	Examples	Direct impact on growth	Direct impact on employment	Catalytic impact on other firms and on overall efficiency in economy
Large	AWCC, Roshan, Hyatt Regency Hotel	Moderate Low	Low Moderate	High Low
Medium	Karizma Construction	High	High	Moderate
Small (dynamic)	Import / Export Firms	Moderate to high	High	Low to moderate
Other small and micro	Carpet Makers	Low	High	Low

larger companies are beginning operations. Examples include the two telecommunications providers (AWCC and Roshan; see below), Coca Cola, and the new Hyatt Regency hotel. Many large firms are funded by foreign investments, but as they are likely to be small in number this group will not make a major direct contribution to employment. Their main contributions are likely to be as: (i) efficient providers of critical services, such as mobile telecommunication or distribution networks, or products, such as cement and fuel, with downstream effects on other enterprises; (ii) major vehicles of foreign investment, whose success will have an important signaling effect; (iii) catalysts for introduction of modern technology, methods of management, and enterprise operation that may have a demonstration effect on other firms; (iv) incubators of newer, smaller, enterprises; and (v) providers of much needed Government revenue.

Medium-sized enterprises typically have 50–250 employees. They are likely to be found in construction and scattered in other services, but would also be expected to emerge in manufacturing. The bulk of their investment is domestic, but with support provided in many cases by expatriate Afghans. This group of enterprises would be expected to be a major source of employment and a base of industrial development and private sector development in Afghanistan.

Small and micro enterprises will be an important source of employment and incomes for the poor, and hence a driver of poverty reduction. Their importance in aggregate means that they will also contribute to overall economic growth. However, relatively few small enterprises will be dynamic and a significant source of efficiency gains in the economy. Such enterprises may graduate into medium scale and some might become large enterprises over time. The extent to which this happens will depend on the degree to which the business environment in Afghanistan encourages successful entrepreneurs to shift into the formal sector.

Finally, a number of private businesses (especially construction contractors) are registered as NGOs, reflecting the peculiarities of the situation in Afghanistan (Box 5.1). While inappropriately registered and benefiting from their non-profit, tax-exempt status,

Box 5.1. A Raisin Factory in Kabul

There were eight raisin processing factories in Kabul in the 1980s. Currently only one of them is operational, which on the day visited was processing raisins for export to Russia.

The equipment is old, bought in 1964 from California, and has worked continuously since then, all the way through the war. Raisins are shoveled onto the conveyor manually. They are washed and winnowed, and then paraffin is sprayed on them. After that, women and boys manually sort the raisins and remove the remaining cap stems, before they are loaded into 12 kg cardboard boxes. Approximately 1/2 of the process requires manual labor. The line can process 4–5 metric tons per hour.

The factory manager claimed to have 250 employees. However, there were only around 30 people working at the time of visit, about 2/3 women and children and 1/3 men. At busy times of the year the factory operates double shifts. The factory operates all year around except for 15–20 days when it is shut for plant maintenance. The factory processes raisins for 15 to 20 exporters during a year. Usually the exporting company pays for everything including labor wages, and the factory owner charges Afs 500 per metric ton of raisins processed. A representative from the Raisin Export Promotion Institute visits to ensure the quality of raisins for export. The factory also has its own small laboratory.

Source: AREU 2004.

these enterprises constitute an important reservoir of technical and management capacity, and could be moved formally into the private sector and thereby become a source of dynamism.

Current Private Sector Activities

Afghanistan possesses a rudimentary manufacturing base with most factories in Kabul and a few major cities such as Herat and Mazar-i-Sharif. A significant component of current manufacturing is in traditional activities, such as carpet weaving, dried fruit production and processing, and other small-scale activities. Transportation services and construction are two major traditional private sector service activities. Private entrepreneurship has recently ventured into a number of areas that are non-traditional in the sense that they either did not exist before in Afghanistan (mobile phones) or were reserved for the public sector (airlines and banks).

Examples of Traditional Activities: Carpets and Raisins. The bulk of Afghanistan's carpets are produced in villages, by women weavers. These find their way to export markets through a network of domestic markets and traders. During the conflict many carpet weavers and traders migrated to Pakistan, mostly to Peshawar. As a result, a large proportion of carpet exports in Pakistan's trade statistics are attributable to the Afghan carpet industry—in Afghanistan, or displaced in Pakistan. Raisins, once the most successful Afghan export, have been hampered by damage to orchards and processing plants, although the recent preferential trade agreement with India has seen Afghan dried fruit exports back in fourth position in that market in 2003—a major recovery. If traditional activities, such as carpets or dried fruits, are to contribute significantly to broad-based growth, it will be important not only to revive production but also to ensure that the smaller players, especially producers, benefit more from these activities. Recent studies of carpet and raisin markets indicate that producers get only a small share of the price paid by the final consumers,[1] for example, 8–15 percent of the final price in the case of carpet weavers. Revival will not necessarily mean going back to old methods of production, processing, and marketing; for some activities, particularly agro-processing, there is much greater premium on quality assurance than 20 years ago.

Construction is booming in Afghanistan and is expected to continue to be an important driver of private sector activity. Most construction of roads and new schools and clinics is being implemented by private firms (many registered as NGOs; see Box 5.2), in the case of roads largely by international contractors. Afghan companies generally do not have sufficient experience, skilled personnel, or equipment to handle larger contracts, although larger Afghan contractors based in Peshawar and Quetta could be encouraged to return. However, many Afghan companies have successfully completed contracts for primary roads and, as sub-contractors to international companies, are increasingly becoming eligible for

1. Studies of the carpet and raisin markets suggest that traditional informal markets are characterized by some non-competitive features. A relatively small group of businessmen may dominate major trading activities, excluding new entrants in various ways including price manipulation, possession of capital (when credit is unavailable to others), political influence, and high levels of vertical integration at the top of the chain (AREU 2004).

Box 5.2. Non-Governmental Organizations (NGOs)

In the absence of an effective state, NGOs have fulfilled a major role in the delivery of both relief and development services in Afghanistan. The centrality of their role was heightened by donors' desire to bypass direct support for the Taliban regime by channeling resources via the U.N. system, or through international and national NGOs. As a result, there are now more than 2,000 NGOs registered in Afghanistan, and a number of international NGOs have over 10,000 employees, working largely in the areas of health and education and provision of humanitarian services. In many ways, NGOs took on *de facto* the state's role in service delivery.

Currently NGOs are operating across Afghanistan in activities as varied as education, health, humanitarian relief services, water supply, refugee return, etc. Initial estimates indicate that in both 1382 and 1383, on the order of $300–500 million per year was being channeled through NGOs.

The legal environment, legal texts, codes, legislation, and decrees do not adequately address the expansion of civil society in Afghanistan. The lack of regulation has also led to a plethora of for-profit organization masquerading as non-for-profit organizations—undermining the legitimacy of the formal economy and displacing the private sector. The Government's development strategy requires greater differentiation between economic and civil society actors.

In 2003 the Ministry of Planning, responsible for registration of NGOs, drafted new legislation that would oversee the work of both national and international NGOs. While not yet promulgated, the law foresees the establishment of a Commission to evaluate NGO capability, quality, and accountability. In principle, existing legislation is currently being enforced by the Ministry of Planning, but in practice capacities are too weak for it to be effective.

The Ministry of Planning believes that a large number of NGOs would probably have their status changed because they do not conform with the new definition. The 2004 mini investment climate survey conducted by the World Bank in Kabul, Mazar-i-Sharif, Kunduz, and Jalalabad found that a number of private companies were registered as not-for-profit organizations.

While the new law needs to protect the rights of legitimate not-for-profit organizations so as to enhance their effectiveness and more generally facilitate a flourishing civil society, it must clearly differentiate between NGOs and contractors—many of which are involved in the construction industry. The law needs to increase the accountability of NGOs through clear management structures, the publishing of annual reports, public access to accounts, and external audit. Profit-seeking organizations should formally register as such, with the Ministry of Commerce and the Afghan Investment Support Agency (AISA). Taking the poor regulatory capacity of the Government into consideration, an NGO Code of Conduct to allow for self-regulation and increased transparency would seem a workable option. In the longer term the economy will benefit significantly if the large number of de facto private concerns currently registered as NGOs are formally incorporated into the private sector.

contracts for secondary road contracts too. The Afghan-owned construction industry is growing rapidly. It is estimated that there are approximately 20–30 medium sized companies with turnover of $1 million or more and another 30–40 companies with turnover of between $200,000 and $1 million. Some donors are trying to ensure greater participation by Afghan companies through policies such as local content requirements.

Construction Materials. The construction boom has led to high demand for construction materials, such as cement and cement blocks, wood, steel and steel products, bricks, aggregate and sand, plumbing products and sanitary fixtures, and glass (Box 5.3). Most demand is met through imports (mainly from Pakistan, Iran, Russia, and to a lesser extent the United Arab Emirates and China), since there is very little manufacturing

Box 5.3. Construction Materials in Mazar-i-Sharif

Mazar-i-Sharif is the economic hub of Balkh province. The province borders Uzbekistan, which connects Afghanistan with the main import routes from Russia and other former Soviet Union countries. The city of Mazar is located 90 km south of Hairatan port on the Afghan-Uzbek border. It is the main commercial center in the north and both a primary market and a distribution point for construction materials imported from Russia. The regional customs office is located in Mazar. Dozens of trucks with imported wood and steel are always parked in the compound of the customs office waiting for paperwork to be completed and duties to be paid before they move on. Drivers usually spend 1–2 days there.

The "bazaars" in construction materials are booming. There are four big markets in the city as well as numerous small shops in the central part of the city. There is some price difference between goods in Mazar and those in other cities. Usually materials imported from Russia are cheaper here than in Kabul or any other city in Afghanistan. Smuggled goods from Pakistan, such as plywood, also reach the markets of Mazar, which is home to many large importing companies. Barakat Construction is among the largest. It has been trading for 45 years and mostly imports steel and wood from Russia and exports raisins to Moscow (AREU, 2004).

capacity in Afghanistan. There are three basic trade patterns: (i) large contractors import materials for their own use; (ii) import/export companies buy from manufacturers and sell to wholesalers, who in turn sell to retailers and large consumers; and (iii) manufacturers export directly and sell to Afghan wholesalers (relatively rare). Some barriers to entry exist at the lower end of the commodity chain. Lack of credit, and vertical integration of the top end of the business, make it difficult for small and medium-sized businesses to expand. Corruption appears to be endemic, and bribes to municipalities, police and, judicial services act as a disincentive to market engagement. The industry currently lacks quality regulations to protect against low-quality materials which often come into the market, and sub-standard construction is common.

Transport. This was an important activity during the conflict, and private transport companies have expanded rapidly since the end of the war. There are a number of flourishing freight and passenger transport companies (the government truck fleet has stopped working). Estimates of the total size of the private truck fleet in Afghanistan range from 47,500 to 80,000. There are 165 registered bus companies with approximately 14,000 buses (the majority of these are minibuses and vans), and the number of registered taxis rose from 17,000 in 2000 to 33,500 in 2002. The Government-owned Millie bus company operates 963 vehicles, mainly in Kabul, and the balance are privately owned and operated. The costs of entry into the market are not high.

Infrastructure. The largest private investment in infrastructure has been in telecommunications. While very modest fixed-line telecom services are provided by the public sector, there are two private mobile operators. The first, AWCC, offers pre-paid GSM services in four major cities. It is a joint venture 20 percent owned by the Ministry of Telecommunications and 80 percent by Telephone Systems International, which is controlled by an Afghan investor providing management. An international competitive tender process in 2002 resulted in the award of a second mobile license in January 2003, to Roshan, owned by a consortium led by the Aga Khan Fund for Economic Development (51 percent),

Monaco Telecom International (35), MCT Corporation (9), and Alcatel (5). Total investment in the two mobile networks is reported at over $180 million, representing most direct foreign investment in the country. The number of connections has increased from 57,000 in 2000 to at least 200,000 by December 2003 (including both mobile subscribers and fixed lines). Total tele-density has increased from 2 per 1000 to at least 8 per 1000, mostly due to Roshan and AWCC. Competition between the two privately owned mobile networks has resulted in prices consistent with international norms.

Currently there is very little involvement of the private sector in the main electricity generation, transmission, and distribution system. However, there are thousands of generators in operation which are privately supplied and maintained. These range from household usage of very small generators to workshops and small businesses using diesel-powered generators of a significant size. Since the end of major conflict in Afghanistan, a private water and sanitation industry has emerged. International agencies typically use either private contractors or a combination of private contractors and their own implementation operations to construct wells, manufacture hand-pumps, and install systems. There are a number of Afghan hand-pump suppliers operating (see Box 5.4 for an example), which provide an illustration of how public sector demand, in this case from international aid agencies, can stimulate Afghan private enterprise.

The growing importance of the construction industry as an area of investment and its potential for the future are reflected in the composition of new investment projects. Box 5.5 discusses recent investment projects benefiting from services provided by AISA. Construction accounts for 25 percent of projects and more than half of expected investment volume.

The primary group of potential foreign investors for Afghanistan currently consists of returning Afghan nationals who left the country as many as 25 years ago for Europe, Australia, North America, and countries in the region. There are also interested investors from countries that have traditionally had trade ties with Afghanistan, such as India, Iran, Pakistan, Turkey, and Uzbekistan, as well from U.S. and European companies. Some foreign investors view Afghanistan as a central business "hub" and vital trade route, where the Middle East meets Southern, Central, and East Asia. In addition, some businesses are striving for "first mover advantage" in establishing a presence in Afghanistan. Moderate interest has been expressed by potential investors in power, telecommunications and internet

Box 5.4. Zam Zam Industries: A Small Water-pump Manufacturer

Zam Zam Industries is a hand-pump manufacturing and metal fabrication business. It was set up in Pakistan four years ago by four former employees of an international NGO and relocated to Kabul in the fall of 2003. It now has 25 employees, including 4 engineers and 10 skilled craftsmen. The factory is currently producing approximately 300–400 pumps per month which sell for between Afs 7,000 and Afs 12,000 ($140–240). The company has two sales channels. Approximately 60 percent of the company's output is made to order for NGOs and international organizations. The remainder of its output is sold to private buyers through a network of eight shops around the country. Zam Zam's competition comes from both Afghan and foreign companies. Zam Zam is diversifying into new products. It is currently working on an order for an international construction company and is also negotiating an order for doors and windows for an international aid agency.

Box 5.5. Characteristics of Recent Investments

According to information submitted to AISA on 84 recent investment proposals, these enterprises together expected an initial investment of about US $120 million and total employment of about 4,000. About a quarter (22) of these projects are in construction, accounting for more than half the total expected investment ($69.3 million, or 58 percent), and half of the total expected employment in the 84 projects (2,000 jobs). Next in importance are 26 manufacturing projects, covering a wide range of activities, with an expected investment of $21 million and employment of about 1,150. Three banks and two hotels account for another $20 million in initial investment but only 140 jobs. The remaining investment proposals comprise a number of service-oriented enterprises and other miscellaneous activities. Only five projects show an initial investment of $5 million or above; these include two construction projects, two banks, and one beverage manufacturing project. Another 17 show an initial expected investment of between $1 million to $5 million. About 50 projects have an investment of $100,000 or less. Only 12 projects are expected to employ more than 100 people; another 11 are expected to employ between 50 and 100 people. A little more than half (58 percent) of the projects, accounting for 24 percent of the investment value, are sponsored by Afghan investors. Sources of foreign investments include Germany (6), Pakistan (4), the UK (4), Iran (3), and the USA (2).

services, banking, business hotels, housing and related infrastructure, agro-business, textiles, steel, and the oil and gas industry. The potential for sizable foreign investments to materialize if conditions are right is illustrated by nine investments newly registered by AISA, which have a total expected investment value of $388 million and an estimated employment once operational of 9,215 people. However, both domestic and foreign investment are severely hampered by a number of serious constraints.

Constraints to Private Sector Development

A rigorous investment climate survey has not been done for Afghanistan. However, a simple survey carried out recently by the World Bank helps identify the major constraints faced by private enterprises. The survey covered about 150 business firms in Kabul, Mazar-i-Sharif, Jalalabad, and Kunduz. Enterprises were provided a list of possible constraints (derived from the World Bank's core investment climate survey questionnaire) and asked to identify if these were severe, moderate, minor, or not constraints on their business operations. The results are summarized in Figure 5.1, indicating the top five investment constraints as: (i) access to land, (ii) lack of water, (iii) lack of electricity, (iv) poor communication facilities, and (v) transportation. Investors were also asked to identify on their own the three most important constraints they faced. Poor security and access to finance were cited as among the three most important problems in all four cities, but security is the number one problem in Mazar and only the number three problem in the other three cities. Transportation and access to roads is among the top five problems in Kabul, Kunduz, and Jalalabad but not in Mazar. Difficulties in getting visas is among the five most serious problems in Mazar and Kunduz but not in Kabul and Jalalabad.

Results also differed by sector (not captured in Figure 5.1). Traders most frequently complained about lack of finance, transportation, non-existent banking services, and visa facilities. Construction companies referred to lack of security and supply of inputs as the

Figure 5.1. Results of Enterprise Survey in Four Cities

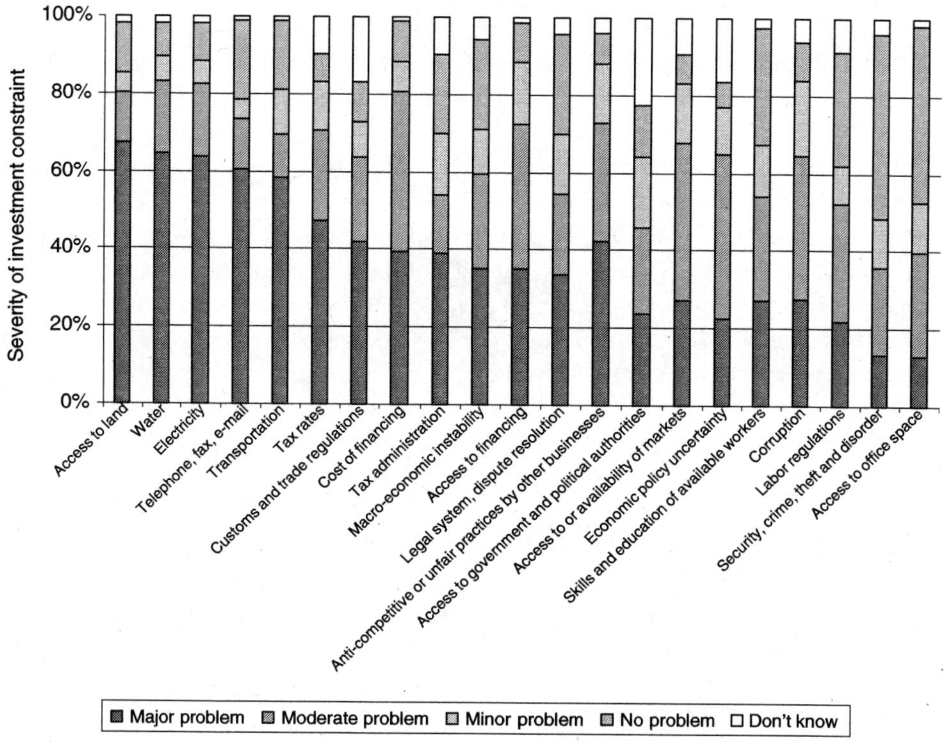

key constraints. Corruption was not seen as a major constraint as investors appear to have classified this as a normal and necessary business transaction. A number of specific constraints faced by the private sector are discussed below.

Land. The scarcity of serviced land, as well as unclear ownership of land, is a major constraint to investment in Afghanistan. Land titling is difficult, and often multiple documents exist for the same piece of land. The return of refugees is compounding the problem, with disputes being common. The scope for resolving disputes through the court system is limited given inadequate court and judicial capacities, lack of necessary legal expertise, and insufficient guidance provided by law (there is no formal company law). Property rights are thus unclear and insecure. Land cannot be collateralized easily and hence cannot be used to generate financial resources or to set up small businesses. To overcome land and other constraints, the Ministry of Commerce (MoC) is establishing an industrial park outside of Kabul.

Electric Power. As in many developing countries, inadequate and unreliable power supply (discussed at length later in this chapter) is a major constraint on private sector activity in Afghanistan—particularly in the industrial sector. Due to a combination of the direct effects of war, lack of maintenance, and theft of spare parts and equipment, power supply is erratic and unreliable. In addition to generation problems, Afghanistan has no national grid and suffers from severe transmission and distribution limitations. Lack of adequate power supply increases costs for private firms who are forced to make alternative arrangements.

Access to Finance. Banking services in Afghanistan remain severely limited. The passage of the Central Banking Law and the Commercial Banking Law in September 2003 and the entry of several commercial banks marks significant progress. Yet, much must be done before financial services are restored to the level required for meaningful trade and investment activities. State financial institutions are largely non-functional. The new private banks have not yet started lending to industry, and it appears that at least some of them will not be inclined to do so in the near future. Local enterprises suffer from a shortage of capital, and trading activity and industrial development have been adversely affected. The absence of a functional formal banking system also prevents the development of a bonding or monetary guarantee system for vehicles or cargo in transit.

Security. This remains a major problem for private enterprises in Afghanistan, although the severity of insecurity may differ across locations. Poor security increases the risks of investment, raises transactions costs, and thereby deters investors, particularly foreign investors who have other places to invest. Poor security also raises the costs for existing businesses, for example, through the need to hire security guards (on the Kabul/Kandahar highway the international contractor employed over 1,000 security guards just to protect the workforce and equipment). It also raises transport costs in general by imposing limitations on operating hours, restricting the flexibility of truck operations, and sometimes requiring the use of convoy systems.

Risk Mitigation. Insecurity as well as other factors increase the perceived political risk of doing business in Afghanistan. The Government strongly encourages foreign direct investment, but without political risk insurance many investors may take a "wait-and-see" approach.[2] Domestically as well, Afghanistan is acutely underinsured. The Afghan National Insurance Company (ANIC), the sole insurance company operating in the country and holding a monopoly on insurance functions, lacks trained staff and has a poor track record in paying out on legitimate claims. Lack of insurance has a significant effect on private sector activity. Most international shipping lines do not allow their containers into the country. Within Afghanistan, cargo moves under either owners' risk or carriers' liability (at much higher freight rates), discouraging trade.

Transport and Trade Logistics. Transit-related trade costs are high in Afghanistan due to inefficiencies in the present transit system, including: (i) non-existent or poor state of trade and transit infrastructure,[3] (ii) very poor condition of the road network, (iii) short

2. Afghanistan is now a member of the Multilateral Investment Guarantee Agency (MIGA), although the total volume of political risk insurance so far provided to foreign investors has been small.

3. Border facilities are mostly run-down, congested, or in many cases only partially functional. Almost all border facilities have no external communication links or IT setups, and have mostly unreliable power supply. Inadequate physical infrastructure also constrains operations at nearly all Inland Clearance Depots (ICDs).

Box 5.6. Quality Certification for Raisins

There are no gazetted grades or standards, cleanliness rules, or public health inspections. The Afghan Raisin Export and Other Dry Fruit Export Promotion Institute, a non-profit body under MoC, has offices in Kabul, which are equipped with a small lab recently fitted out by the Japanese government, as well as offices in Kandahar, Mazar, and Jalalabad. Its role is to provide services to producers and regulate the quality of exports. It issues a certificate of "quality control" after carrying out laboratory tests, a procedure for which they charge Afs 50 per metric ton. Provincial departments of the Ministry of Agriculture and Animal Husbandry (MAAH) also provide a certification service to exporters of raisins. But such certification is rarely based on laboratory testing.

internal hauls on transit routes, (iv) insecurity, and (v) numerous checkpoints along the routes. With the limited exception of some direct road transport from Karachi to Kabul, all of Afghanistan's foreign trade is transshipped, which raises costs directly (handling charges) and indirectly (loss and damage). Because international shipping lines do not allow their containers into the country, most cargo, subjected to multiple handling, is thus break bulk cargo, vulnerable to handling loss and damage. Coordination between transporters in Afghanistan and transit countries, and between shippers and customs officials, is poor because of the lack of professional transit agents and poor communications. A local freight-forwarding industry was very active prior to 1975 but is non-existent today. There are no norms of accreditation for freight-forwarders.

Quality and Standards. Afghanistan has no metrology, standards, testing, and quality (MSTQ) infrastructure; as a result the country is often a dumping ground for sub-standard goods. Export development also is inhibited given the high quality standards demanded by international markets, especially for agro-based products. Without a proper MSTQ system, enterprises are unable to access information on standards, calibration, and product testing facilities. Existing limited arrangements for quality control are generally ineffective (see Box 5.6).

Regulatory Burden. Although there have been improvements in the regulatory regime, including streamlining business registration, customs procedures, and trade licensing systems, there are still numerous excessive regulatory burdens. For example, the transaction costs of transporting goods within Afghanistan are raised directly by multiple fees and taxes, and indirectly by delays and uncertainties due to multiple checkpoints along the routes. Provincial agencies interfere by imposing informal procedural requirements. Dealing with municipalities remains a big hassle. (See Box 5.7 on the regulatory problems faced by Roshan, a private mobile telephone operator, which pre-date recent improvements.) While business registration and overall trade licensing have been streamlined, obtaining specific licenses (for example, for operating in certain sectors such as pharmaceuticals) may still take considerable time.

Corruption by public sector employees is considered a major constraint to business (see Chapter 4). Private sector operators state that bribery to police, judicial services, municipal, and other sector Ministry staff is almost a daily affair—and often $3–4,000 is paid in bribes to municipal staff just to gain access to land. Anecdotal evidence

Box 5.7. Constraints Faced by a Private Mobile Telephone Operator

Despite its success Roshan, one of the two private mobile telephone operators in Afghanistan, encountered many obstacles along the way, ranging from poor physical infrastructure to insecurity and excessive Government bureaucracy. While not unexpected, these constraints added to the time and cost of doing business for the company.

Infrastructure. Establishing a mobile telecommunications operation throughout Afghanistan requires significant amounts of personnel and equipment to be transported around the country. The poor state and lack of security on the roads and unreliable local air service meant that Roshan found it necessary to lease a plane to transport its staff and equipment within the country.

The lack of reliable electricity supply in Afghanistan has been a source of difficulties for Roshan. The company had to install power generators at all of its sites. Every base-station has two 16kW generators, and there are pairs of larger 250kW and 350kW generators at its major switch and control center sites. To date, Roshan has spent $3 million on generators as a result of the unreliable electricity supply. By the end of 2004, the company expects to have 220 sites operational in Afghanistan, by which time the annual maintenance costs of Roshan's electricity generation capacity will exceed $1 million. In order to reduce the cost of generation, Roshan is considering solar power solutions for its base sites.

Bureaucracy. Dealing with the Government bureaucracy has been a challenge in some respects. For example, three licenses were required from the Government before Roshan could begin operations—an investment license, a trading license, and a telecommunications license. The investment license required 19 signatures of Government Ministers and officials, and it took 18 months to obtain a trading license. A similarly laborious process was involved in registering the "Roshan" name, which also required 19 signatures. The company has also had to deal extensively with municipal authorities for everything from general permission to operate in a town to specific authorization to carry out even very simple civil works such as repairing drainage channels. In Jalalabad, for example, Roshan found that permission was required from the municipal authority to operate in the city.

Roshan's experience provides clear evidence of improvements over time, however. Customs clearance delays have been reduced considerably, for example. More generally, Roshan's interactions with various Government agencies appear to have led to improvements in policies and processes, improving the business climate and demonstrating the value of private sector feedback.

suggests that municipal Construction Commissions are involved in corruption and bribery.

Labor. Because of low literacy levels and the lack of training facilities, qualified management and service staff are scarcely available, and most labor training takes place on the job. The lack of qualified employees is exacerbated by the barriers against women being employed in certain jobs, as well as a dysfunctional education system in terms of preparing students to exploit future labor market opportunities. Since formal employment opportunities are very limited, further skill enhancement does not occur to any significant extent.

Legal Framework for Private Sector Development. Afghanistan has inherited many laws, regulations, and procedures that inhibit trade and investment instead of encouraging it. A legal framework that allows businesses to start up easily, to function efficiently while they are in operation, and to exit the market in a timely and efficient manner is needed. An active program of legal reforms is currently underway in Afghanistan with donor support, although the proposed investment law has faced considerable delays in gaining approval. The adaptation of foreign laws to the Afghan context and translations of English drafts are important challenges to legislative reform in Afghanistan.[4]

Assets Locked Up in State-Owned Enterprises (SOEs). Afghanistan has about 70 SOEs, many of which are defunct and none are operating at full capacity. Most SOEs lack resources to carry out major restructuring. Moreover, many are overstaffed and lack management capability to increase capacity utilization. Many SOEs have considerable surplus land attached to them that is not required for their operations.

Government Strategy and Implementation Priorities

The Government has placed the private sector at the center of its development strategy. Two of the three Pillars of the NDF relate to the private sector—one directly as private sector development itself and the other indirectly in terms of infrastructure for private sector development. Beyond general pronouncements and strategy documents, the Government has been actively pursuing pro-private sector policies and has generally avoided actions which would adversely affect the private sector, such as resurrecting state-owned enterprises or restoring public sector procurement and trade in certain commodities. On the structural reform front, good progress has been made in trade reform and in liberalizing the financial sector. Nevertheless there is a long way to go in improving the investment environment and in providing more adequate infrastructure for the private sector, two key prerequisites for strong private sector development, and in shifting incentives in favor of the formal economy in the interest of greater competitiveness, efficiency, and growth.

Improving the Investment Climate

The Government recognizes that a sound investment climate is essential if private enterprise is to be the driving force for broad-based and sustainable growth in Afghanistan. Key elements include: (i) security and law and order (see Chapter 4); (ii) macroeconomic stability (see Chapter 3); (iii) the policy, legal, and institutional framework; and (iv) availability of critical production inputs (for example, land, labor, and infrastructure—discussed in the following section). Private sector development requires an enabling policy framework that is clear and predictable. The Government has made a strong commitment to such policies and has taken a number of steps in this regard. A conducive legal framework and a fair and effective judicial system—to settle disputes, enforce contracts, and protect property rights and investments—is required, and a program of legal reforms is currently underway with donor support. Non-viable state-owned enterprises need to privatized or liquidated. The Government is involved in preparation of a privatization program, which needs to be based on an appropriate legal framework and handled in a transparent manner with due consideration to the social implications of privatization.

4. Several important pieces of legislation relevant for private sector development are at an advanced stage of preparation: the Foreign Investment Law; the Decree on the Transfer of Government Property; the draft Decree on Corporatization of Telecommunications; the draft Company Law; and sectoral laws such as those on telecommunications, petroleum, and mining.

The Government is looking to the High Commission for Investment to provide improved coordination across the different Ministries and agencies. The Government also established the Afghanistan Investment Support Agency (AISA) with a mandate to promote foreign investment and facilitate business. Operational since August 2003, AISA helps investors secure necessary permits, licenses, and clearances; provides general information on investment opportunities, regulations, and standards; and provides support in the acquisition/leasing of land. A draft Presidential decree on the transfer of government property gives the High Commission the authority to allocate government land earmarked for industrial use to private investors. The High Commission will need strengthening in order to fulfill the roles assigned to it.

An institutionalized mechanism for obtaining regular feedback from the private sector about the constraints that it faces would be very desirable, conducted through an effective, regular dialogue with private sector associations. The Afghan Chamber of Commerce, which has existed for many years, is essentially a government agency with several regulatory functions. A number of independent private sector collective bodies have emerged and are active, including the Afghan-American Chamber of Commerce (AACC) and the Afghanistan Traders and Industrialists Center (ATIC). There are plans to consolidate these and a number of other private sector associations into the Afghanistan International Chamber of Commerce (AICC). The future role of the Afghanistan Chamber of Commerce will need to be delineated, given that many of its functions as a quasi-government entity no longer exist or should be abolished. The Government is considering streamlining its functions and converting it into a truly private sector chamber.

Greater export orientation is a very important aspect of the Government's private sector development vision. This will require a successful export promotion effort with collaboration between the public and private sectors. It will also require development of an effective quality and standards system. The Export Promotion Department in MoC has an explicit mandate to promote and facilitate exports. However, it suffers from weak capacity, including lack of many basic skills, and has lost contacts in developed countries after the shift in trade flows away from these countries since the mid-1970s. The Government is seriously considering revamping its export promotion efforts and is starting to establish a quality and standards system. The Government's export promotion efforts should focus on activities of a public good nature. This will require adoption of an appropriate policy and regulatory framework and institutional structure, with adequate capacity. While the Government may take the lead in setting up this system, important parts of it, such as laboratories, would be private sector activities.

The Government is planning to set up Industrial Parks to provide access to serviced land and other critical basic services. There are currently plans to set up three small industrial parks in Kandahar, Mazar-e-Sharif, and Bagram. Another 19 potential sites have been identified. The Government is developing an institutional framework to oversee the development of industrial parks. Options being considered include an independent agency or a department within AISA. Private participation in the development and management of industrial parks is envisaged. Industrial parks, with an appropriate policy, legal, and regulatory framework, can be a powerful instrument to encourage entrepreneurs to shift into the formal sector. They are only a partial solution to the land access problem, however. Over the medium term, appropriate actions will need to be taken to clarify and strengthen property rights, especially in land.

Expanding Infrastructure on a Sustainable Basis

Infrastructure is a critical input for the private sector, and Afghanistan's basic infrastructure, such as existed prior to the war, was badly damaged by the conflict itself and severely run down due to lack of maintenance. As emphasized in Chapter 3 of the SAF report, indicators of infrastructure availability in Afghanistan are in most respects the worst in the world, well below the corresponding figures for Sub-Saharan Africa (Table 5.2).

The Government, fully recognizing the centrality of infrastructure for growth, has developed a major investment program most notably in roads, but also in electric power and urban water supply. Just as important as the investments and the mechanics of infrastructure provision will be the institutional and policy framework, which will be essential for appropriate incentives and accountability for performance, and for financial sustainability (see the model of accountability for public services presented in Chapter 8, based on World Bank 2004g). Key directions for reform, starting from the highly centralized model of government service delivery that Afghanistan has inherited, include (i) separation of the service provider (public utility) from the government and its operation on an autonomous, commercial basis with accountability for performance; (ii) business-like relationship between service provider and service recipient, with a service orientation on the part of the former; and (iii) financially sound and sustainable operations, based on cost recovery.

Particular attention should be given to cost recovery from service recipients, which is not necessary only for financial sustainability and demand containment (the reasons usually cited). Paying for services changes the incentives of both clients (increased stake and vigilance and making better choices) and service providers (better provider behavior, increased and sustained supplies). Thus cost recovery, with appropriate lifeline tariffs or other mechanisms to ensure access for the poor, can be an effective instrument for accountability and sustainability objectives. Given the public good dimension and targeting issues relating to the poor, cost recovery is not possible or desirable in all cases. Figure 5.2 presents guidance on this issue based on the inherent characteristics of a service, its usage by the poor, and ability to target the poor. These guidelines need to be tempered by consideration of the costs and distortions arising from government funding of a service (for example, through taxation), if cost recovery is not resorted to.

Institutional and service delivery issues for two key infrastructure sectors—electric power and highways—are discussed below. Detailed investment requirements for major infrastructure sectors were presented in the SAF report (Afghanistan Government 2004, Chapter 3).

Electric Power

Sector Situation. Very limited quantity (only 6 percent of the population has access to power from the grid) and poor quality (low voltage, intermittent supply, black-outs) of electric power supplies are severely constraining Afghanistan's economic development. This dire situation reflects lack of investment, insufficient maintenance, and loss/damage of infrastructure due to conflict, looting, etc. In addition to grossly insufficient generation capacity (which is being augmented by imports of power from neighboring countries), the system is plagued by inadequate transmission, poor distribution, and lack of back-up

Table 5.2. Infrastructure in Afghanistan and Selected Other Countries

	GNP per/cap 2000	Total kms road per sq km area 2000	Percent of road paved	Motor vehicles per 1,000 people 2000	Electricity consumption per capita kwh	Telephones per 1,000 people	Access to water 2000	Access to sanitation 2000
Armenia	520	0.531	96	5	957	152		
Azerbaijan	600	0.287	92	49	1750	104		
Bangladesh	370	1.441	9	1	89	4	97	53
Congo Republic	570	0.037	10	18	48	7	51	
Guinea	450	0.124	17	4		8	48	58
India	450	1.010	46	8	379	32	88	31
Indonesia	570	0.180	47	25	345	31	76	66
Nepal	240	0.090	31		47	12	81	27
Pakistan	440	0.320	43	8	321	22	88	61
Sri Lanka	850	1.465	95	34	255	41	83	83
Tajikistan	180	0.194	83		2163	36		
Turkmenistán	750	0.049	81		944	82	58	100
Uzbekistán	360	0.183	87		1650	67	85	100
Zimbabwe	460	0.047	48		894	18	85	68
Afghanistan (2003)	186	0.032	16	14	12.16	1.6	13	12

Source: Afghanistan Government (2004b).

Figure 5.2. When and How to Levy User Fees

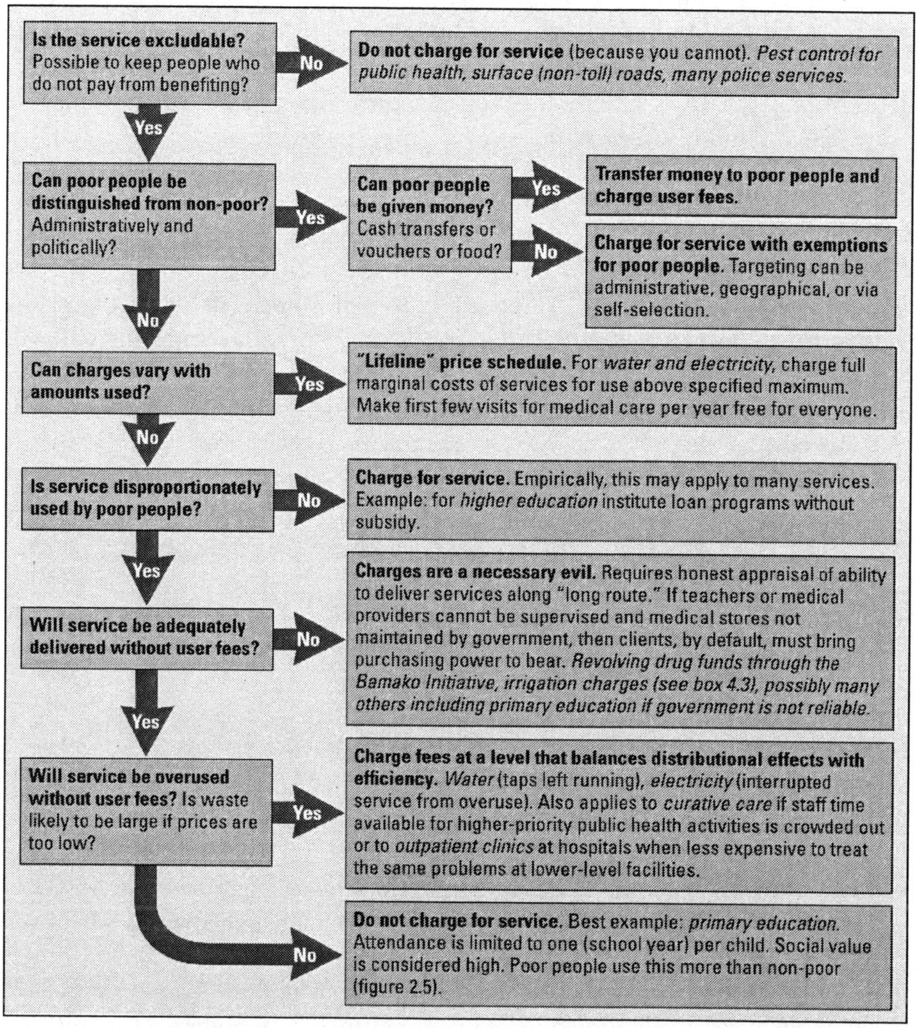

Note: Numbers for Boxes and Figures refer to those in the World Development Report 2004.
Source: World Bank (2004g), Box 4.4, p. 71.

equipment, which results in losses. Most of the equipment in the power sector is old, dilapidated, and failing. Although the population demonstrates willingness to pay for power supplies when the costs are transparent (imported power or diesel generation), in Kabul and some other large cities like Kandahar electricity is priced at levels far too low to recover the costs of O&M—overall the average cost recovery rate (ratio of power tariff to cost of supply) is estimated at just over 50 percent.

Organizational Structure. The Ministry of Water and Power is in charge of the power sector in Afghanistan, which it operates through a number of departments and public enterprises—the latter function as parts of the ministry however. The state power utility, Da Afghanistan Breshna Moassesa (DABM), is in charge of generation, transmission, and distribution of electricity and has nearly 7,000 employees, most of whom are in some 14 regional electricity departments responsible for running electricity facilities in different parts of the country. DABM has neither an appropriate governance structure nor financial resources to improve electricity services. Until recently its staff were paid from the ministry's budget, and funds for maintenance, fuel, spare parts, etc. are lacking.

Government Strategy. The Government's key objective is to expand coverage of electric power supply while improving quality, through rehabilitation of existing facilities and expansion (including in the short run power imports where appropriate). The goal is to increase coverage of the electricity grid in urban areas to 90 percent by 2015, which translates into an overall national electricity access ratio of 33 percent, compared with an estimated 6 percent at present. The capacity of the Ministry of Water and Power will be enhanced, and a program management approach will be taken with establishment of a Project Implementation Support Unit within the ministry. DABM is to be corporatized as a first step toward transforming it into an autonomous, commercially-oriented business entity with special focus on power distribution. Emphasis will be given to improving billing and collections, and a process of tariff enhancement has begun in Kabul.

Improving Service Delivery. While major investments will be required to achieve power sector objectives, institutional and policy changes that improve incentives and enhance accountability of service providers also will be essential.

i. An early focus on improving billing and collection is necessary.
ii. A relatively ambitious power tariff reform could be embarked upon as the quality of power supply is improved and the network is expanded. While this is essential for covering O&M costs and thereby ensuring the financial sustainability of the system, it will also yield dividends in terms of the power utility's incentives to provide good service and consumers' incentives to restrain their own power usage and demand good service.
iii. As power tariffs are rationalized, consumer protection mechanisms and feedback channels need to be developed to help ensure that there are adequate levels of service.
iv. Corporatization of DABM is an essential first step, but it will need to be accompanied by appointing a new Board of Directors and commercially-oriented managers, building capacity, instilling a more business-like corporate culture, and better commercial cash management and pricing practices, among others.

Highway Network

Sector Situation. Afghanistan's pre-war paved highway network, although of limited length (some 2,000 km) was excellent in terms of quality in relation to the relatively low traffic levels, reflecting large investments in main roads funded by aid from the USSR and USA. Protracted conflict and lack of maintenance left this network largely dilapidated—road trips that took hours 30 years ago took days by the end of the war. Secondary, tertiary, and farm-to-market roads were neglected in the pre-war period with for the most part no improvements subsequently. Rehabilitating the road network has been a top priority for the Government during the past 2½ years, and despite delays work is well underway, with concomitant improvements in travel times already beginning to materialize. Widespread efforts also have been made to repair and improve smaller roads, primarily through public works employment programs (most notably NEEP). Nevertheless there is still a long way to go in rehabilitating the highway system and completing its segments including the remaining "ring" connection in Northwest Afghanistan.

Organizational Structure. The Ministry of Public Works is responsible for the national highway system, with a centralized administrative structure. Although the ministry traditionally was supposed to handle construction and maintenance, capacity and equipment for the former are lacking, and maintenance has suffered greatly from grossly inadequate financial resources. Technical and managerial capacity are very weak, making it difficult to oversee and coordinate the major donor-funded road investment program underway, and to prepare and evaluate bankable major road projects for future investments.

Key Sector Issues. In addition to the deteriorated road network and centralized organizational structure described above, the highway sector faces a number of serious problems:

i. Security is an important constraint adversely affecting the pace and cost of road construction and rehabilitation.
ii. The financing of recurrent costs of the road sector is far from adequate, and funding mechanisms for cost recovery are undeveloped. Toll collection is irregular, unsupervised, and un-audited, and much of the revenue does not go to the Government.
iii. There is little effective regulation of road use, and freight loads exceeding appropriate weight limits damage roads and shorten their usable life.
iv. Road maintenance appears to be to a large extent reactive to significant deterioration, with insufficient attention to routine maintenance which is more cost-effective.
v. The Afghan private sector is growing but still lacks capacity to handle sizable road construction projects, although it handles smaller roads and often is subcontractor in major road projects. Thus capacity building in the private sector is extremely important.

Government Strategy. The Government has developed a large investment program for major highways, including rehabilitation of the existing network, completion of the network, and, over time, construction of new roads. The Government plans to establish a Program Management Unit in the Ministry of Public Works to support implementation of this program. The role of the ministry will shift away from direct responsibility for constructing and maintaining roads to setting policies, network planning, setting and enforcing standards and regulations, and overseeing the major highways (for which construction and rehabilitation works would be contracted out). Over the longer term, the Government envisions that: (i) major roads will be overseen by an autonomous road agency; (ii) the preservation and further development of the highway network will be financed by road user charges, through some form of "road fund"; (iii) road construction and maintenance will be undertaken primarily by private contractors contracted on a competitive basis; and (v) donor assistance would be directed mainly at rural roads.

Improving Service Delivery. Key priorities from the accountability standpoint include:

i. Phasing out the ministry's direct involvement in road construction and maintenance will focus its role on sector policies and oversight, competitive contracting to the private sector, sector planning, and so forth. This change will avoid conflict of interest between these roles and the ministry's existing (not well-fulfilled) role in construction and maintenance.
ii. Developing appropriate financing mechanisms whereby road users directly (via registration fees, tolls, and so on) and indirectly (through a fuel charge or similar levy) pay for their usage of roads will be critical for the sustainability of road investments. Good governance arrangements will be crucial for the success of a road fund.
iii. In addition, participation by user groups (truckers' associations, vehicle owners) in oversight and monitoring of road management can enhance accountability for services.

Conclusions

The Government views private sector-led development as the key to Afghanistan's longer-term economic development and poverty reduction. Concerted efforts will be needed to create a suitable enabling environment for the private sector and to push forward with public sector reforms redefining the State as the regulator of the private sector—not its

Table 5.3. Priority Areas for Support to the Private Sector

	Description	Priority action
Policy framework	Clear role of public and private institutions	▪ Clearly define the mandate, roles, and responsibilities of key ministries, bringing them into line with the new economic policy of the Government. ▪ Establish an institutional framework to oversee the privatization and liquidation of non-viable state-owned enterprises. ▪ Establish a mechanism for regular and effective dialogue between Government and the private sector.
	Legal and Judicial Framework	▪ Pass the draft Investment Law. ▪ Review the legal framework for private sector development in order to identify areas where gaps, inconsistencies (between different laws), and contradictions (between the overall government approach and provisions of specific laws) exist. ▪ Develop a company law.
	NGO Registration Trade	▪ Conduct a thorough review and re-registration of NGOs. ▪ Continue trade policy improvements, and support for trade facilitation, and provide export promotion services.

Table 5.3. Priority Areas for Support to the Private Sector (*Continued*)

	Description	Priority action
Institutional framework	Governance	▪ Strengthen the High Commission for Investment. ▪ Strengthen capacity in Government to provide research and policy support.
	Regulation and Certification	▪ Continue the simplification of business registration processes and the streamlining of customs clearance procedures. ▪ Develop a metrology, standards, testing and quality (MSTQ) system.
	Access to Factors of Production	▪ Reform/privatize the state-owned commercial banking system. ▪ Develop collateral systems to increase the incentives for banks to provide loans. ▪ Conduct an assessment of the prospects of micro-finance institutions to scale up and serve small enterprises.
	Capacity Building of the Private Sector	▪ Develop a strategy for the effective provision of capacity building services to the private sector. ▪ Work toward market-oriented provision of capacity building services to ensure they reflect the needs of private firms.
	Export Promotion	▪ Strengthen and reform the Export Promotion Department of MoC and ensure it has high-quality staff—perhaps through the PRR process. ▪ Adopt an appropriate policy and regulatory framework and institutional structure for export promotion development.
	Taxation	▪ Continue registration of major companies for tax purposes and provide further support for revenue collection. ▪ Enhance the capabilities of the MoF Large Taxpayers Office.
Other	Security and Risk Mitigation	▪ Expansion of ISAF into regional cities. ▪ Focus on measures which can help mitigate perceived risks arising from both political and non-political sources. ▪ Further development of investment guarantee facilities (MIGA etc.) to provide political risk insurance to foreign investors. ▪ Develop the insurance industry to provide insurance coverage on a commercial basis.
	Utilities	▪ Continue the expansion of power and water utilities. ▪ Provide investment support for reform of Municipalities to develop their role as a service provider. ▪ Develop a clear and consistent policy framework for private sector participation in provision of utilities.
	Land	▪ Develop a policy, regulatory, and institutional framework for development of Industrial Parks with private sector participation.

competitor. The goal is a dynamic and well-regulated economy with a substantial formal component.

It is clear that trade, both within the region and more globally, will need to be a driving force in Afghanistan's economy over the medium to longer term (see Chapter 3). Afghanistan has joined the World Customs Organization. Development of the financial sector will be critical; on September 15, 2003 the Government approved new laws for central banking and the regulation of all other banks. The Government is further developing the legal framework, with new laws on investment, trade in goods and services, and economic governance (including bankruptcy, competition, and land use).

The Government, with support from the international community will need to focus on overcoming the many constraints faced by the private sector, among which the challenges of continued insecurity and lack of infrastructure remain key. A focus on institutional capacity building for both public and private sectors; improved public sector management; formulation of a sound enabling regulatory framework for businesses; development of banking and insurance services; introducing standards, metrology testing, and quality certification services; labor market training and skill enhancement; land titling; infrastructure development for trade and investment; trade, transit, and transport facilitation; and private sector capacity building are vital if high growth rates are to be sustained (Table 5.3).

CHAPTER 6

Agricultural Development Priorities and Prospects

Contributing an estimated 53 percent to GDP (excluding drugs) and 67 percent to the labor force in 2003, agriculture (crops, livestock, forestry, and fishery) is central to the Afghan economy. Agricultural performance strongly influences overall economic growth, evident in the recent recovery after three years of drought. With most poor people living in rural areas, many depending either directly or indirectly on agriculture, improved agricultural performance would have major impacts on poverty reduction through direct effects on producer incomes, indirect effects on consumer welfare through changes in food prices, employment and wage effects, and growth-induced effects throughout the economy.[1] Agriculture and related activities are a major vehicle for women's participation in the economy. Agricultural development is part of the Government's core program of promoting efficient and sustainable use of natural resources, promulgated in the NDF and reiterated in the SAF report. The first section of this chapter provides an overview of agricultural performance, structure, policy framework, and key issues. Reform priorities in four key areas—irrigation, research and extension, marketing, and credit—are then discussed in the second section. The chapter ends with a look at agricultural prospects.

1. This is not to downplay the contribution of the rural non-farm economy which will also be important in combating rural poverty and improving livelihoods. However, agriculture continues to be a primary occupation in rural areas and is a catalyst for rural non-farm activities.

Overview and Policy Framework

Recent Performance

Afghan agriculture has suffered badly for nearly 25 years. Main drivers of agricultural growth and rural poverty reduction—technology, roads, irrigation, education—have all suffered extensive deterioration due to conflict, lack of maintenance, and most recently the severe drought. Trend growth in agricultural output, as measured by an index which includes all crop and livestock products (but not opium poppy), slowed dramatically from 2.2 percent per year in the pre-conflict period of 1961–78 to 0.2 percent during 1978–2001. Cereal output actually declined by 2.0 percent per year between 1978 and 2001, after growing at 1.3 percent annually during 1961–1978 (Table 6.1). Since 2002 there has been a strong recovery with the return of normal precipitation in much of the country and improved availability of seeds and fertilizers. Total cereal production (primarily wheat) increased by 82 percent in 2002 and by a further 50 percent in 2003, reaching 5.4 million tons—roughly the aggregate level Afghanistan needs to meet its foodgrain consumption needs. Production of fruits and vegetables and livestock products has also increased in the past two years but will take longer to reach pre-conflict levels given the sharp reduction in livestock herds and destruction of orchards in recent years.

Table 6.1. Agricultural Growth Rates (percent per annum)

	1961–1978	1978–2001
Agricultural Production Index	2.2	0.2
Cereals production	1.3	–2.0

Note: Growth rates are trend rates calculated using a log linear regression.

Source: Staff estimates using data from FAOSTAT (2003); ADB (2003a).

Cereal production growth is expected to slow down from its accelerated pace of the last two years, since the area under cereals has probably reached its upper limit within the current capacity.[2] It is extremely important, however, that agriculture continue to grow at an average rate of at least 5 percent per year over the next decade to enable faster overall economic growth and to make a substantial dent in rural poverty. Developing a facilitating environment for this to be achieved with the right mix of public policies, institutions, and investments is a major challenge.

Main Structural Features

Although Afghanistan's economy is primarily agricultural, only 12 percent or 7.9 million hectares of the country's total land area is classified as arable (FAO/WFP 2003). Geographically, nearly 75 percent of the arable area is concentrated in three of the eight

2. While area increase was responsible for only 9 percent of increased cereal production in 2002, it was responsible for 55 percent of increased production in 2003 – virtually all land left fallow during the drought was brought back into production.

agricultural planning regions of the country—north, northeast, and west (Figure 6.1). Of the total arable area, not more than half is actually cultivated annually, mainly because of water availability problems.

The agriculture sector is composed mainly of cereal crops which account for an estimated 75 percent of agricultural value added, non-cereal crops 15 percent, and livestock 10 percent. These numbers should be treated with caution as they are subject to revision.

Figure 6.1. Regional Distribution of Arable Land, 2003

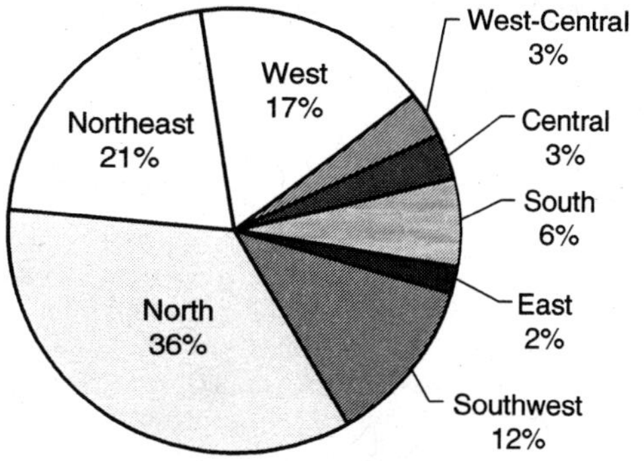

Source: Maletta and Favre (2003).

Cereals. Wheat is the main cereal crop, covering about 2.4 million hectares or 68 percent of total cultivated area in 2002 (Figure 6.2). It is grown by most farmers, largely for subsistence and animal fodder, on irrigated as well as rain-fed land. Most (75–80 percent) wheat production is from irrigated land, with rain-fed wheat area (and yield) varying with climatic conditions. Nearly 70 percent of wheat is produced in the three main arable regions (north, northeast, and west) of the country. Other cereals cultivated include rice, maize, and barley.

Figure 6.2. Cropwise Distribution of Area Cultivated, 2002

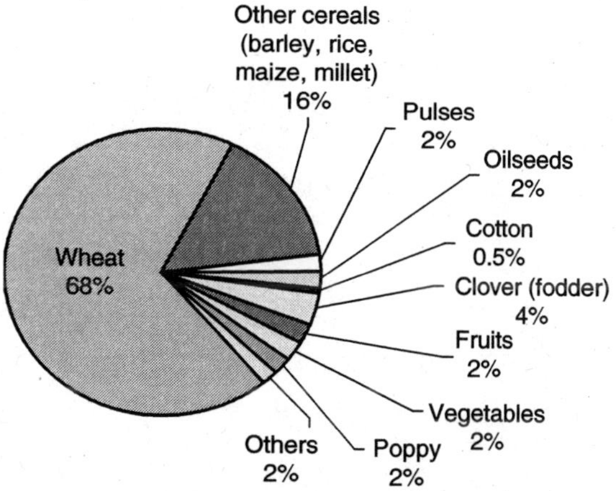

Source: Staff estimates using data from Maletta and Favre (2003); Afghanistan Government (2004b), UNODC (2003b).

Non-Cereals. The important non-cereals are pulses, oilseeds, fruits, vegetables, fodder, and opium poppy. Area under poppy has risen sharply since 2001, reaching an estimated 80,000 ha in 2003, about 2 percent of cultivated area or 1 percent of arable area (Chapter 7). Financial returns to cultivating poppy appear to have been marginally higher than for the most lucrative alternatives in the late 1990s (Box 6.1), but rose dramatically following the Taliban ban in 2000/01. Among other non-cereal crops, fruits and vegetables are important because of their past significance and potential future prospects. The fruits sub-sector (grapes, almonds, apples, apricots, pomegranates, and so forth), which in the 1970s was a significant part of the Afghan economy contributing over

Box 6.1. Comparative Returns from Crop Cultivation

Assessing relative profitability of different crops in Afghanistan is hampered by lack of reliable and representative data. Apart from some recent farm-level estimates of costs and returns to wheat cultivation, there is little information available on costs of production for the other main crops. Estimates from 2000 are available on the gross value of output per hectare for different crops (ICARDA, 2003, shown in Chart), but since the costs per hectare are not known, it is difficult to draw any conclusions about relative profitability

Nevertheless, available information suggests that, first, opium poppy has the highest gross value of output per ha. In 2000 it was estimated at eight times that of wheat, but by 2003 with the steep increase in the farm-gate price of poppy it had risen to 28 times that of wheat. Even after adjusting for higher production costs, the difference in profits per ha is enormous. Second, most important fruits (almonds, apples, grapes, pomegranates) and vegetables (potatoes, onions, tomatoes) also offered better gross revenue per hectare in 2000 compared to wheat, but not poppy. Third, in 2003 the gross value of output per ha from wheat cultivation increased substantially as a result of improved yields, from around $450–500 per ha to $700 per ha.

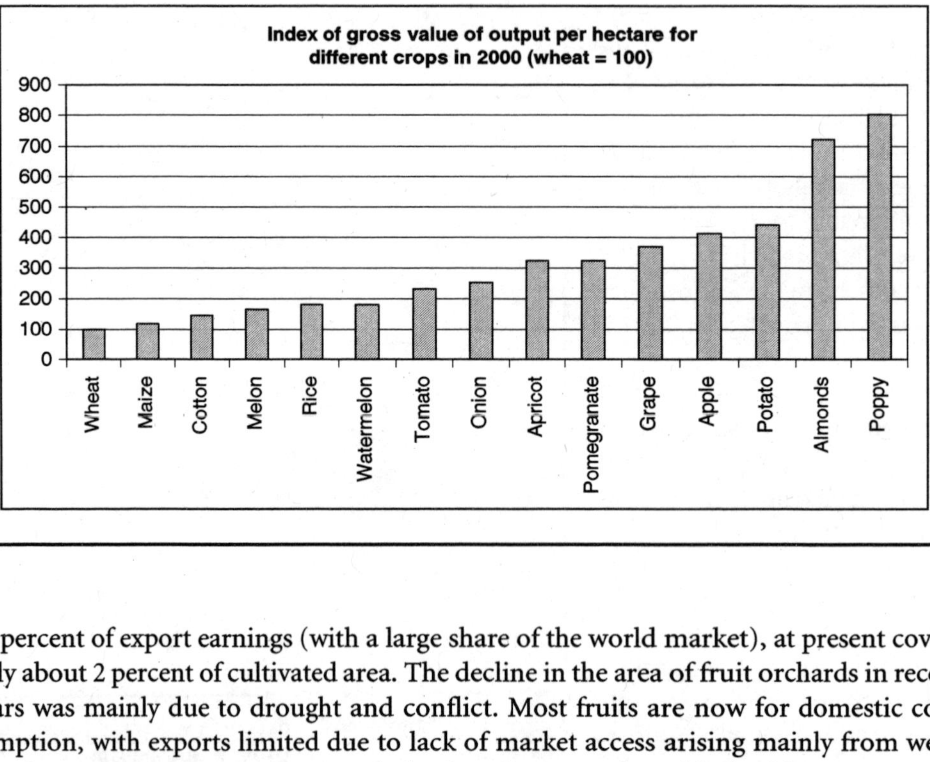

40 percent of export earnings (with a large share of the world market), at present covers only about 2 percent of cultivated area. The decline in the area of fruit orchards in recent years was mainly due to drought and conflict. Most fruits are now for domestic consumption, with exports limited due to lack of market access arising mainly from weak post-harvest management practices, lack of quality control, and lack of finance. Vegetables, increasingly preferred because of their short growing cycle in an uncertain environment, also cover about 2 percent of cultivated area; the main products are melons, watermelons, potatoes, onions, and tomatoes. Fruits and vegetables are major cash crops, with marketed proportions in the range of 50–70 percent of production. Cotton, significant in the 1970s, has declined to negligible levels with the collapse of the domestic cotton textile industry.

Livestock is a major source of food and income for Afghan farmers, traditionally being an integral part of most farming systems in the country. Range pasture land covering

Table 6.2. Livestock Population Per Family

	1995	1998	2003
Cattle	3.7	2.5	1.2
Sheep	21.9	14.2	2.9
Goats	9.4	5.8	2.4
Donkeys	1.1	0.7	0.5
Camels	0.4	0.2	0.1
Poultry	11.6	6.8	4.0

Source: FAO (2003b).

about 45 percent of the total land area has traditionally supported a large livestock population, with animals being the only source of income for some groups like the Kuchi nomads. The livestock population declined in the 1980s but had recovered to pre-war levels by the mid-1990s. However, the drought years of 1999–2001 had a devastating impact. As per a 2003 census the estimated livestock population is about 34 million (including 12 million poultry), a major decline from the 1990s. The number of cattle and poultry per family had fallen to one-third of the 1995 figure, with numbers of sheep and goats per family suffering an even steeper decline.

Input Use. According to a farmer survey covering 30 provinces in 2002/03, use of improved seeds, fertilizers, and tractors in Afghanistan is significant. Nearly 54 percent of wheat area in 2003 was sown with improved seed released in the last 10 years (through FAO and other sources), while the rest was sown with local seeds or improved seeds introduced more than 10 years ago. There are regional variations, however, with less than 30 percent wheat area using improved seeds in the southwest and southern regions but over 75 percent in the east and northeast. Fertilizer use is also substantial, with a national average of about 180 kg/ha for irrigated wheat and regional variations ranging from an average of 345 kg/ha in the central region to 80 kg/ha in the southwest. Fertilizer is also commonly used for fruits, vegetables, and other crops. Use of tractors is also significant, and in 2002/03 about 46 percent of land was cultivated using a tractor compared to 39 percent in 2001/02. This increased use may have been partly prompted by the decrease in the number of oxen due to the prolonged drought, although significant income for many farmers from opium (e.g. in Helmand where more than 98 percent of land was cultivated using tractors) is also a factor contributing to increased use of tractors.

There is a large degree of unanimity on the main constraints facing agriculture in Afghanistan, based on recent studies and farmer surveys. These include:

i. lack of assured and timely irrigation;
ii. inadequate knowledge of improved production and post-production technologies;
iii. access to markets;
iv. access to credit; and
v. weak institutional capacity in both public and private sectors.

Policy and Institutional Framework

Unlike in many other countries, Afghanistan's agricultural sector does not suffer from major price distortions arising from input subsidies or price support policies. The trade environment is relatively undistorted—without high import tariffs, quantitative restrictions, or

Box 6.2. Typical Regulatory Requirements of a Modern Agricultural System

- Legal and business regulation (with low costs of compliance for doing business), transparency, adjudication of contract disputes, contract enforcement, market regulation.
- Food safety regulations and standards (especially in processing facilities), and testing for contamination (including microbial) and chemical residues.
- Natural/environmental and common property resource (waterways, forests, air, fauna) protection, and land and water use management including tenure administration.
- Intellectual property rights (IPR) regulations to provide incentives for innovation, enforcement of IPR laws and patents, balancing security of property rights with technology accessibility for smallholders.
- Verification and certification of seeds and plant propagation materials and registration and regulation of agrochemical use.
- Inspection services and issuance of phytosanitary certificates, and verification and certification of products for satisfying relevant grades and standards.
- Labeling requirements and their enforcement.

Source: World Bank (2004a).

export subsidies. In sum, the incentive structure is largely market driven, and furthermore, the Government is committed to keeping it this way.

The main challenges to developing Afghan agriculture are institutional. Public and private institutions are ill-equipped in terms of physical infrastructure, regulatory framework, human skills, or concrete knowledge of what a modern and competitive agricultural sector looks like (Box 6.2). Three core ministries have been involved in agriculture and natural resource management—the Ministry of Agriculture and Animal Husbandry (MAAH), the Ministry of Irrigation, Water Resources, and Environment (MIWRE), and the Ministry of Rural Rehabilitation and Development (MRRD). Water-related issues have been entrusted to MIWRE, agricultural research and extension to MAAH, and rural development/employment/poverty programs to MRRD. Within this broad division of labor, areas of overlap/gap are being identified and addressed. At the farm level, water, technology, and livelihoods are inextricably linked, so effective coordination between the three ministries is critical for efficient delivery of public investments and support services in rural areas. The agricultural sector may be affected by consolidation of ministries, which is under consideration (mentioned in Chapter 4).

The structure of the ministries also reflects a centralized form of administration inconsistent with current rural development thinking which calls for decentralized decision making and implementation. At present more than one-third of the roughly 13,500 staff employed in the three ministries are located at headquarters in Kabul. Also, the long period of conflict has weakened all government institutions—buildings and equipment have been destroyed, existing staff are poorly paid, they lack appropriate technical and managerial skills, and ministries generally lack the capacity to effectively carry out their functions. The PRR, an interim public administration reform program which includes capacity building, higher pay, and staff retraining, has been initiated in some ministries.

Although there is as yet no formal national agricultural policy or strategy, a draft Policy and Strategic Framework (PSF) for the Agriculture and Natural Resources Sector has recently been prepared by MAAH in consultation with MIWRE, MRRD, and major development partners. It identifies the main issues and problems to be addressed, outlines a broad sectoral vision with strategic objectives, lists major interventions needed, and prescribes following NDF principles for developing detailed sub-sectoral policies and programs to guide future sector development. The PSF represents an encouraging beginning, particularly in its adoption of the NDF division of roles and responsibilities between the public and private sectors. The next step is to prepare a set of detailed sub-sectoral policies and strategies. These should address, inter alia, roles of public and private sectors (including NGOs) in performing particular functions, appropriate regulation to foster development of a modern food and agricultural system, institutional reform and inter-ministerial collaboration, and development of human resources.

Priority Areas for Reform

While there is a large degree of consensus on the main problems and constraints in agriculture, what is less clear is a road map to effectively address these constraints within underlying boundaries of fiscal sustainability, environmental sustainability, and political acceptance. The rest of this chapter discusses four priority areas where immediate Government action is necessary to accelerate agricultural growth: rehabilitation and management of water resources; effective generation and dissemination of agricultural technology; facilitation of modern post-harvest handling and marketing systems; and enhanced access to rural finance. One other constraint that has been identified as very serious is land tenure insecurity (Box 6.3). While recognized as important, this is part of a larger governance agenda, not only related to agriculture. Experiences elsewhere suggest that resolving land tenure issues can be complex and controversial, and for this reason it may be prudent to carry out more research in the area and for the Government to adopt an incremental and learning by doing approach that involves local communities, before scaling up. International experience suggests that building on the best traditional practices can be an effective way to move forward (De Soto 2000).

Water Resources

Water is central to Afghanistan's agriculture. Lack of assured and timely irrigation water supply at the farm level is perhaps the most important constraint to agricultural growth. Irrigation infrastructure, as well as many supporting community-based and government institutions, have seriously deteriorated or broken down due to years of conflict, lack of maintenance, and more recently drought. Addressing irrigation problems is high on the Government's agenda.

Present Status of Irrigation Systems. Traditional surface systems, with intakes from rivers and streams, account for about 80 percent of the irrigated area. While these systems have generally survived, their community-based mechanisms for water management and

Box 6.3. Land Tenure Issues in Afghanistan

Information about how rural land is distributed and under what conditions is incomplete, but there are important regional differences. Disturbed settlements and tenure insecurity render information unreliable beyond the short term. High rates of sharecropping by both landowners and landless and the ambivalent status of mortgaged plots make precise definition of owners difficult.

- Years of conflict have seriously disturbed land relations, de-securing farm and pasture rights in some areas, and jeopardizing the ability of administrators or courts to manage or uphold rights fairly.
- Landlessness and indebtedness in the farming sector have been longstanding features of Afghan agriculture. Population growth and land shortages, opium poppy production, ethnic tension, insecurity, and more recently the drought remain potent drivers to land grabbing, landlessness, and destitution.
- Pasture land is a principal source of conflict. Competition over this valuable resource engenders conflict among settled and nomadic land users and ethnic and territorial interests. Issues of common property rights also arise.
- A plural legal basis to land rights exists, in the form of customary, religious, and state law, and with a great deal of overlap, some inconsistency, and much uncertainty as to norms in each body of law. Landowners variously use custom, Shariat, or evidence from the land register to demonstrate their rights.
- A clear system for land tenure administration does not exist. Administration (such as the formalization of routine transfer of rights) falls, by default, to judges.
- There is currently no institutional focus for dealing with land tenure. The main discernible land policy of the Government is to restore land to those who owned the land in 1978. However, adoption of this strategy without addressing underlying grievances associated with how land was acquired will not provide a lasting resolution. A second main policy is to pursue registration and entitlement, mainly to encourage investment. This deserves more thought in light of the failure of registration approaches to deliver tenure security.

Source: Wily (2003).

maintenance have been adversely affected by local commanders who frequently have not respected water rights or the authority of the farmer elected and employed *mirabs* (water masters). This has had a significant impact on water distribution, both within some of these systems, and across irrigation systems along the same river. Next in importance are larger modern irrigation systems, accounting for about 10 percent of irrigated area. Managed in the past by parastatal agencies, these have been gravely affected during the past twenty years as maintenance was neglected due to lack of staff, equipment, and finances. Consequently only the upstream parts of the roughly 325,000 hectares of their command areas now receive proper irrigation. Karezes (a traditional irrigation system using underground tunnels), accounting for roughly 5 percent of irrigated area, have also suffered due to the war; some were deliberately destroyed, sabotaged, or mined to make rehabilitation difficult. The recent drought, coupled with a gradual disintegration of community responsibility, has led to indiscriminate groundwater pumping by some farmers, leading to declines in groundwater levels in some areas and jeopardizing traditional springs and kareze fed supplies. Springs and wells constitute the remaining types of irrigation systems.

Water Availability and Use. Recent estimates indicate that Afghanistan has about 70 billion cubic meters (BCM) of annual water resources, of which 55 BCM is surface water and 15 BCM is groundwater. Annual water use, of which over 95 percent is for irrigation, is estimated at about 20 BCM, which means that not more than 30 percent of water resources are being utilized. Actual irrigated area has been considerably lower in recent years than earlier. It is roughly estimated that 1.3 million ha were intensively irrigated in 2003, with a slightly larger area under "intermittent irrigation." There is also considerable regional variation in water availability and use, with the north, northeast, west, and southwest regions accounting for about half of estimated surface water resources and three-fourths of irrigated area (Table 6.3).

Table 6.3. Regional Composition of Surface Water Resources and Irrigated Area

	Percent distribution of	
Region	Surface water resources	Irrigated area (FAO satellite maps)
North	6	21
North East	25	12
West	10	15
South West	11	25
West Central	6	3
Central	20	15
South	4	5
East	18	5
Total	**100**	**100**

Source: Sheladia Associates (2004).

Government Strategy. There is substantial scope for improving the quality (timely delivery) and expanding the quantity (area under assured irrigation) of irrigation, thereby reducing vulnerability to droughts and increasing yields in Afghanistan. Recognizing the centrality of water, the Government plans to invest about $2.35 billion between 2004 and 2015 in four sub-programs related to water resources and irrigated agriculture (Table 6.4). On the investment

Table 6.4. Estimated Irrigation Potential in Afghanistan

	Hectares ('000)
Area irrigated before the war to be brought back to permanent irrigation through rehabilitation works	240
Area under irrigation that require potentially improvement/rehabilitation works to allow more intensive cultivation	1,310
Area under intermittent irrigation that can be brought to intensive irrigation mainly through development of storage infrastructure	953
Area never irrigated that could be brought to intensive irrigation through development of new irrigation schemes	1,035
Total	**3,538**

Source: Afghanistan Government (2004b).

side, it is estimated that a total of 3.54 million hectares of irrigation potential could be developed through rehabilitation and development of new infrastructure such as storage. Projects currently funded by external assistance focus on the first three categories and provide funds to rehabilitate infrastructure serving about 0.43 to 0.55 million ha. Another 0.5 million ha., mainly in the third and fourth categories, is planned to be developed by 2015 under the National Long Term Irrigation and Power Program.

On the policy and institutional front, the proposed strategy contains three main elements. First is the adoption of a river basin approach to manage water resources. Two pilot river basin management organizations are to be established by the end of 2004, and three more by 2006. These will be autonomous bodies that will administer all water resources related matters within their boundaries, including water allocation to different subsectors (such as drinking water, irrigation, and industry). Second, as part of the Priority Reform and Restructuring (PRR) program underway in most ministries, MIWRE is to be restructured, with retraining of all staff by 2008, reduction (about 40 percent planned by 2006) and redeployment (from Kabul to the provinces) of staff, and privatization/liquidation of Helmand Construction Company, Deep Wells Drilling Department, and Metal Works by 2006. Third is the adoption of a participatory approach involving water user groups in rehabilitation and O&M of all irrigation schemes in the future.

Recommendations for Consideration. Overall, the irrigation strategy appears to be on the right track, although there are significant implementation issues. Given conditions prevailing in Afghanistan, the initial focus on rehabilitation of irrigation infrastructure is appropriate. There is a risk, however, that MIWRE's efforts may become so focused on rehabilitation/development that other critical aspects with potentially large multiplier effects in terms of delivering sustainable growth outcomes may be neglected. Selected recommendations include:

i. *Attention to operation and maintenance (O&M) and cost recovery.* International experience demonstrates that while creating assets can be relatively easy, ensuring timely and adequate O&M is much more difficult. Although the MIWRE plan is that water user groups (WUGs) will be involved in O&M of irrigation systems, a number of actions are needed to ensure that this happens. First is appropriate legislation that formalizes the roles and responsibilities of WUGs, MIWRE, and other stakeholders. While the traditional mirab system worked well without written rules and agreements, there are increasing reports of challenges to it from local commanders and the system breaking down as a result, so providing legal protection to resolve disputes is essential. Second, WUGs need to be involved as early as possible in rehabilitation/development work, ideally from the design stage, which creates ownership and facilitates smooth handover of O&M. Third, cost estimates of annual O&M requirements should be prepared early and discussed with WUGs prior to any significant capital investment. While detailed project-wise estimates of rehabilitation costs are available with MIWRE, there is relatively little information available on expected O&M costs.

ii. *Dissemination of improved agricultural techniques and management practices.* Productivity and income effects of irrigation can be fully realized only by adopting improved agricultural technologies. Because agricultural technology is primarily an MAAH responsibility, efforts need to focus on: (i) revitalizing MAAH's capacity for technology generation and transfer; (ii) incentives for effective field-level coordination between MIWRE, MAAH, and other government/NGO staff; and (iii) using WUGs and other forms of farmer groups as a cost-effective instrument of technology transfer.

iii. *Environmental considerations.* While MIWRE is currently focusing on surface water irrigation, groundwater resources need to be looked at closely and their indiscriminate exploitation curbed. Groundwater tables need to be regularly monitored, especially in vulnerable areas, and appropriate actions taken if necessary, through pricing and other instruments. While enacting regulations on groundwater extraction is an option, implementing such regulations would be difficult, especially in the prevailing situation of insecurity. International experience suggests that community participation and peer pressure can often be more effective in managing groundwater resources than policing by government staff. Attention also needs to be paid to integrating watershed development with irrigation improvement (little work has been done on integrated watershed development in Afghanistan).

Research and Extension

Productivity growth in agriculture is based largely on application of science, technology, and information. Studies consistently show high returns to investments in agricultural research in developing countries, averaging over 40 percent (Table 6.5). A recent paper on comparative returns to public investments in R&D, irrigation, roads, education, and electricity in China and India showed that public investment in R&D contributed the most to promoting agricultural growth in both countries (Fan, Zhang, and Zhang 2002). While complementary investments in infrastructure are necessary, investment in agricultural research and extension is a key element in enhancing a country's competitive advantage by reducing production costs, improving product quality, and generally increasing efficiency along the commodity chain.

Table 6.5. Estimated Rates of Return to Investment in Agricultural Research

Region	Number of estimates	Median rate of return (%)
Africa	188	34
Asia	222	50
Latin America	262	43
Middle East/ North Africa	11	36
All Developing Countries	683	43
All Developed Countries	990	46
All	1772	44

Source: Alston and others (1998), cited in World Bank (2004a).

Present Status. Prior to the conflict Afghanistan had a substantial agricultural research system which, at its peak, carried out its functions through 24 research stations and over 1,000 staff, of whom 25 percent were technical research staff. This system is now largely dysfunctional as a result of widespread infrastructure destruction and loss of skilled staff. The agricultural extension system, which used to operate through about 400 extension units spread across the nation, is in a similar state of disrepair. Although there are still large numbers of staff on the MAAH payroll (about 10,000), most have little exposure to modern agricultural management practices. Capacity building efforts need to focus on updating technical skills but also on developing new skills related to management, monitoring and evaluation, participatory approaches, and marketing.

Government Strategy. Part of the problem with revitalizing the agricultural research and extension system is that there appears to be little consensus on the way forward. Opting for an army of centrally controlled staff who also double as input supply agents is neither a desirable nor a sustainable option. Increasingly global trends are toward public-private partnerships and decentralized systems that can identify and respond nimbly to changing farmer demands.

The Government's strategy for revamping agricultural research and extension is less developed than in the case of irrigation. The initial step in strategy development is a review planned for 2004 of the policies and institutional structure needed to establish and operate an efficient agricultural research and technology transfer system that will respond to farmers' identified priorities and to future farming needs. This exercise could be the basis for a national research strategy and a national extension strategy, which is a recommended second step. In this context it should be noted that policy planning and analysis in MAAH needs to be strengthened.

Recommendations for Consideration. Establishing an effective and sustainable research and extension system is a high priority. Key directions on the research side include:

i. *Focus on adaptive research, not basic research.* There are many new technologies available internationally from which Afghan agriculture could benefit—including not just new varieties but also improved practices in nutrient management, pest management, water management, conservation farming, and integrated crop-livestock production. Efforts should be made to form partnerships with regional research institutions/systems to access these technologies, validate them in local conditions with the help of the domestic research system, adapt as necessary, and then spread them to farmers through the extension system.
ii. *Strengthen demand for research products.* Past investments in research have mostly focused on supply of research products rather than farmer demand. Research systems need to be responsive and accountable to client demands. This can be fostered by encouraging farmer participation in priority setting, execution, and evaluation of research programs through rapid appraisals and participatory on-farm research, farmer representation on research governing bodies and advisory panels, decentralizing/deconcentrating research, and linking research to demand-driven extension.
iii. *Align research priorities to needs.* While research priorities will emerge from development strategies and client demand, likely priority areas include: (i) post-harvest research, product quality, and food safety—horticultural exports, for instance, have good potential but will require substantial adaptive research to meet international quality standards; (ii) environmental conservation; and (iii) social science and policy research.

On the extension side the following considerations are important:

i. *Define public and private sector roles.* Because there is frequently a mix of public and private elements in an extension system, it is important to delineate the roles of the public and private sectors in provision of specific services. For instance, generic farm advisory services, market price information through mass media, advice on environmental conservation practices, and control of major contagious diseases are legitimate public sector responsibilities. Establishing and enforcing quality parameters for agricultural inputs also is a public sector responsibility, that needs to be handled through appropriate regulation. However, supply of inputs such as seeds or fertilizers or farm equipment, apart from demonstrations, should be left to the private sector.

ii. *Contract out extension services where possible.* There is growing recognition internationally that even in situations where public financing of extension is justified, private service delivery is often the more efficient way to serve clients (Box 6.4). Good-practice examples of contracting out extension include Chile (introduced in 1978), Bangladesh, and India. Contracting out extension programs works best when community or producer organizations are closely involved in selecting extension agents, evaluating services, determining program content, and deciding how services are allocated.

iii. *Adopt participatory approaches.* Extension strategy needs to emphasize development of capacity for farmers to express their demand for services and increase their influence over programs, strengthening accountability for service delivery (see Chapter 8 for a conceptual framework in this regard). International experience confirms that working with client groups makes extension services more accessible to small farmers by exploiting economies of scale in service delivery and by providing a mechanism for producers to express their demand for services.

Box 6.4. Outsourcing Extension Services

Advantages:

- Reduces permanent staff requirements and allows deployment of resources to high-priority areas.
- Allows for accessing providers with special skills to provide specific services.
- Promotes partnerships and working relationships with other providers.
- Enhances flexibility in responding to special needs of diverse clientele.
- Tests innovative and higher risk "new" systems.
- Increases provider accountability and forces more attention to financial management.

Disadvantages:

- Institutional memory may be lost; some private providers may not pass on new skills and lessons learned.
- Increases the need for skills of contract negotiation, supervision, and monitoring performance.
- High initial costs (if not offset by staff reductions).

Source: Rivera, Zijp, and Alex (2000).

Two concrete lessons emerging from these approaches are: (i) working with existing groups is often more successful than starting new ones—in Afghanistan the elected village Community Development Councils (CDCs) being established under the National Solidarity Program (NSP) could provide an appropriate entry point, eventually paving the way for specific farmer interest groups to emerge and farmer-to-farmer extension to take root; and (ii) promoting farmer groups requires specialized skills which are often lacking in traditionally trained public extension workers—calling for appropriate training, but also extensive use of private community facilitators (including NGOs) to fill the gap.

iv. *Decentralize/de-concentrate agricultural extension services.* User participation and response to local needs can be facilitated by decentralizing governance, administration, and management of extension programs. Extension systems in industrialized countries have long been decentralized, with responsibility devolved to local governments, often in conjunction with local producer organizations. This approach is now spreading to many developing countries. However, decentralization raises complex political and administrative issues, and would be premature in Afghanistan given the governance environment in many parts of the country. Nevertheless, in preparing for the future, there are a few salient lessons. First, decentralizing extension will work best when it is part of an overall public sector reform program transferring responsibilities from national to local governments. Second, de-concentration is nearly always the first and necessary step, which puts staff from centralized administrations in closer contact with local people and problems, although it does not change the central line of authority and control. There should be adequate central support, especially for capacity development, monitoring and evaluation, establishing quality control systems, training, subject matter specialists, and production of extension materials.

v. *Reach out to women.* Women play an extremely important role in all dimensions of agricultural production (Box 6.5), yet they have not figured prominently enough in agricultural policies and past extension initiatives. As part of a demand-driven and community-based approach, women should be explicitly targeted which will reap major benefits in terms of agricultural production and incomes.

vi. *Expand the scope of extension services beyond production.* While re-establishing an effective extension system, care should be taken that it is not restricted to production as has traditionally been the case. Advice to farmers would be particularly important, especially for horticultural crops. This could include guidance on market acceptability, post-harvest handling techniques, marketing methods, and calculation of marketing costs.

vii. *Develop sustainable financing mechanisms.* The planned MAAH review of the agricultural research and technology transfer system should look closely at staff and skill requirements and at levels of salary and non-salary expenditures that can be supported over the long term, and take appropriate decisions on staff levels.

Agricultural Marketing

Well-functioning agricultural markets improve competitiveness and increase incomes to farmers, laborers, and entrepreneurs. In Afghanistan, prospects for a sustained horticultural

Box 6.5. Agriculture and the Gender Division of Labor

Recent research highlights the extent to which land tenure arrangements, ownership, and the social dimensions of production in Afghanistan need to inform the agricultural development strategy (see Wily 2003 and Maletta 2003).

As the recent NRVA results highlight (see Chapter 9), female-headed households are among the poorest members of society. Security of tenure and security of other social and economic assets for women are most often less than those for other groups. It is therefore vital to understand the extent to which gender aspects impact on ownership, cultivation patterns, division of labor, post-harvest processing, livestock raising, and dairy production. Future extension work should acknowledge women's input at various stages of cultivation (with regional variations), and their significant responsibilities in post-harvest processing of crops. Moreover, livestock extension must focus on women as far as veterinary services are concerned.

While there are no exhaustive surveys of the division of labor within rural households nor of women's contribution to the agricultural economy, evidence from a number of scattered local surveys highlights that women's and girls' contribution is very significant but remains largely

Main Characteristics of Villages

	Village A (mainly Pashtun)		Village B (Pashtun)		Village C (Pashtare)	
Women's production activities	Household activities—cheese, embroidery, sewing		Household activities, farmingfarm labor, migration (piecework/farm labor)		Household activities, wood collection, farming, farm labor	
	Women	Men	Women	Men	Women	Men
Crop planting	x	x	X	xx	x	x
Crop Main-tenance (mainly weeding)	x	x	Xx	xx	x	xx
Irrigation		xx	X	x		xx
Crop Harvest	x	xx	Xx	xx	xx	xx
Crop Process	x	x	X			
Wild Plant Collection	x	x	X	x	xxx	x
Fodder Management	xxx	x	Xx	x	xxx	
Livestock Management	xxx	x				
Shepherd		x			x	x
Farm Labor		x	X	x		x
Non-Farm Labor		x		x		x
Transport					x	x
Other	xxx		Xx	x		xx

x: less than 10% of positive respones; xx: 10% or more positive respones; xxx: more than 25% positive respones

Source: Kerr-Wilson and Pain, 2003: Table 1, p. 8 and Table 11, p. 16.

(continued)

Box 6.5. Agriculture and the Gender Division of Labor (*Continued*)

unrecorded and un-monetized. A significant portion of households in all surveys are female-headed. Women and girls undertake a wide range of farm-based activities ranging from seed bed preparation, weeding, horticulture, and fruit cultivation to a wide range of post-harvest crop processing activities such as cleaning and drying vegetables, fruits, and nuts for domestic use and for marketing. The chart at right, showing three villages with different conditions, demonstrates the centrality of women's involvement in all stages of the production of crops and livestock. Better applied research, a more focused policy that acknowledges women's central contribution to agriculture, and associated investment instruments geared toward women are therefore needed.

revival, in particular, depend to a large extent on improving market efficiency and an environment that encourages greater private sector investment.

Present Status. Agricultural markets and support services are not well developed in the Afghanistan. The most serious constraint has been the absence of a well-maintained road network, although fears about security, poor market facilities, and telecommunications also are important issues. Wholesale market infrastructure, even in major urban centers, is sub-standard, lacking in many cases basic services such as water, electricity, and sewage. There is no organized management of these markets, most of which are on land nominally owned by municipalities, as a result of which trading is done in unhygienic conditions and no money is spent on maintenance. Facilities for sorting, cooling, packaging, and storage are poor or non-existent (and cold storages will require reliable supplies of electricity). Support services like market information systems do not exist. Food safety regulations, grades and standards, quality control, and testing and certification services are lacking or weak.

Government Strategy. While investments in roads and other market-related infrastructure will help address the "hardware" side of market development, capacity in MAAH and the Ministry of Commerce to support the equally if not more important "software" side is lacking. Not enough attention is being paid to strengthening this aspect, despite a general consensus that addressing marketing constraints is essential for accelerated and sustainable agricultural growth. This could have adverse consequences for development of an export-led horticulture sector.

Recommendations for Consideration. Strategically, and to keep the task manageable, it would be appropriate to focus in the short term on improving market prospects for horticultural products. Afghanistan has a long tradition in horticulture, so most Afghan farmers and traders are already familiar with many horticulture crops and are likely to be receptive to measures that improve product quality and marketability. Second, some of the high-value horticultural commodities, if properly marketed, could generate large farm-level profits and employment. These could include spices (small amounts of saffron and cumin are already being exported), medicinal herbs, flowers, fragrances (like rose oil), and the more traditional dried fruits and nuts. Third, fuelled by rising consumer incomes, international demand for income-elastic horticultural products is growing rapidly, notably in Russia, Eastern Europe, India, and East Asia.

International markets for horticultural products are very competitive and demanding in terms of quality. The challenge for Afghanistan is to stimulate private sector-led initiatives, backed by public investment in critical infrastructure and an appropriate regulatory environment (such as for sanitary and phyto-sanitary measures). Actions to stimulate private investment economy-wide are discussed in Chapter 5. Establishing an appropriate regulatory environment and support services for modernizing horticultural markets would include:

i. Public investments in roads, including those linking farms to markets, and availability of other basic infrastructure like electric power to run cold storages and other marketing facilities.
ii. Establishing minimum standards for different wholesale agricultural markets to provide basic amenities and marketing facilities, and developing a system for management and operation of these markets by elected representatives of the main market players (farmers, traders, processors, and so forth) that is financially sustainable through collection of marketing fees, with Government oversight limited to ensuring fair trading practices.
iii. Developing and enforcing a grades and standards system that reflects market requirements. Private stakeholders need to take a lead role in the development of these standards, with Government facilitation and enforcement of an agreed system. Information on sanitary and phyto-sanitary standards in different countries is needed.
iv. Supporting strategic market research to assist the Government in deciding which crops should be supported in terms of research, extension and other facilities.
v. Emphasizing marketing issues in agricultural extension to: (i) help farmers and others better understand markets and become more commercially numerate; and (ii) link farmers to agribusiness. Adoption of a farmer group approach to agricultural extension will also facilitate group marketing, which can significantly enhance the negotiating power of farmers and the prices they receive for their produce.
vi. Piloting a publicly funded market information system to test its usefulness and cost effectiveness; if successful the model can be scaled up with private funding/partnership.

Rural Credit

A functional rural financial system is necessary to enable farmers to better manage their activities, improve technologies, and increase productivity. Based on the lessons of international experience with directed lending to agriculture through publicly-owned institutions, and in line with current development thinking, the Government has decided to dissolve the state-owned Agricultural Development Bank. Currently, traditional sources (moneylenders, traders, family, friends) are the main source of agricultural credit, together with various NGO-led micro-finance initiatives. The Micro-Finance Support Facility of Afghanistan (MISFA) is seen as the primary apex facility for micro-finance, with a target of reaching 80,000 people in its 18-month pilot phase. The program has started well and by March 2004 had an estimated 25,000 clients. At this early stage the main issue is related to cost-effectiveness—administrative costs in the first year of operation have been high, reportedly as much as 1:1 for each dollar lent as substantial expenditures went into establishing new facilities. The lower population density in Afghanistan's rural area as compared with the cities and with many other countries also affects costs. Administrative costs have to be controlled for financial sustainability of the program.

Establishing a viable rural financial system in Afghanistan should be seen as a medium-term objective rather than a short-term goal. Creative solutions for filling the gap between micro-finance at the low end and nascent larger-scale commercial lending need to be explored, in order to respond effectively to farmers' credit requirements. This will be especially important in the case of marketed horticultural products and exports. Rural credit also needs to be seen as part of a wider financial systems approach within which financing for agriculture is viewed as part of the broader rural finance market. Key priorities put forward in a recent World Bank report on this subject include the following:

i. In the short term, establish an effective system of NGO and micro-finance registration and monitoring, and facilitate entry and expand outreach.
ii. Adopt new NGO legislation that encompasses micro-finance activities and other savings and credit associations; encourage larger, well managed institutions to expand their range of products, including deposit taking among members.
iii. Eventually consider transformation of some of the larger micro finance entities into banks or non-bank financial institutions.

Prospects for Afghan Agriculture

Future agricultural prospects in Afghanistan depend to a large extent on how speedily and effectively public and private institutions can respond to challenges and provide an appropriate environment that can stimulate market-driven agricultural growth. The last two years have seen a strong recovery from the drought of 1999–2001. Sustaining and further building on this recovery in the medium term will depend on weather and security conditions but also on investments and institutional strengthening in the key areas discussed above.

Expanding the scope and effectiveness of irrigation is the best option to raise yields and reduce the vulnerability of the agricultural economy to drought. However, benefits from irrigation investments could be modest if agricultural technology and market-related services are not strengthened concurrently. These are critical gaps in the current strategy.

On purely economic grounds, opium poppy is the most profitable crop and is likely to remain so (Box 6.1). Poppy cultivation in Afghanistan in many respects represents a model of contract farming—inputs, extension advice, and credit are provided to farmers under a firm buyback arrangement at an attractive price. Finding alternative crops to match these arrangements will be difficult if not impossible. Thus a combination of agricultural and rural development with effective law enforcement will be necessary (Chapter 7).

Wheat will continue to be the most widely grown crop in Afghanistan for some time, partly for subsistence reasons and partly because diversification will take time to materialize to a substantial degree. Prior to 2003 wheat yields in Afghanistan were much lower than in neighboring countries. In 2003 irrigated wheat yields in Afghanistan increased significantly to an average of 2.8 tons/hectare, close to levels in neighboring countries, based on good precipitation and improved availability of seeds. Rainfed wheat yields rose to an average

1.1 tons/ha, also comparable to yields in neighboring countries. However, there is no structural reason for wheat yields (and incomes) to be trapped at these levels. In the medium term, national average irrigated wheat yields of 3.0 to 3.5 tons/ha and rainfed yields of around 1.5 tons/ha would be feasible with improved on-farm management and appropriate inputs. Already in 2003, average irrigated yields of more than 3.5 tons/ha were recorded in four wheat producing provinces.

Among horticultural crops, raisins, apricots, pistachios, almonds, melons, and pomegranates appear to have relatively greater economic potential. Less is known about some of the spices, medicinal herbs, fragrances, and flowers, although some of them (such as saffron, roses) may have very good potential. Key challenges relate to improving product quality and access to export markets. In addition to investments in roads and other infrastructure, steps to modernize research, extension, and marketing will be critical in addressing issues related to varietal improvement, improved post-harvest practices, and export market access.

In the livestock sector, restoring the size of animal populations, severely affected by the drought, is the priority. This requires investments and institutional strengthening in animal health services and in meeting animal nutrition demands. Even so, recovery in the livestock sector is likely to be gradual.[3] In the longer run, breed improvement is likely to become a focal area for which national level data on different breeds, currently unavailable, will be a prerequisite.

Given its nature and scale and the many challenges faced, the process of rebuilding the agricultural sector in Afghanistan will take time. Success will also require coordination between Government ministries, a large and varied donor community, the private sector, and the farming community. With the right leadership, commitment, and sustained prioritization of agriculture, there is no reason why the challenges cannot be successfully met.

3. According to one estimate, based on a return to normal weather patterns and technical assumptions about fertility/mortality levels, it could take five years for small ruminants to return to pre-dought levels and up to 10 years for cattle numbers to recover.

CHAPTER 7

Understanding and Responding to the Drug Economy[1]

Heroin, made from opium, is an extremely dangerous drug, with some 15 million addicts worldwide and strong links to HIV/AIDS and crime. Global output of opium shot up from 1,000 tons in 1979 to some 4,500 tons in 2002 (equivalent to about 450 tons of heroin). Afghanistan currently produces the bulk of the world's illicit opium. The impact of the drug industry on Afghanistan's economy, polity, and society is profound, including some short-run economic benefits for the rural population and macro-economy but major adverse effects on security, political normalization, and state building. Hence responding effectively to the drug economy will be essential. This chapter first describes and analyzes Afghanistan's opium economy and its key economic and other implications. Lessons from international and Afghan experience with efforts to curb the drug industry are discussed, and the Government's National Drug Control Strategy is then summarized. The main options and instruments for strategy implementation are outlined and their respective advantages and drawbacks assessed. Given the magnitude, complexity, and profound implications of the drug industry in Afghanistan, the emphasis is not on hard-and-fast solutions but rather on gaining a better understanding of the issues and trade-offs.

1. This chapter, which consolidates recent analysis by the World Bank, draws on the excellent work of UNODC (in particular UNODC 2003b), and on micro-level fieldwork by the UK and others. However, it should be emphasized that quantitative data on the drug economy are by their nature rough estimates and hence should be used with caution.

The Opium Economy in Afghanistan

Growth and Spread of Production

In conditions of lawlessness and impoverishment, and starting from a tiny base in the late 1970s, opium has become Afghanistan's leading economic activity, having now spread to all of Afghanistan's 34 provinces. Opium production (measured at farm-gate prices) is estimated to have generated close to one-sixth of total national income in 2003, and the subsequent trade and processing of opium into opiates (heroin and morphine) generated a somewhat greater amount of income within Afghanistan. The proportion of opium refined in-country appears to be continuing to rise, and reportedly most recent drug seizures at Afghanistan's borders have been of opiates. As can be seen from Figure 7.1, growth of opium cultivation and production was substantial in the 1990s and was interrupted for only a single year by the effective ban imposed by the Taliban.

Although the proportion of Afghanistan's land and labor resources used for opium production is relatively small—only about 7 percent of total irrigated land area even after a large increase in opium poppy cultivation in 2004, as many as two million people are involved in opium production, earning higher incomes than in other activities. In 2003 the

Figure 7.1. Opium Cultivation and Production Trends, 1990–2004

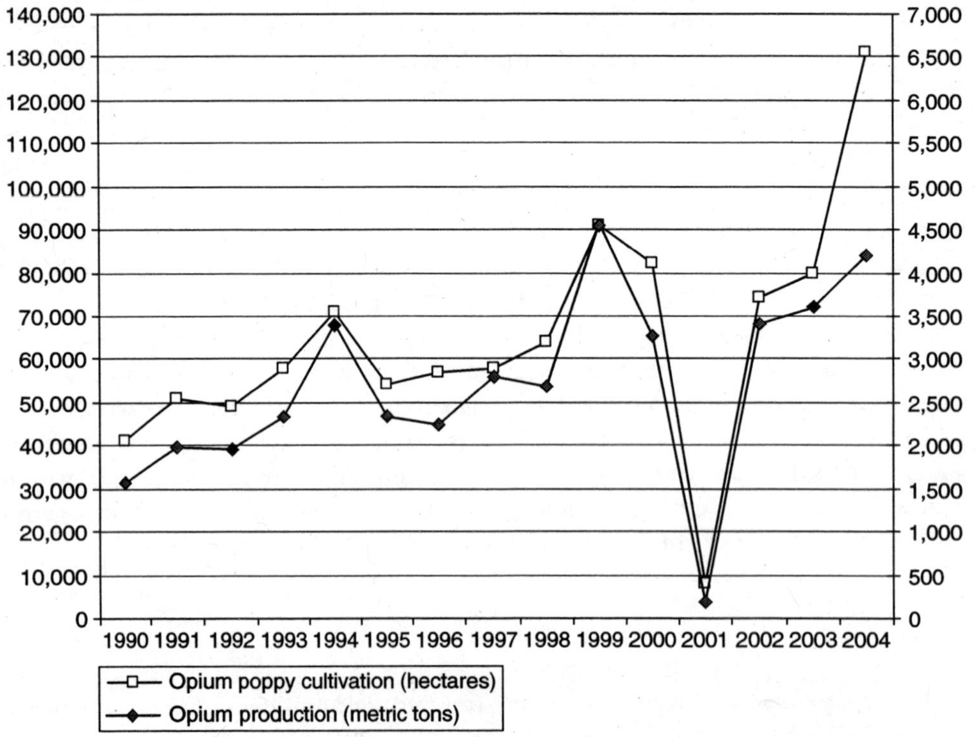

Note: Data for the earlier years up to 1994 are considered less reliable than data for more recent years.
Source: UNODC (2003a, 2003b, 2004).

average gross income per hectare from opium cultivation exceeded that of wheat, the main alternative crop, by as much as 27 times. In some parts of the country where poppy cultivation is concentrated, wage rates of as much as $11–12 per day for opium harvesting work have been reported, five times the market wage rate for rural unskilled labor. Although incomes declined in 2004, they remain far higher than those in other agricultural activities.

The rapid growth of the opium economy in the past two decades demonstrates that it is very attractive to farmers—a durable commodity commanding a high price, having a guaranteed market, with credit and other inputs available from traffickers, easy to transport, and non-perishable. The phenomenal rise of the opium economy can be in addition attributed to:

i. *Exit of other suppliers and growing world demand.* Three opium producers (Iran, Pakistan, Turkey) stopped opium cultivation, opening up a supply gap in the world market that Afghanistan could fill. Growth of demand in neighboring countries, especially Pakistan, and in Europe starting in the mid-1980s further enhanced growth prospects for Afghanistan's opium production.

ii. *Collapse of governance and law enforcement.* During the conflict Afghan governments effectively lost control of the countryside, and there was no credible law enforcement.

iii. *Drugs and arms.* Drugs provided a ready source of cash to pay for arms, and an opium for arms trade arose which various actors involved in successive conflicts encouraged.

iv. *Rural pauperization.* The conflict led to extreme rural impoverishment—more than half of Afghanistan's villages were bombed, livestock numbers dwindled, irrigation networks were destroyed or run down, and over a third of land went out of production. A modest agricultural recovery in the mid-1990s was wiped out by the severe drought of 1999–2001. Under these dire circumstances, and despite religious and cultural aversion, opium production came to be widely accepted as a coping mechanism and livelihood strategy.

v. *Comparative advantage.* Based on its natural conditions, weak security environment, and experience with large-scale production, Afghanistan now has a strong comparative advantage in opium production.

vi. *Market development.* Market organization is excellent, well adapted to the characteristics of the product and to the nature and intensity of risks. Markets extend from the farm gate to the frontier and beyond, and there is working capital financing available at all stages, as well as credit and other inputs for producers.

Given the small share of Afghanistan's land and labor resources now devoted to opium, modest requirements for other inputs, and the level of know-how and market organization, there is ample potential for further increases in production. Price declines (resulting from market saturation), wage increases for skilled labor used in opium harvesting, disease resulting from overextension of production, and changing expectations with respect to law enforcement could moderate further growth of the opium economy. However, the most recent UNODC survey indicated that farmers planned to further increase the area under poppy cultivation for the 2004 crop, and in the event there was an estimated 64 percent increase in the total poppy area (Table 7.1).

Table 7.1. Estimated Opium Cultivation, Production, and Incomes 1995–2004

	1995	2000	2001	2002	2003	2004
Production (tons)	2,300	3,300	185	3,400	3,600	4,200
World Market share (%)	~52	70	11	74	76	87
Number of provinces producing opium	n/a	23	11	24	28	34
Area under poppy prod (ha)	54,000	82,000	8,000	74,000	80,000	131,000
Area under poppy/Area under cereals (%)	2.0	3.2	n/a	3.2	2.8	5.9
Gross farm income per ha (US$)	1,000	1,100	7,400	16,200	12,700	4,600
Value of opiate exports (million US$)	n/a	850	N/a	2,500	2,300	2,800
Gross farm income from opium (million US$)	50	90	60	1,200	1,000	600
Gross downstream domestic income (million US$)	N/a	760	N/a	1,300	1,300	2,200

Note: Estimates have considerable margins of error; there have been some changes in estimation methods over time.

Source: Afghanistan Government (2004b, Table 1.2); UNODC (2003a, 2003b, 2004).

Prices and Incomes

Farm-gate prices of opium were low in the 1990s, but a nearly ten-fold rise occurred when the Taliban banned opium production in 2000 (Figure 7.2). High prices of $300/kg or above were maintained in 2002–03 despite the recovery of opium output, but prices declined in late 2003 and have fallen more sharply in 2004, to an average of around $90/kg by late summer before a modest recovery post-harvest. It is clear that margins between farm-gate prices and border prices of opiates are very large, on the order of double in 2002/03 and well over four times in 2004 (based on the gross income estimates in Table 7.1).

The lion's share of opium income in the 1990s went to traffickers rather than farmers, and several other crops were financially competitive with opium. This pattern changed dramatically after the Taliban ban, and close to half of annual gross income from the opium economy appears to have gone to the farm level in recent years, although this share has declined as farm-gate prices fell in 2004. The share of opium output refined within Afghanistan appears to have been rising, leading to higher domestic value added accruing to traders and processors. The following groups benefit from the opium economy:

i. *Better-off farmers* (characterized by significant landholdings and capital resources), cultivating poppy on their own land (typically as part of a diversified cropping pattern including other food crops and cash crops) and in many cases letting out part

Figure 7.2. Opium Farm-gate Prices 1994–2004

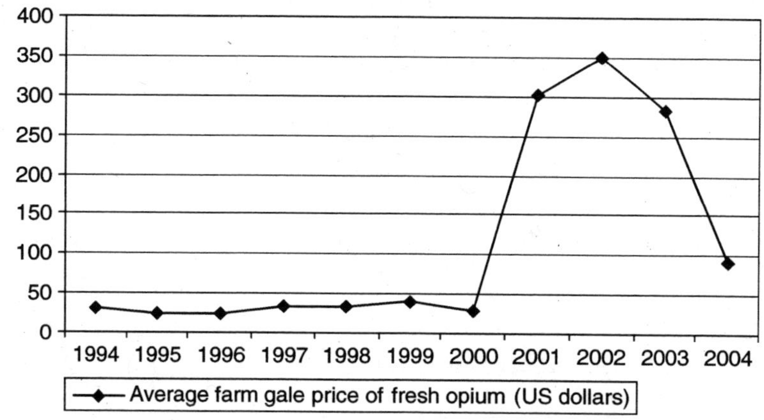

Source: UNODC (2003a, 2003b, 2004).

of their land to sharecroppers and getting part of the poppy crop in return. These farmers have been major beneficiaries of the opium boom and many of them have become rich.

ii. *Poor farmers* (probably most of the roughly 350,000 farm households estimated to be involved in poppy cultivation), typically with little or no land and often burdened with debt, cultivating opium poppy on tiny amounts of their own land or as sharecroppers (with opium cultivation normally required by the landlord). For these farmers, the benefits of high opium prices in recent years may have been to a large extent dissipated by servicing high-interest debts and by unfavorable sharecropping arrangements.

iii. *Rural wage laborers*, as many as half a million, the bulk of them poor, who harvest the poppy crop which is a highly labor-intensive activity. Large numbers of itinerant laborers move seasonally following the poppy harvest in different areas. Wage laborers have benefited from the opium boom, although many of them also may be mired in debt.

iv. *Small opium traders*, very roughly estimated by UNODC (2003b) at around 15,000, who buy and sell raw opium at the farm gate and at "opium bazaars," and typically handle small volumes (as little as 100 kg per year or less) and in many cases are often involved in the trade on a part-time basis.

v. *Wholesalers and refiners*, much smaller in number, who trade in large quantities, organize processing, move product across the border, and so forth.

vi. *Local warlords and commanders*, who receive "protection payments" and in turn employ substantial numbers of militia fighters, and may "sponsor" processing facilities.

vii. *Government officials*, at various levels, who receive bribes from the drug industry in return for favors in law enforcement or other aspects.

The gender dimension of the opium boom also is noteworthy. Women play a very important role in poppy cultivation in northern and eastern Afghanistan, being involved in planting and weeding; thinning; lancing the capsules; collecting the opium; clearing the fields; breaking the capsules and removing the seeds; cleaning the seeds; and processing by-products like oil and soap. In the southern, generally more conservative region, women do not participate directly in opium poppy cultivation but rather indirectly by preparing meals for hired laborers. Although women's labor in poppy cultivation traditionally has been unpaid, local labor shortages in some areas have led to women in Badakhshan and Takhar provinces, often for the first time, being paid wages. This is in addition to women's traditional right in many areas to make a final pass at already harvested opium fields and glean what is left. Tragically, daughters are often used to settle opium-denominated debts.

Drug Industry Structure and Market Organization

What we know about the opium business in Afghanistan suggests that it more closely resembles a competitive market than a criminal cartel. Entry and exit seem to be relatively easy for both production and trafficking, and the number of participants is high. Opium is openly bought and sold on various markets. Parts of the drug industry are more concentrated, with relatively few and more powerful actors involved in opium refining and cross-border trading. There is, however, evidence of new entrants joining even at these stages of the business, and the existence of a number of trading routes going out of Afghanistan to the North, West, South, and East facilitates competition nationally if not necessarily locally. Increasing refining of opium into heroin within Afghanistan, to the extent that it is occurring, may be accompanied by drug industry consolidation. Opium production has been responsive to prices and has shifted locations in response to eradication campaigns, demonstrating that it is "footloose." Prices have been flexible at the micro level.[2]

Some implications of a competitive drug industry are explored in Box 7.1. In addition the criminal nature of the drug business—and consequent ability and tendency to use armed force in the conduct of business—needs to be taken into account. In the Afghan context where government military power and law enforcement have been weak, and where local conflict is conducted mainly with small arms, entry into the military sphere by small actors with limited resources would be easy. Moreover, it would be difficult for one or a few actors to dominate militarily on a sustained basis. Under such circumstances a fragmented, competitive drug industry could emerge, leading to fragmented capture of the state apparatus at the local level by drug interests, which would be inimical to the emergence of an effective, unified state.

2. The maintenance of opiate exports apparently at near normal levels during the year of the Taliban ban, and then the persistence of high farm-gate prices for two years after large-scale opium production was restored, may be explained by the existence of large inventories in the late 1990s, which were sold off to maintain supply during the year of very low production and then were rebuilt when production resumed. The recent sharp decline in farm-gate prices reflects the impact of oversupply in the face of already high inventories by the end of 2003. But more work is needed to better understand opium price trends.

Box 7.1. The Competitive Model of the Drug Industry

If the number of actors in the drug industry is great enough that there is no opportunity for strategic behavior, or if anti-competitive behavior is deterred (at least over time) by new entry or its threat, a competitive model of the drug industry may be applicable to Afghanistan. This would have the following implications:

i. Opium prices would adjust to the point where marginal cost is equated with demand (as opposed to marginal revenue in the case of a monopoly producer). Thus prices would be lower than in a monopoly situation, and production in a static sense would be higher, unless demand is completely price inelastic.
ii. Over time the supply curve would adjust through expansion, new entry, etc. to the point where "excess profits" in the drug industry are eliminated. This does not mean no profits, just a normal level of profits competitive with what can be earned in other sectors (factoring in a risk premium and the cost of avoiding law enforcement).
iii. Production could increase quite sharply (at least from season to season) in response to foreign demand.
iv. Once there is full adjustment to the perfectly competitive equilibrium, further growth of total opium production would tend to track world demand rather closely.
v. Thus the nightmare scenario under the competitive model is one of an efficient, competitive drug industry increasingly embedded in Afghan society and with low opium prices stimulating world demand. Heroin demand is growing slowly in Western European markets but very rapidly in Asia and the former USSR.

The perfectly competitive model suggests that resources for political influence and destabilization would be under fragmented control. Hence there would likely be a pattern of fragmented capture of the state apparatus at the local level and exercise of power by illegitimate drug-financed local and regional authorities.

Economic and Poverty Implications

The sheer size of the opium economy means that it has very important economic implications and linkages (Box 7.2). It is a key part of the "informal equilibrium" of the economy as a whole, discussed in Chapter 1. From a macroeconomic perspective, the opium economy stimulates aggregate demand and has a positive effect on Afghanistan's balance of payments but does not contribute to government taxes except indirectly, for example through Customs duties on imports financed by drug proceeds. The very large size and potential volatility of the opium economy constitute a significant risk for the Afghan economy as a whole (Chapter 1).

The impact of Afghanistan's drug economy on household incomes is of central importance from a poverty perspective. In recent years Afghan farmers have received in the range of half a billion dollars annually from opium production, with another several hundred million dollars probably going to wage laborers (see Ward 2004, Table 1). This constitutes an enormous injection of income into Afghanistan's battered rural economy. Income from opium appears to be unevenly distributed. For the better-off it has been a source of wealth creation, for the poor it has been a coping mechanism for survival and in many cases for gaining access to credit and land, albeit on unfavorable terms. In sum, the opium boom in recent years appears to have been a potent force in generating incomes in rural areas.

Box 7.2. Key Economic Linkages

Income: The income accruing to the Afghan population from both production and trade in opium is quite high in relation to the GDP of a very poor country. This income is allocated to a very large number of participants in the farm and trading sector, and also through protection payments to others.

Consumption: Even allowing for leakages from expatriation of opium revenues, it is clear that a large share of drug receipts is spent in Afghanistan, mostly on consumption expenditures for goods and services.

Domestic production: A substantial percentage of consumption expenditures from drug receipts would appear to be on domestically-produced goods and services. This is especially true of farm and wage incomes.

Investment: A significant part of drug receipts goes into re-investment, since the drug business itself absorbs working capital and fixed investment in processing and transport facilities. Surplus funds may be invested mainly in building construction (helping finance building booms in Kabul and other cities), transport, and trade.

Balance of payments: It is likely that a considerable share of gross drug proceeds (roughly estimated at $2.3 billion in 2003) stays in Afghanistan. Although estimates are highly uncertain, taking into account the propensity to import from drug industry proceeds (e.g. for durable goods like vehicles and televisions), the net positive effect on Afghanistan's balance of payments could be in the range of $1 billion annually.

Fiscal linkages: Opium revenues largely escape the official tax net. It is reported that opium farmers pay the *ushr* tithe, which in some regions may be paid to the local mullah, in others to the local administration or commander. More important, a large share of opium farm gate receipts and downstream income goes into levies of various kinds by local interests, outside the budget. (For example, the most recent UNODC Farmer Intentions Survey reported that farmers pay local commanders between 10 and 40 percent of the opium harvest, and that in some areas opium traders pay local commanders for the right to enter producing villages and purchase opium there.) An indirect fiscal linkage is that Customs duties are levied on many imported goods paid for with drug receipts.

Asset prices: The real estate market in Kabul and in other large cities is booming, and rural land prices also appear to be on the rise. This may reflect to some extent an influx of drug money.

Wage rates: The drug economy also appears to be driving up rural wage rates. Wage rates have gone up to peaks of $11–12 a day for a skilled worker during the harvest period. Rural unskilled wages in the winter of 2003/04 were in the range $2.50–3.00 per day, compared to $1.50–1.75 in the previous winter. There are signs of insufficient labor coming forward for government public works programs at the offered wage of $2 per day. However, wages may moderate with the recent decline in the farm-gate price of opium.

Finance and credit: The opium economy provides considerable amounts of credit to the rural economy, which is attractive to farmers who often have no other sources of credit. However, implicit interest rates are very high, and advances tend to be denominated in opium, exacerbating the long-term dependency of farmers on opium.

An understanding as to why farmers grow poppy is essential for design of effective strategies to respond to the drug economy. Available information suggests the following:

i. Poppy cultivation is an important element in poppy farmers' strategies for crop mix and risk management, with some farmers specializing in opium (particularly highly indebted small farmers) but many cultivating poppy as one among several crops.

ii. For most poor rural households wage income is more important than farm income. Thus they benefit from high demand for labor for poppy cultivation and harvesting.
iii. The majority of households have to buy most of their food from the market. Opium production or associated wage labor provides assured cash with which to purchase food.
iv. High levels of risk associated with opium production encourage landowners to sharecrop out some of their land for poppy cultivation, which spreads risk and at the same time provides access to land and water (and often credit) for the poor through sharecropping.
v. Many poorer farmers report that they are obliged to cultivate poppy, even if they have misgivings about doing so, due to high debts or sharecropping requirements.
vi. There is variation among regions, and even among communities in a local area, in the mix of rich and poor opium farmers, the relative importance of farming and wage labor, land tenure arrangements, and access to opium markets.

These stylized facts provide an indication of the complexity of farmer and household motivations and of the rural livelihood impacts of opium. Poppy has enabled some people, not necessarily poor in the first place, to grow rich, but for many more people the opium economy has become an important source of income enabling them to cope better with the poverty and vulnerability that they remain mired in. Abrupt shrinkage of the opium economy or falling opium prices without new means of livelihood would significantly worsen rural poverty. Finally, although the rate of addiction to opiates in Afghanistan is believed to be relatively low it is likely to be rising, facilitated by the increasing trend of refining opium into heroin in-country and the return of heroin-addicted refugees from neighboring countries.

Security and Political Implications

The opium economy has profound adverse implications for security, politics, and state building in Afghanistan. It contributes to a vicious circle whereby the drug industry financially supports warlords and their militias, who in turn undermine the Government—which is also corrupted and captured at different levels by bribes from the drug industry. As a result the state remains ineffective and security weak, thereby perpetuating an environment in which the drug industry can continue to thrive. The linkages between drugs, warlords, and insecurity add up to a vicious circle of mutually-reinforcing problems, shown in Figure 7.3 (see also Chapters 1 and 4).

There is also some anecdotal evidence of linkages between drug money and terrorist networks. Warlords, drug interests, and terrorists work together to promote insecurity and weaken the state, even if their interests do not coincide in other respects. In fact many warlords and local commanders directly sponsor or are otherwise involved in the drug industry, and the same may be true of some terrorist groups. All in all, the security and political implications of Afghanistan's opium economy present a grave danger to the country's entire state building and reconstruction agenda.

Figure 7.3. A Vicious Circle

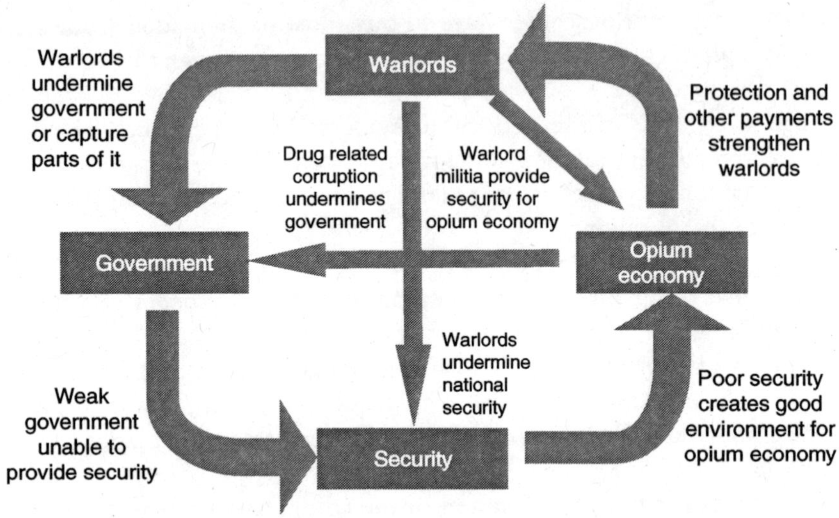

Lessons from Experience in Fighting Drugs

International Experience

Drug consuming nations have invested heavily in drug control, but success has been elusive. Law enforcement and interdiction of international drug shipments have raised the risks associated with drugs, increased prices, and interrupted supply. Demand-side interventions such as treatments can mitigate some of the adverse effects of drugs, including crime and HIV/AIDS. But there has been no large, sustained reduction in global consumption of illicit narcotics.

There is also rich international experience with supply-side interventions to reduce drug production, primarily eradication of poppy fields. A key lesson is that eradication alone will not work and is likely to be counterproductive, resulting in perverse incentives for farmers to grow more drugs (for example, in Colombia), displacement of production to more remote areas, and fueling of violence and insecurity (Peru, Bolivia, Colombia), which in several cases forced the eradication policy to be reversed and led to adverse political outcomes. Neither does the approach of making eradication a condition for development assistance work—without alternative livelihoods already in place, premature eradication damages the environment for rural development.

The most successful case of speedy and sustained drug eradication was in Iran, where the Khomeini government quickly brought down opium poppy cultivation from 33,000 ha prior to 1979 to zero. However, there arose a major problem with transit of drugs produced in Afghanistan through Iran, and the country's strong interdiction efforts have been responded to with violence and terror—since 1979 more than 3,000 Iranian law enforcement officers have been killed in confrontations with heavily armed drug traffickers. Moreover, Iran has been left with the highest opiate addiction rate in the world—nearly

2 percent of the population are regular drug abusers. Mexico succeeded in eradicating poppy by spraying in the mid-1970s, but the drug industry responded by dispersing cultivation to smaller fields hidden in remote areas, and by the early 1980s Mexico was supplying as much heroin to the US market as before eradication.

Thailand and Pakistan succeeded in eliminating opium production on a sustainable basis. Their approach has been gradual, taking decades rather than months or years. In both cases, eradication was undertaken only following the implementation of comprehensive alternative development programs which raised incomes in the target areas through development of profitable cash crops. In both cases, poppy cultivation was localized and constituted a small percentage of total national economic activity. Moreover, opium production boomed in neighboring countries (Myanmar in the case of Thailand and Afghanistan in the case of Pakistan), suggesting that the drug industry moved its activities elsewhere rather than shutting down.

Afghanistan's Experience

Afghanistan has had more than a decade of experience with efforts to reduce opium production. All of these initiatives failed to achieve their objectives (Box 7.3), except for the Taliban ban which succeeded in drastically reducing opium production for a year—but with questionable sustainability, worsening poverty, and no apparent effect on the flow of

Box 7.3. Counter-Narcotics Experience in Afghanistan

Since the early 1990s, there has been a series of attempts to control opium production in Afghanistan, each of which has been in its own way unsuccessful.

Alternative development without security and political support: Starting in 1989 several projects were initiated following the model of "alternative development" used in Pakistan and the Andean region. These projects were in areas where opium production was entrenched and there was insecurity and lack of political support. Benefits were offered to communities (through their councils of elders or *shuras*) in return for a commitment to phase out opium cultivation, but there was no impact on production. An evaluation concluded that the *shuras* were unrepresentative, there was too little connection between project benefits and farmer motivations and constraints, the better-off captured the benefits, and offering benefits with "conditionality" created perverse incentives.

A simple ban vigorously applied: In 2000 the Taliban imposed a complete ban on opium cultivation, severely enforced, which resulted in production in Taliban-controlled areas falling to negligible levels. No restrictions were imposed on trade, however, and the flow of opium out of Afghanistan did not much diminish. Border and consumer prices remained high, while farm-gate prices shot up, suggesting that operators may have maintained turnover by running down large inventories. The eradication campaign pauperized many farmers, requiring them to incur debts which they are still repaying. The ban also promoted a shift in cultivation to northern areas outside the Taliban's control, and shifted trade to the northern trafficking route through Tajikistan.

Eradication with promised cash compensation: The post-Taliban government quickly banned the cultivation, production, abuse, and trafficking of drugs, and in the spring of 2002 an eradication campaign was carried out on about 17,500 ha. Compensation was offered but apparently only actually paid to one tenth of the farmers whose crops had been destroyed. In many areas eradication seems to have involved opportunistic local power plays, with factions trying to destroy the economic power base of other factions. Failure to honor promises of compensation impoverished smaller and highly-indebted farmers and harmed the credibility of the program. Only 12 percent of respondents to a UNODC survey said that the eradication campaign would deter them from planting.

(*continued*)

Box 7.3. Counter-Narcotics Experience in Afghanistan (*Continued*)

Eradication with promise of reconstruction support: In 2003 more than 21,000 ha of opium was reportedly "eradicated," and opium production was "foregone" through persuasion on 5,000 ha more. Some was eradicated by local authorities who promised that rural development assistance would follow, but this has come slowly if at all. Although there were marked reductions in poppy area in Helmand and Kandahar provinces, elsewhere production grew and spread to new districts and provinces, and the total poppy area increased by 8 percent to 80,000 ha.

opiates into consumer markets. Moreover, the Taliban ban resulted in a sharp rise in the farm-gate price of opium and stimulated a multi-fold increase in opium production in areas outside the Taliban's control. After the Taliban were removed total national output rebounded to near-record levels.

Recently a new approach has been developed—"alternative livelihoods"—which takes a holistic rural development perspective in implementing projects intended to enable those whose livelihoods currently depend on poppy production to find other, sustainable livelihoods (through a combination of on-farm and off-farm activities). Some relatively small projects have already been initiated and are generating valuable experience with this concept. Except in that it may be associated with law enforcement measures, the alternative livelihoods concept resembles any good integrated rural development project and in that sense is not controversial. There are however some important issues. First, no matter how well designed and implemented, relatively small interventions cannot be expected to make much of a dent in the enormous opium economy. What is really needed is generalized economic growth and rural development—"alternative livelihoods for Afghanistan as a whole"—which can only be accomplished through reforms, policies, and substantial programs implemented nationwide. Thus the alternative livelihoods approach needs to be integrated into the national rural development and poverty reduction strategy. Second, the sequencing of alternative livelihoods initiatives with law enforcement actions is extremely important for the effectiveness of both and needs delicate management.

Some General Lessons

Perverse Incentives Associated with Targeting. Providing development assistance in return for a locality's commitment to stop opium production, paying farmers compensation for destruction of poppy fields, and implementing alternative livelihoods projects or other development projects in poppy-growing localities—all involve targeting of farmers or localities currently cultivating poppy and providing them with benefits for stopping. This can generate perverse incentives for others, not currently producing opium, to get into the business in order to be eligible for benefits. In order to minimize the risk of perverse incentives, assistance should not be targeted solely or primarily at farmers and localities currently cultivating poppy.

Price Effects. Eradication and other actions to reduce the supply of opium (including successful alternative livelihood projects) will likely result in higher farm-gate prices, increasing incentives for farmers to cultivate poppy. The very large, lasting price rise after the Taliban ban on opium cultivation is a notable example. Such price effects need to be taken into account and may influence the mix and sequencing of actions. For example, interdiction against trafficking and refining, by disrupting downstream stages and at least temporarily reducing demand for opium at the farm gate, may have a lesser (or even negative) impact on farm-gate prices.

Short-term versus Longer-term Implications. Experience has shown that the short-term and longer-term effects of actions against drugs can be quite different, making sustainable success elusive. For example, eradication even if successful tends to result in shifting of opium production elsewhere, so the outcome over the medium term is that total production has not been much affected but is now dispersed in more remote areas where it is more difficult to root out.

Prioritization and Sequencing. The impact of different actions against drugs can depend very much on how they are combined with other actions and how they are sequenced. For example, eradication in the absence of alternative livelihoods being available does not work, and eradication followed by assistance does not seem to work well, yet eradication (and its threat) can help reinforce alternative livelihoods development if the former follows the latter.

Effects of Poor Security and Governance. Implementation of development programs and law enforcement in conditions of poor security and weak governance is extremely difficult, and distortions inevitably emerge. The credibility and effectiveness of recent eradication campaigns have been weakened by local responsibility for implementation and associated perceptions of factional bias, corruption, and favoritism in the selection of which fields to eradicate. Anecdotal evidence suggests that the poor have been disproportionately affected by eradication.

Strategic Interactions. From a dynamic perspective the drug industry, which has very large interests at stake, can be expected to respond vigorously to efforts to curb opium production, refining, and trade. The more effective the Government's actions, the more vigorous the likely response from the drug industry. It has a formidable arsenal of instruments, including: (i) *pricing*—given the huge margins beyond the farm gate there is scope for the drug industry to raise prices almost to any level necessary to provide adequate incentives to opium cultivators; (ii) *location*—the drug industry is "footloose" in shifting the location of refining, trade routes, and cultivation; (iii) *inputs and extension services*—these contribute to the attractiveness of opium cultivation; (iv) *corruption*—the resources of the drug industry can be used for bribery on a massive scale to undermine efforts against drugs; and (v) *armed violence against the authorities*, and against others (for example, coercion of farmers).

Need for Innovative Approaches. Limited success in past experience with fighting drugs does not give much ground for optimism, especially in view of the unique aspects of the opium economy in Afghanistan (most notably its sheer size). No single approach is likely to be effective and sustainable; a combination of different measures, well-designed and well-sequenced, will be essential to have any hope of success. There is also a need to think "outside the box" and explore innovative approaches. Some illustrative examples are listed in Box 7.4.

Box 7.4. Examples of Possible Innovative Approaches

A broader approach to alternative livelihoods. The alternative livelihoods approach as implemented so far runs the risk of being ineffective due to the small size of interventions and offsetting responses by the drug industry. Blanketing the entire country with alternative livelihoods projects in theory could deal with these problems but is not feasible and in any case underlines the need to get away from a project focus. What is really needed is sustained growth of the rural economy as a whole—both agriculture and off-farm activities—which will generate livelihoods that those displaced by the shrinking of the opium economy can take up.

Using cost-benefit and/or cost-effectiveness criteria for prioritizing actions. Although such assessments inevitably would be crude and subject to margins of error, they would nevertheless be useful in addressing questions like whether to devote limited law enforcement resources more toward interdiction or toward eradication.

A strong public communications campaign, enlisting support of religious leaders and others respected by rural communities, could be an important part of the national effort against drugs if backed up by other actions. This is called for in the National Drug Control Strategy but so far appears not to been fully exploited.

Going after abusive behavior by the drug industry, for example credit at extremely high effective interest rates (over 100 percent) and denominated in opium. Legal and practical approaches to cancellation of opium-related debts could be explored, although it should be recognized that the tradition of advances carrying very high implicit interest rates is well-entrenched in Afghanistan's rural areas, and other forms of rural credit would need to be available.

Interdicting shipments of chemical precursors into Afghanistan. It takes about four liters of acetic anhydride to yield a kilogram of heroin, so large amounts of precursor chemicals are currently being imported into the country.

Combining anti-money laundering efforts with "grandfathering" of assets from past drug revenues. This could help co-opt parts of the drug economy that are already shifting into other businesses and give them a stake in the legitimate economy. The obvious risk of perverse incentives would need to be taken into account.

Preventing spread of opium cultivation to new areas. Past eradication campaigns focused on the provinces with the highest levels of opium production, where the greatest reduction in production could be achieved in the short run. The dynamic effect, however, has been the growth and spread of opium cultivation in other provinces—making it more difficult to attack subsequently and spreading the adverse political and security impacts into additional parts of the country. A strategy of containing opium production in traditionally important areas and giving high priority to preventing its spreading into new areas could be explored.

Tactical uncertainty and incomplete information. Strategic considerations suggest that maintaining some degree of uncertainty vis-à-vis the major actors in the drug industry—about the Government's plans as well as about next moves and specific actions—may be useful.

Government's National Drug Control Strategy

Institutional Framework. The Government established the Counter Narcotics Directorate (CND), which reports to the National Security Council, in October 2002. CND is responsible for counter-narcotics strategy development and coordination but not for implementation, which is the responsibility of line agencies. The main tasks of CND are to: (i) develop the national counter narcotics strategy; (ii) coordinate counter-narcotics activities in the Government including budgets and programs; (iii) liaise with internal and external partners; (iv) coordinate drug interdiction programs with neighboring countries; (v) act as a clearing house for projects related to drug control; and (vi) set benchmarks and timeframes and monitor progress. CND has about 50 staff in total. Present activities include policy and strategy development, demand reduction and public awareness activities, legal and judicial reform (including drafting the new Anti-Narcotics Law that was adopted in 2003), coordination of alternative livelihoods efforts (with the Ministry of Rural Development), and coordination on law enforcement with the Interior Ministry. Further strengthening of the counter-narcotics institutional structure is under consideration.

National Drugs Control Strategy (NDCS). Promulgated in May 2003, the NDCS sets a cautious and gradualist tone: the approach "should be realistic" and "take account of the economic and social causes of illegal cultivation." "Attention is first needed to establish security and the rule of law, and to create a stable environment to accelerate reconstruction and build institutions." There is also awareness of the political risks—"in carrying out law enforcement interactions it will be important to balance the political risk of instability caused by counter-narcotics measures with the political desirability of projecting central authority over the entire country and of eliminating the cultivation and production of narcotic drugs." On the other hand, the NDCS sets ambitious goals: (i) a 70 percent reduction in opium poppy cultivation by 1386 (five years) with total elimination by 1391 (ten years); (ii) interdiction and prosecution of trafficking, processing, and distribution of narcotics and precursors; (iii) forfeiture of drug-generated assets and checking money laundering; and (iv) enhancing regional and international cooperation.

The alternative livelihoods concept is central to the NDCS and is considered as an essential condition for eradication. It is seen as part of a broad-based economic and social development strategy, to proceed *pari passu* with "phased law enforcement." A poppy cultivation ban will be enforced where "rural reconstruction has already produced tangible results and alternative livelihoods are sufficiently available." The NDCS includes an implementation plan, which has been translated into five action plans for judicial reform, law enforcement, alternative livelihoods, drug demand reduction and treatment, and public awareness, approved at an international conference on counter-narcotics strategy in February 2004.

Some Questions. The NDCS provides a good strategic framework for action. It acknowledges the difficulties and proposes many sound and necessary actions. It has provisions for action plans, coordination, monitoring etc. The proposals (such as on alternative livelihoods) link to existing activities and programs rather than proposing yet more initiatives for an already overloaded system. Moreover, the purpose of the NDCS is not to put forward a detailed blueprint for all actions but rather to present a coordinated framework including key principles and strategic elements. Some questions that arise related to the strategy are posed below.

i. *Ownership and implementation*: The Government is embarking on an important process of generating broad-based ownership through conferences, publications, etc. But questions remain about ownership and implementation capacity for the NDCS.
ii. *Strategic targets*: The targets are ambitious, in contrast with the cautious language in much of the document. Are the targets realistic? Are the measures as ambitious as the targets? The strategy lists numerous steps that appear to add up to a broad and integrated attack on the drug problem, yet many of them are already ongoing

and have not made an impact. Is much greater concentration of resources and effort needed? In the light of experience, are the measures proposed the right ones, or is a "paradigm shift" needed?

iii. *Institutional architecture and capacity*: The role assigned to CND of coordinating and catalyzing other institutions rather than implementing programs itself seems appropriate. But does the architecture provide for adequate high-level decision taking? In Thailand, for example, the Cabinet meets once a year on drugs, deputy ministers meet quarterly, and the directors of all concerned departments and institutions meet monthly. A second, practical question relates to the capacity of the CND.

iv. *Legal framework and law enforcement*: Law enforcement for both eradication and interdiction is problematic. Despite the recent law, the legal framework is unclear, institutional responsibilities are confused, and implementation capacity is in its infancy.

v. *Judicial and penal process*: There are questions about the judicial and penal process for drug criminals. The strategy does not discuss the key steps of prosecution and punishment, or measures to get a working judiciary and penal system established.

vi. *Focus on production or trafficking*: Actions against production, processing, and trafficking are included in the NDCS, but there is no discussion of prioritization. Should limited law enforcement capability be directed toward eradication or toward interdiction?

vii. *International support*. Will direct international involvement in law enforcement be necessary, particularly in the short run while domestic capacities are being built?

viii. *Alternative livelihoods concept*: The alternative livelihoods concept that is so prominent in the strategy is left vague and general and is not clearly defined.

ix. *Priority areas for alternative livelihoods*: The NDCS states that priority will be given to poppy growing areas because the farmers are poor, and to source areas for poppy labor. However, as discussed earlier "favoring" poppy areas may generate perverse incentives.

x. *Sequencing of alternative livelihoods programs and eradication*: There appears to be a lack of consensus about the appropriate pace and phasing of alternative livelihoods and eradication. The NDCS appears to endorse the "alternative livelihoods first" approach. Yet there is pressure on the Government to vigorously pursue eradication quickly.

xi. *Controlling financial flows*: The question of controlling the monetary proceeds of the drug trade, which are transferred through the informal *hawala* financial system, is important. The subject is mentioned in the strategy but no specific actions are proposed.

Options and Trade-offs in Strategy Implementation

Broader Strategic Framework

Breaking the vicious circle of drugs, warlords, and insecurity, which is so inimical to Afghanistan's state-building and reconstruction agenda, requires a multi-pronged approach. Drug control measures alone will not be effective. Thus the response to the drug

Figure 7.4. Strategic Framework for Breaking the Vicious Circle

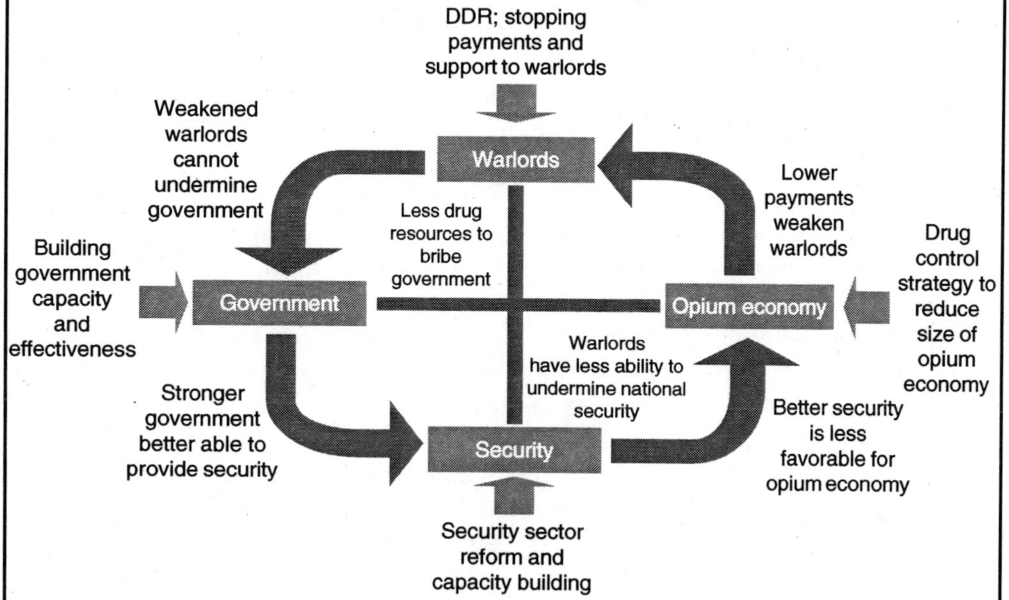

economy must occur within a broader strategic framework including state building and improving security as well as curbing warlords, similar to the strategy for breaking out of the "informal equilibrium (Chapter 3). As shown in Figure 7.4, in addition to drug measures this framework includes (1) curbing warlords' power by stopping payments and other support to them, DDR to take away their militias, co-opting them into the Government where appropriate, etc.; (2) building state capacity and resources; and (3) security sector reform and capacity-building. All this needs to happen in an environment of rapid economic growth which allows the drug economy and other forms of illegal activity to be eventually replaced by legitimate economic activities. The rest of this chapter focuses on the right-most part of Figure 7.4 relating directly to the opium economy.

Strategic Objectives, Implementation Options, and Trade-offs

The overall strategic objective of the NDCS is to progressively reduce the size of Afghanistan's opium economy and eventually eliminate it. This challenging and ambitious goal needs to be accomplished in a way that (1) is technically feasible and sustainable and builds required capacity; (2) does not increase rural poverty; (3) avoids pushing the Afghan economy into a recession and handles any macroeconomic fall-out—for example a worsening of the balance of payments; (4) manages the political risks associated with fighting drugs; and (5) takes into account the dynamic longer-term implications and strategic responses by the drug industry.

Capacity and resource constraints mean that it is not possible to do everything, which brings issues of prioritization and sequencing to the fore. Different options need to be assessed on the basis of the above criteria and in light of the lessons of experience, and choices made. Four options involving the three main counter-narcotics instruments are reviewed below.

Option 1: Interdiction. This would involve pursuing drug traffickers and seizing their product, enforcing closure of opium bazaars, and destroying processing facilities. It might also involve sanctions against officials who condone and benefit from the drug trade, seizure of drug-related assets, and legal action against drug money balances and flows. The technical rationale for interdiction is strong, as the trafficking and processing business is more concentrated, more evidently criminal, and has fewer participants than the production stage. Interdiction also does not result directly in rural impoverishment, at least not to the same degree as actions against resource-poor farmers. It is likely that some proportion of the drug trade will be suppressed; risk premia will increase sharply; and the drug business will become increasingly aggressive and well organized in its response. The costs of trafficking and processing could be expected to increase. This will increase the border price of opiates, and it may lower farm-gate prices at least temporarily due to disruptions in the downstream supply chain. In sum interdiction, if vigorously pursued, has the likely *economic advantage* of reducing the trade and decreasing its profitability (after risk premia are taken into account) and disrupting the supply chain; it has the *moral advantage* of attacking what is more evidently criminality; it has the *technical* advantage of focusing on a much smaller number of actors than eradication; and it has the *political advantage* of directly addressing the nexus of drugs and illegitimate political and military power

Three issues arise with respect to implementation. *Enforcement* requires political will, adequate money, and institutional changes (reinforcement and reorganization of the interdiction forces, judicial reform). The *effectiveness* of this approach has its limits: neighboring Iran—a well organized, affluent, and committed state with a well-functioning police force and judicial system—has struggled for years in a bloody war on trafficking. Even with this caveat, vigorous interdiction would certainly make a difference. *Political risk* is significant, given that so many people at every level benefit from the drug trade. Thus if the Government opts for an interdiction-led strategy, political consensus would be required, and sustained external support would be essential. The likelihood that the drug industry will respond aggressively with violence and political manipulations has to be anticipated, and the risks and responses taken into account.

Option 2: Eradication. Eradication, involving destruction of opium growing in the fields and sanctions against poppy farmers, attacks the problem where it starts and destroys the most visible evidence of illegality. While eradication can reduce opium output locally, production can quickly shift to other producing areas and spread to new areas quickly (stimulated by the higher farm-gate prices caused by eradication), and cultivation can resume in eradicated areas in the following year if there is no follow up. Moreover, the governance and poverty impact of eradication can be problematic. The fairness and consistency of recent eradication campaigns in Afghanistan has been questioned, and poorer farmers appear to have been disproportionately affected (the better off may escape eradication by means of political connections and/or bribes). Total national production has not fallen as a result of eradication, and a UNODC survey indicates no difference in planting intentions between areas where eradication took place and those where it did not.

Overall, an eradication-led strategy could face severe problems with implementation, poverty impacts, and political damage. *Implementation* is very difficult where the authority of the central government is fragile, and experience indicates that it will lead only to changes in the location of opium production. *Poverty impacts* will be negative, given the dependence of large numbers of poor people on opium for their livelihood as well as the distortions in implementation noted above. *Political risk* is daunting, but in a different way than for interdiction. The Government wants to win over the rural poor through inclusive development processes, not aggressive destruction of their livelihoods. Existing rural development and governance initiatives in the countryside, which comprise an important part of the state-building agenda, may be compromised. Finally, there is a moral, political and economic case for having alternative livelihoods programs in place before commencing eradication.

Option 3: Alternative Livelihoods. Alternative livelihoods programs, which have a central place in the NDCS, include components of comprehensive rural development, farming, and off-farm income generation. Whatever their impact on drug production, they should contribute to development and poverty alleviation (through creation of assets, markets, and livelihoods) and are non-confrontational. But important issues remain to be resolved. Conducting alternative livelihoods programs only or mainly in areas currently growing poppy runs the risk that poppy cultivation will move elsewhere, encouraged by perverse incentives. Implementing these programs first in areas currently not growing poppy would have an appropriate incentive effect (for both opium cultivating and non-opium cultivating farmers) but would require programs of a different order of magnitude given that poppy currently is not grown on 93 percent of Afghanistan's irrigated area. Or programs could be targeted toward areas "at risk" of getting involved in poppy cultivation, but how should such areas be defined? More generally, alternative livelihoods initiatives cannot be separated from the broad-based rural economic growth and income generation that will be critical in phasing out Afghanistan's dependence on the opium economy.

Alternative livelihoods approaches are attractive, but as the primary instrument of a drug reduction strategy they suffer from critical weaknesses in time, scale, cost, and effectiveness. Completing such programs will take many years and large resources, without visible reduction of drug production in the interim. Moreover, opium would remain the crop of choice particularly for resource-rich farmers, and poorer farmers may continue to be bound to the opium economy by debt and their need to access land and credit. Thus sole reliance on persuasion through alternative livelihoods approaches would not succeed in reducing drug production.

Option 4: Alternative Livelihoods Programs Coordinated with Eradication. The weaknesses of stand-alone eradication and alternative livelihoods programs suggest that the two approaches need to be pursued together. This is consistent with the national strategy, where broad economic and social development is to take place in tandem with "phased law enforcement." The key issue with such a combined approach is the need for appropriate sequencing. Eradicating first runs the risk of alienating farmers and reducing their receptivity to rural development efforts in general (including alternative livelihoods programs). On the other hand, implementing alternative development programs first means a delay in eradication, which at the extreme could be quite long. Yet there is pressure on the Government for quick results.

Strategic Trade-offs. The following discussion is intended to pose questions and suggest options rather than to make hard-and-fast recommendations.

i. *Balancing economic measures and law enforcement.* Both are essential, and close coordination is needed between law enforcement and development instruments, taking into account incentives and sequencing issues.
ii. *Interdiction, eradication, alternative livelihoods.* The Government may want to initially give priority to interdiction over eradication, as trying to do both equally would disperse scant political capital, energy, and capacity. Alternative livelihoods programs—and more generally measures to promote broad-based economic growth and employment generation—could be put in place, with the threat of law enforcement measures to follow in due course. Eradication measures could then be planned once implementation capability and political support are mobilized. It is the combination and phasing of the three elements that will be most effective.
iii. *Prioritization.* Given capacity and budget constraints, prioritization is essential. The possibility of using a cost-benefit tool to analyze different options was discussed above. In the immediate future, giving priority to action against larger participants in the drug industry would seem to be the most cost-effective approach, and also would have potential for a strong positive public reaction. A focus on new areas with little or no history of poppy cultivation could make sense, as it is easier to roll back the practice where the technology and networks are not yet entrenched.
iv. *Monitoring progress and impacts and adjusting plans.* The NDCS emphasizes the need for good monitoring, and there needs to be a thorough assessment of the economic and social situation of opium farmers and wage laborers.
v. *Law enforcement capability.* Clarifying institutional responsibilities with respect to law enforcement is a priority. Exceptional measures are needed to strengthen capacity.
vi. *Legal framework and judicial and penal process.* The justice system as it relates to drugs needs strengthening. The legal framework is under review. Consideration could be given to devising a fair but easily implementable legal, judicial, and penal process for drug offenders, perhaps including special mobile courts dedicated to narcotics cases.
vii. *Need for international support.* The Government is seeking sustained international support and cooperation in its efforts against drugs, and in controlling the trade in both transit and consuming countries.

CHAPTER 8

Delivering Basic Social Services with Gender Equity

In 2001, levels of basic services and social indicators in Afghanistan were among the worst in the world, reflecting very limited coverage pre-war and the effects of protracted conflict. Considerable progress has been made in the past three years, but Afghanistan still lags far behind other poor countries in terms of basic social services (education, health, water supply), and quality is problematic. Delivering public services is critically important for Afghanistan because:

i. *Services contribute to economic growth* by augmenting human capital, and to a lesser extent by directly contributing to total GDP (see Chapters 1 and 3).
ii. *Public services improve human welfare,* especially that of the poor who cannot afford expensive alternatives.
iii. *Delivery of public services helps reduce poverty,* through both of these channels.
iv. *Effective service delivery enhances the Government's credibility and legitimacy* in the eyes of the public, thereby strengthening public support for the Government and facilitating political progress and necessary reforms (see Chapter 4).[1]

This chapter analyzes issues and constraints faced by Afghanistan in expanding the coverage and improving the quality of basic social services, and puts forward some approaches and strategies in line with the Government's development vision and policy framework. The chapter focuses on accountability relationships, incentives, and the institutional

1. As noted in the *National Development Framework* (Afghanistan Government 2002), this does not mean that government can or should deliver all services itself, but the government does bear ultimate responsibility for service delivery outcomes and in that sense must be "in charge," whether or not it is directly involved in financing or provision.

framework—without which financial and human resources and technical solutions alone will not deliver the desired results on a sustainable basis. The pre-war situation, the impact of the conflict, and recent progress are first briefly reviewed in the first section. The second section presents a conceptual framework for analyzing public service delivery, highlighting key issues and general recommendations for Afghanistan. The final section focuses on specific sectors including education, health, and water supply and sanitation.

Background

Pre-War Situation and Impact of Conflict

In the late 1970s, Afghanistan had a highly centralized system of social service delivery by government organizations, primarily for a small elite group of the urban population. Most Afghans, who lived in rural areas, were not beneficiaries of any public services. The bulk of people did not have telephones, electricity, or piped water, and most were not reached by modern education and health facilities. Afghanistan's pre-war social indicators not surprisingly were very low, reflecting the extremely limited coverage of public services. Table 8.1

Table 8.1. Public Service and Social Indicators

	Pre-war	Year	1999 or 2000[a]	2003	Target 2015
Primary education (gross enrollment %)	30	1974	15	54	100
Primary for girls (gross enrollment %)	9	1974	0[b]	40	100
Primary for boys (gross enrollment %)	51	1974	29	68	100
Access to basic health services (% population)	24.1[c]	1974	n/a	40	95
Immunization, DPT (% of children under 12 months)	4	1980	35	30	n/a
Immunization, measles (% of children under 12 months)	11	1980	40	n/a	n/a
Maternal mortality ratio (modeled estimate, per 100,000 live births)	N/a		n/a	1600	205
Infant mortality rate (per 1,000 live births)	190.5	1975	165	115	55
Under-5 mortality rate (per 1,000 live births)	300	1975	267	172	130
Life expectancy at birth, total (years)	39	1975	43	43	n/a
Improved water source (% of population with access)	5[d]	1977	13	13[e]	80[f]
Improved water source, rural (% of rural population with access)	n/a		11	n/a	n/a
Improved water source, urban (% of urban population with access)	n/a		19	n/a	n/a

a. Data quality during the conflict is weaker.
b. Some girls were enrolled in schools in areas not controlled by the Taliban and in rural areas.
c. percent of population with access to Basic Health Centers.
d. percent of population with potential access to public water supply systems.
e. No updated data available.
f. For Kabul.

Source: World Bank (2004f); UNICEF and CSO (2003); Afghanistan Government (2004b); staff estimates.

presents rough estimates of service availability and social indicators for Afghanistan in the late 1970s, 1999–2000, 2003, and targets for 2015.

Afghanistan's social services were gravely damaged by the long conflict and associated flight of human capital, lack of funding, and neglect of maintenance. While the government structure remained in place along with many public servants, actual service delivery to a large extent ceased, and where activities continued quality deteriorated. Rural social service provision was largely wiped out (rural schools destroyed, teachers killed or driven away); urban social services bore the brunt of Taliban retrogressive social policies in the late 1990s, with many facilities closed, girls forbidden to go to school, and female professionals dismissed except to some extent in Health. Salaries of public sector service providers became so eroded by inflation as to be nearly meaningless.

There were some positive developments however. Millions of Afghans became refugees or were displaced to cities in Afghanistan (and thereby exposed to urban environments), helping kindle demand for social services, education in particular. NGOs stepped in with limited humanitarian funding, helping some failing public facilities to stay in operation with salary supplements (especially in the Health sector) and non-salary support. Thus while government capacity sharply deteriorated, some capacity was maintained in the NGO sector, which had been virtually non-existent before the war. In a few cases like rural drinking water supply in many areas and girls' primary education in rural Pashtun areas, the coverage of services most probably was greater than before the war. These modest achievements under very difficult conditions had a limited impact quantitatively and could not offset the deterioration in government service delivery. All in all, in terms of service delivery outcomes Afghanistan was essentially left out of a quarter-century of development (Table 8.1).

Recent Progress

Inheriting a dire situation with public services largely non-functional, the Government emphasized in its NDF in April 2002 the critical importance of ensuring adequate basic social services for the population. Remarkable progress has been made in a number of areas during the past three years. For example, through extraordinary efforts supported by international partners, more than three million children were enrolled in school in 2002 and more than four million in 2003, one third of them girls. This far exceeds past peak levels and rates of school enrollment. Another notable example is immunization, which had been pursued with limited resources and great difficulty during the conflict but which achieved considerable success during the past two years, with positive outcomes like the number of reported new polio cases dwindling to near zero.

Despite these achievements, coverage of most services remains very low (Table 8.1), and serious quality problems are evident. Afghanistan still lags well behind other countries at similar levels of development in school enrollment, literacy rates are very low, and large gender disparities persist especially in rural areas. The Basic Package of Health Services (BPHS) is estimated to cover only 40 percent of the rural population, and effective coverage is much less than that due to capacity and resource constraints. The bulk of Afghans still do not have reliable electric power supply and clean water. Thus the situation that prevailed in the 1970s and during the long period of conflict—basic social services not

Table 8.2. Rural Households' Access to Basic Services

Access to basic infrastructure	% of households	Service facilities in community	% of households
Electricity	16	Primary school	48
Non-traditional lighting[a]	10	Secondary School	13
Non-traditional cooking[b]	0.1	Health facility	9
Covered drinking water[c]	24	Public transportation	34
Adequate toilet facility	7	Food market	5

a. Electricity, generator, gas.
b. Kerosene, gas, electricity.
c. Handpump.
Source: Afghanistan Government (2003).

reaching most of Afghanistan's people—has not yet been fundamentally changed with the partial exception of primary education. This is illustrated by the National Rural Vulnerability Assessment (NRVA), which collected rural household survey data on access to various basic services, some of them privately-provided (see Table 8.2).

International experience demonstrates that achieving better social service delivery on a sustainable basis, especially to the poor, requires more than just human and financial resources and good technical solutions. The key actors that relate to public service provision need to be accountable to each other, which requires appropriate incentives and institutional relationships.

Conceptual Framework

A conceptual framework for analyzing public service delivery issues is provided in the World Bank's *World Development Report 2004: Making Services Work for Poor People* (World Bank, 2004g). The main actors associated with public service delivery can be categorized in three groups: the *public* (with particular focus on the poor) in their dual roles as citizens and clients; the *government* (at different levels in sizable countries) in political and policymaking guises; and the *service delivery organizations* themselves, including management and the front-line professionals directly providing services (teachers, public health providers, utility technicians, etc.).

The accountability relationships between these actors form an "accountability triangle" (Figure 8.1). The "long route" of accountability includes two stages, whereby service providers are supposed to be accountable to government policymakers (through explicit contracts or other forms of "compact") and the government in turn is supposed to be politically accountable to the people as citizens (through the electoral process and other political mechanisms). The "short route" of accountability is directly from service providers to service recipients (clients), whereby through choice of providers (if possible) and participation (monitoring and other activities), clients seek to make service providers more accountable directly to them. This framework can be used to analyze service

Figure 8.1. Accountability Relationships in Public Service Delivery

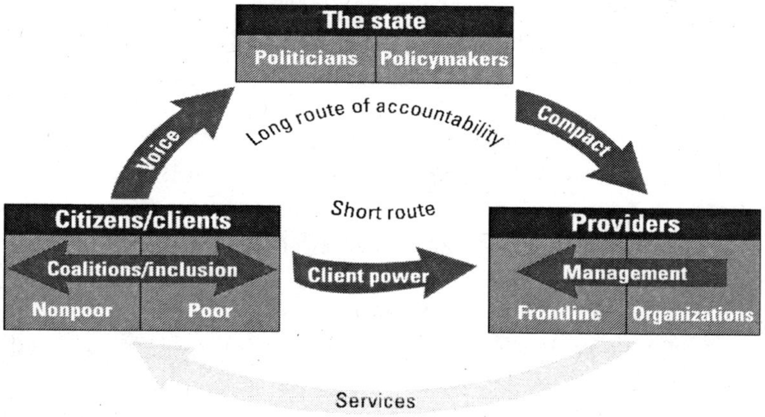

Source: World Bank (2004g), Table 3.2, p. 49.

delivery breakdowns and actions to make services work better, depending on different political contexts and characteristics of the public services concerned. Key dimensions include whether the clients are heterogeneous or homogeneous and whether the public service is easier or more difficult to monitor. Services that are both transactions-intensive and discretionary on the part of the frontline service provider—such as education—tend to be more difficult to monitor than those which do not have one or both of these characteristics.

This framework implies that there is often scope to improve public service delivery by enhancing the accountability of service providers directly to clients (including the poor)—the "short route" of accountability. In the context of Afghanistan, the long route of accountability also is very important as it can help build citizens' loyalty to the Government (Chapter 4).

This conceptual framework also sheds light on the financing of public services. The financial flows are similar to the accountability arrows in Figure 8.1—that is, payments from clients to service providers (cost recovery); from citizens to government (taxes and levies); and from government to service provider (subsidies or, if the service is provided by a government department, budget expenditures). Financing is critical for long-term sustainability of social service delivery. In the case of elementary education, and only to a slightly lesser extent for basic health services, cost recovery (discussed in Chapter 4) is not an option due to the intended poverty impact of the services (and major externalities in the case of immunization and certain communicable disease programs). However, community contributions, for example to construction or maintenance of rural school buildings, can be pursued both on grounds of financial cost-effectiveness and to promote community ownership of the service. In any case, it is essential to program adequate budget allocations for recurrent expenditures in social sectors, especially the non-salary portion which is chronically neglected in many countries (see Chapter 4).

Key Issues for Afghanistan

This framework helps in understanding the key issues that affect basic social services in Afghanistan and lead to gaps and quality problems in service delivery. These include overall human and financial resource constraints, institutional weaknesses, inadequate financing mechanisms, and weak accountability relationships.

Limited Human Resource Capacity in Afghanistan. While constraints are most salient in the public sector due to low salaries and loss of professionals during the war, Afghanistan overall is very short of educated, skilled, and professional human resources, reflecting the breakdown of the education system and other effects of conflict. Competition among different actors (Government, NGOs, private sector, international agencies) for this very limited pool tends to bid up wages without eliciting additional supply from domestic sources (see Chapter 4 on the "second civil service"). Capacity constraints affect both the state and providers and are especially severe at management levels. There is also a very serious gender imbalance, reflecting mainly the disproportionately low supply of educated women, aggravated by the Taliban's dismissal of the bulk of female civil servants, many of whom have not returned.

Financial Resources and Sustainability Issues. Social services have been starved of funds for a long time, and domestic fiscal resources are still much lower than in other countries despite recent revenue mobilization efforts (see Chapter 4). This situation is expected to improve, but demands on limited domestic revenues will continue to be large and growing, necessitating difficult trade-offs.

De jure Highly-Centralized Government Service Delivery Structures and Mindsets. The existing system in Afghanistan is based on the view that the state itself has to deliver services. Management of service delivery and policymaking are combined within the same central ministries. The first instinct when Afghanistan emerged from conflict, in the government bureaucracy but also among many others, was to restore centralized government service delivery, without consideration of the implications, costs, and sustainability of this approach in the context of the required quantum leap in the coverage of public services. Moreover, the geographic and bureaucratic "distance" between frontline service delivery personnel and departmental management in Kabul is often very great, so the managerial relationship tends to be weak and easily can break down altogether. The lack of separation of service delivery management from government policymaking also makes it more difficult for the Government to hold service delivery organizations accountable for their work, and leads to patronage which detracts from the necessary focus on service delivery.

De facto Local Political Control. In many areas, the national government has relatively weak control in practice (Chapter 4). This reflects difficulties in communicating between Kabul and provinces (poor security, lack of roads and telecommunications), as well as a tendency on the part of the center to neglect liaison with the provinces, lack of availability of approved non-salary budget allocations, and delays in salary payments to provincial officials. The weakness of central authority also reflects the political power structure—in particular the "capture" of some provincial administrations by regional powerbrokers. In general, local powers have very limited direct accountability to the clients, and therefore local control does not lead to better service delivery. In particular women tend to be completely excluded from political influence at the local level, and have a limited presence at national level.

Lack of Information and Monitoring. Information flows can promote accountability and better service delivery. However, good information on service delivery was not generated in the past but rather bureaucratic reporting within the government hierarchy. Even these information flows to a large extent broke down during the conflict. While the reporting system from government service providers to government policymakers (and then onward to citizens) can be difficult to make work well, there are ways to promote information flows between service providers and clients in support of the short route of accountability.

Disconnect with Households and Communities. The centralized service delivery entities did not interact closely with the people and communities they were intended to serve. The approach was top-down and one-size-fits-all, with little client feedback or provider responsiveness to client needs and preferences. "Client power," the short route of accountability, was very weak as a result. While such an approach may not have worked too badly in urban areas prior to the war, its shortcomings are obvious in trying to scale up and expand coverage throughout a far-flung country with difficult logistics and communications, particularly in view of the high expectations among the rural population as a result of their contacts with NGOs.

Sustainability Issues Related to Heavy Reliance on Donor Funding.[2] Most funding for social service delivery in Afghanistan today comes from external assistance. In addition to the need for domestic resource mobilization to replace donor funding over time (see Chapter 4), there are concerns that the heavy reliance on external assistance in the short run will:

i. Build in higher costs of delivery that will turn out to be unsustainable in the long term when donor funding tapers off and the burden has to be taken up by domestic resources.
ii. Entrench parallel networks and capacity that will prove difficult to integrate into national programs and delivery mechanisms.
iii. Postpone and render more difficult the hard trade-offs that need to be made in the interest of cost-effective service delivery in a fiscally constrained environment.

2. These concerns relate especially to external assistance outside budget channels and without transparent cost control incentives such as competitive contracting. Recent Government initiatives try to address many of these issues.

Improving Basic Social Service Delivery in Key Sectors

From a medium-term perspective, getting institutional relationships and incentives for different actors right so there is meaningful accountability will be critical for effective social service delivery in Afghanistan. This is true despite the imperative to respond to enormous problems of narrow coverage, problematic quality, insufficient human resource capacity, and limited funding. In sectors where there has already been a significant degree of success in expanding coverage of services (e.g. primary education), addressing institutional and policy issues is all the more urgent because they will be a major determinant of service quality, whether people continue to utilize the services or drop out, sustainability, etc. Where the expansion of service delivery has not yet gotten very far, it is important to build in considerations of institutional relationships, incentives, and accountability from the start. Box 8.1 has examples of options for improving service delivery, grouped in five general categories—improving management, strengthening accountability, better use of information, financial incentives and fiscal sustainability, and donor engagement. The focus is on doable options in the Afghan context which do not entail drastic changes in the structure of government.

The remainder of this chapter discusses selected social services including elementary education, basic public health services, and urban water supply and sanitation. There are major capacity and investment requirements in each sector, as well as recurrent expenditure needs, all of which are discussed in *Securing Afghanistan's Future* (Afghanistan Government 2004b). Here the focus is on the institutional, policy, and financing arrangements that will help enable the resources and capacity in these sectors to work effectively in delivering services, especially to the poor.

Elementary Education

Sector Situation and Key Issues. Great success has been achieved in bringing primary school enrollments (including for girls) up to unprecedented levels not seen before in the history of Afghanistan (Figure 8.2). Over four million children are now in school, one-third of them girls, but this still represents only a little more than half of school-age children and 40 percent of girls. Moreover, these figures hide dramatic regional disparities, with girls representing less than 15 percent of total enrollment in nine provinces in the east and south. Besides gender disparities, such figures also reflect the persistent huge urban-rural disparity. The challenge will be to sustain and further expand enrollments and progress toward universal primary education, in line with the national objective of reaching 100 percent gross primary school enrollment (including for girls) by 2015 (see Table 8.1). A critical prerequisite both to keep children in school, notably girls who have higher drop-out rates than boys, and to further expand enrollment is adequate content and quality of education, which are in urgent need of improvement.

Obstacles to expansion of education and better quality include (i) constraints on numbers and skill levels of teachers, particularly in under-served rural areas where it is difficult to deploy female teachers; (ii) poor or non-existent school infrastructure, with many classes held in tents; (iii) outdated curricula—including in their portrayal of gender roles—and shortages of teaching materials; (iv) a variety of constraints affecting

Box 8.1. Examples of Approaches to Improving Social Service Delivery in Afghanistan

Improving Management

1. De-concentration within the government departments responsible for overseeing service delivery, i.e. enhancing the role of provincial and district government officials. Local governments as they build capacity will be in a better position to oversee and monitor front-line providers, which is impossible to do effectively from the center.
2. Enhancing the management role and autonomy of service provision facilities where appropriate, e.g. in the case of hospitals and educational institutions. This will permit the managers of these facilities to act more like managers as opposed to bureaucrats in a long chain of administrative hierarchy.

Strengthening Accountability

1. Clients (individually or through their communities) monitoring local service delivery facilities and providing feedback on their performance. This needs to be built into programs.
2. Organizing service-specific beneficiary groups to provide monitoring and feedback, e.g. parents' associations in the case of elementary schools, transport associations in the case of roads, water or power user groups, etc.
3. Giving the Community Development Councils that are part of the National Solidarity Program a broader role in monitoring local service delivery and giving voice to communities' concerns and priorities.
4. Ensure female beneficiary involvement in monitoring and feedback on service delivery, particularly in the health, education, and water supply and sanitation sectors.

Using Information to Improve Management and Strengthen Accountability

1. Radio.
2. Posting resource allocations, which was done in the Kabul University Block Grant project, supported by IDA.
3. Use of local languages to improve outreach to clients/beneficiaries, especially women.

Financial Incentives and Fiscal Sustainability

1. Pushing out the non-salary budget so that provincial and district governments can function, with further installments contingent on proper accounting and reporting of initial installments. The Government intends to implement such a mechanism in the current financial year (1383).
2. Modest enhancement of spending discretion (within the budget) at lower levels of government administration.
3. Maintaining a hard budget constraint for lower levels of administration through observance of budget allocations and standards (with flexibility for reallocations within categories as noted above).

Donor Engagement

1. Move assistance through the government budget, thereby strengthening budget accountability channels.
2. Reinforce service providers' domestic accountability relationships and avoid trying to duplicate them.
3. Maximize consistency of approaches across donors.
4. Coordinate TA and build domestic capacity, avoid "enclave" approaches.

Figure 8.2. Education Enrollment Figures

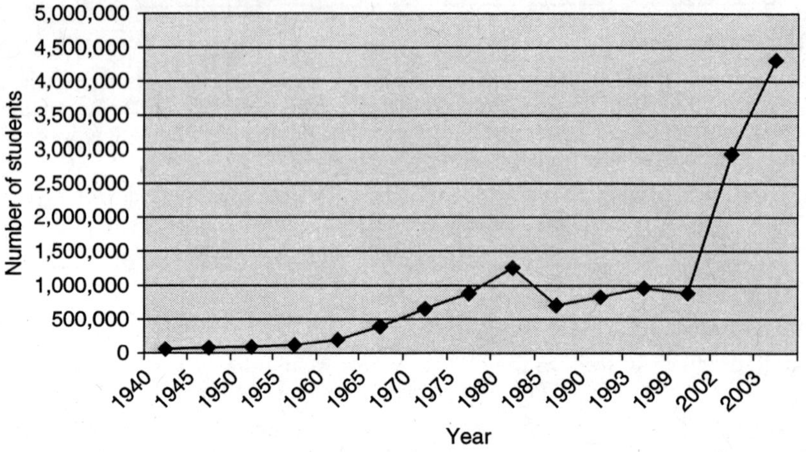

Source: Afghanistan Government (2004b).

access to education in remote areas and especially for girls, such as distance, lack of security, and lack of toilets at schools; (v) low retention rates especially for girls; and (vi) financial resource constraints.

Organizational Structure for Service Delivery. Education, before the war and recently, has been delivered mainly through a highly centralized government apparatus in the Ministry of Education. As noted recently: "Almost all key decisions are made in Kabul. Even the provincial and district offices have very limited decision-making authority...With few exceptions, a culture of dependency on the center pervades the education sector in Afghanistan" (Evans and others 2004a, p.116). Another prominent feature has been the past emphasis of the Ministry of Education on its role as primary, even sole provider of educational services and inputs, including school construction and textbook production. This approach is beginning to change for non-educational activities. But overall, unlike in the case of other post-conflict countries where the collapse of the state and of government-provided education led quickly to local and community-based schooling, in Afghanistan the main thrust has been to revive and expand the centralized government system. Given experience, the ability of this approach to deliver the coverage, quality, and sustainability needed in order to achieve universal primary education in Afghan conditions is questionable.

Government Strategy. The Government's vision is good-quality education for all, regardless of gender, ethnicity, language, religion, or location. This objective, which amounts to achieving the MDGs for Education, has been translated into a development program emphasizing (i) teacher development (increasing the numbers of teachers and improving their qualifications); (ii) infrastructure investments (school repairs and construction); (iii) curriculum and textbook development and provision; and (iv) special measures to increase and maintain enrollment of girls. Deployment of more male and female teachers in rural areas is of particular importance.

Improving Service Delivery. The Government recognizes that modifications in the traditional centralized, government dominated approach to providing education will be required: "The goal is to gradually put in place systems of mutual accountability between levels of government and communities for ensuring well performing schools. An accompanying goal is to incrementally delegate greater decision making and spending authority to districts, communities and schools" (Afghanistan Government 2004b, Education Annex). This implies several concrete reform directions:

i. Getting the Ministry of Education at the central level out of direct provision of education and production of inputs, and focusing on its role of policymaking, regulating and monitoring service delivery, facilitating others' work, and contracting for goods/services.
ii. Delegating (de-concentrating) decision making authority and management roles vis-à-vis schools and teachers to provincial and district levels of government, which will entail building the capacity of Provincial Education Departments and District officials.
iii. Giving schools more flexibility in day-to-day management and authority over non-wage O&M resources at the school level.
iv. Involving communities (parents' associations or Community Development Councils) in monitoring and overseeing schools and holding them accountable for performance. A special effort to involve mothers in parents' association could positively impact on girls' enrollment and retention. Innovations like community contracting of NGO education providers are being tried out.
v. Greater roles for schools and communities will not work unless the Government delivers on its obligations. This means paying salaries on time, providing funds for non-wage O&M, providing necessary teaching materials, etc.
vi. Better information flows at the local level also will be very important.

Basic Health Services

Sector Situation and Key Issues. Afghanistan's health indicators are among the worst in the world with large gender gaps—under-five mortality rate of 172, infant mortality rate of 115, and estimated maternal mortality rate of 16 (all per 1,000 live births); rate of chronic malnutrition (moderate or severe stunting) around 50 percent; and very high rates of disability due to polio, cerebral palsy, and conflict (including landmines). Recent surveys have revealed that almost half of all deaths among women of reproductive age are a result of pregnancy and childbirth—and that more than three-quarters of these deaths are preventable. Among children diarrhea, acute respiratory infections, and vaccine preventable illnesses likely account for 60 percent of deaths, and among adults tuberculosis results in an estimated 15,000 deaths per year, with 70 percent of detected cases being among women. Life expectancy is estimated at 43 years. Only something like 40 percent of the rural population is in the coverage areas of basic health facilities, and moreover these are inadequately staffed with female health personnel in particularly short supply. With the prevalent reluctance of women to seek medical assistance from male health workers, the lack of female staff greatly obstructs women's use of health facilities. Only 9 percent of rural households surveyed in 2003 reported a health facility in their village (Table 8.2), although it is possible that a larger percentage may have had a health facility in the locality. While immunization coverage has expanded including for measles and polio (only seven confirmed polio cases reported in 2003), routine immunization coverage (DPT3) is estimated to be only 30 percent.

Key issues include, in addition to financial resource constraints, (i) inadequate numbers of skilled health staff in rural areas, particularly women; (ii) lack of managerial capacity especially at provincial level; and (iii) managerial and organizational structures that do not provide incentives or accountability for results. Many health professionals (doctors, nurses, technicians, immunizers, etc.) get incentive payments or "top-ups" from NGOs and donor agencies. While helping retain such staff, these payments, especially their ad-hoc nature, raise concerns about sustainability and also that staff may become more responsive to their financiers than to the Government. Planned standardization of top-ups should help reduce this latter tendency.

Organizational Structure for Service Delivery. In the pre-war period the Health sector had a centralized mode of government service delivery management similar to that of Education. There have been significant changes during the conflict and more recently, however. Government health services were gravely affected by conflict, flight of talent, and lack of funding. In the 1990s, NGOs using humanitarian funding came on the scene and provided modest levels of service in some areas. They also became the repository of most of the remaining professional capacity in the Afghan health sector, through employment of these professionals or through top-ups for those who remained in government service. This pattern of NGO and NGO-supported service delivery has continued since 2001, as has the heavy reliance on donor funding.

Government Strategy. With the ultimate objective of improving health outcomes for all Afghans and achieving corresponding progress toward health MDGs, the Government has developed a Basic Package of Health Services (BPHS), including maternal and newborn health, child health and immunization, public nutrition, and communicable disease control. The goal is to deliver the BPHS to 90 percent of the population within seven years and 95 percent within 12 years. In addition, the Government will continue to strengthen vertical programs to achieve blanket coverage of simple yet effective interventions such as salt iodization, polio, measles, and tetanus immunization, and vitamin A distribution. The Government intends to ensure that every health facility in the country has sufficient female staff, and that all staff are properly trained and independently certified to have the required skills and knowledge. Finally, organizational and managerial reforms to improve health service delivery will be implemented and management capacity built up within the Government, particularly at the provincial level. The Government is pursuing different ways of generating incentives and accountability for results, including working with the private sector and NGOs. One example is Performance-Based Partnership Agreements (PPAs), whereby service providers are contracted on a competitive basis to deliver the BPHS in a province, with per capita cost an important consideration and independent monitoring of performance. So far PPAs are in effect for seven provinces.

Improving Service Delivery. The PPA approach has potential to provide an appropriate accountability relationship between Government and service providers, with incentives for cost-effective service provision. The Government is keeping its options open as to whether this will be the dominant mode of delivery of basic health services or whether the government service delivery network will be rebuilt, depending on experience with different modes of service delivery. Irrespective of this choice, strengthening the management and oversight capacity of provincial health departments, part of the reform plan, will be critical for success. Options for enhancing the role of service recipients and communities in promoting accountability of service providers for results also should be explored. Special efforts should be made to involve female service recipients, as women and children comprise by far the largest number of potential health beneficiaries. This is particularly important for non-standardized services provided to individuals at basic health facilities. Options for augmenting outreach, for example training for traditional birth attendants, could be explored. Some health services lend themselves to standardized delivery to easily identified target groups (e.g. children), with effective top-down monitoring. Examples include immunization, vitamin A supplementation, certain types of screening, etc., which are handled through vertical programs in many countries including Afghanistan.

Urban Water Supply and Sanitation

Sector Situation. The proportion of Afghanistan's urban population that has access to modern water supply systems is estimated at less than 20 percent, the lowest figure in the world. This reflects minimal investment in urban water supply and sanitation (WSS) for decades and running down of systems through damage and lack of maintenance, aggravated by sharp increases in urban population in recent years. A large majority of urban residents draws water from wells or traditional canals and streams, which is at great risk of contamination from sewage and other pollutants. (According to recent surveys, 50–70 percent of the tube wells tested in Kabul were unsafe.) The situation with respect to sanitation is even worse, with virtually none of the urban population served by modern sewerage systems, and much solid waste not collected or properly disposed of. There are serious adverse implications for health and risk of epidemics. Continuing rapid urbanization and massive building (re)construction in urban areas (which generates large amounts of rubble and debris) further aggravate the crisis of urban sanitation.

Organizational Structure for Service Delivery. The Central Authority for Water Supply and Sewerage (CAWSS) is responsible for urban water supply and piped sewerage. It was previously part of the Ministry of Public Works but is now under the Ministry of Urban Development and Housing. CAWSS was established in 1978 as a quasi-autonomous government-owned company, but its present legal status is not clear and it has not been operated on a commercial basis. CAWSS manages the water supply system in Kabul and has networks in 12 other cities. Communications and other difficulties during the conflict gave rise to de-facto regional management of urban water supply in several parts of the country. Solid waste collection and disposal is the responsibility of municipal governments.

Key Sector Issues. Beyond severely limited coverage, poor quality of supply, and major funding requirements, the urban WSS sector faces difficult institutional and policy issues: (1) lack of institutional capacity for sector policymaking; (2) lack of a clear legal and regulatory framework; (3) grossly insufficient cost-recovery in relation to O&M requirements—for example in Kabul the ratio is about 15 percent—and lack of a tariff policy including subsidy mechanisms; and (4) over-centralization of CAWSS formal responsibilities with respect to cities other than Kabul.

Government Strategy. The Government's short-run strategy has been to focus on rehabilitation and revival of existing water supply and sanitation services while initiating capacity building, institutional strengthening, and developing plans for system expansion. It is recognized that as the system is restored and expanded, managerial and technical capacity will need to be sharply augmented to run operations. The Government has also initiated increases in user charges—it is estimated that the O&M costs of running the rehabilitated and expanded urban water supply system over the next seven years will be some $65 million, and the funding of these expenditures needs to be put on a sustainable basis.

Improving Service Delivery. The large investments required for WSS need to be complemented by institutional and policy changes to ensure actual delivery of services, adequate quality, and financial sustainability. Donor support for urban WSS cannot be expected to continue indefinitely, and budgetary resources also will be constrained, so sustainable sources of financing for O&M and eventually for investments need to be found. The following actions would enhance incentives for good service delivery by strengthening accountability:

i. Corporatization of CAWSS so that it can be run on an autonomous, commercial basis.
ii. Establishment of autonomous, commercially-oriented water supply entities in other cities, in a gradual, phased manner as their capacity and operations expand.
iii. Phased decentralization of government oversight of urban WSS to municipalities, while getting the central government out of direct involvement in operations.
iv. Increasing reliance on cost recovery, which will promote financial sustainability, encourage a more commercial orientation on the part of the provider, contain demand, and give users more of an incentive to hold providers accountable.
v. Ensuring convenient access to safe water for the urban poor, through well-located and well-maintained standpipes.

Solid waste disposal is a municipal function and presents different issues. Contracting out of garbage collection and disposal functions is already occurring and can be expanded, with municipal governments playing a monitoring and regulatory role. There is scope for greater community participation in and monitoring of solid waste disposal, to enhance accountability. Water supply, sanitation, and solid waste disposal all require strategies which specifically address and involve the female members of communities and households, with women and children in urban and rural areas being the primary water collectors. Community participation in sanitation and solid waste disposal would also need to focus on women in particular.

Conclusions

The above discussion highlights that each sector has its own specific characteristics which influence and constrain choices with respect to institutional relationships and accountability mechanisms. Table 8.3 below brings out some of the key dimensions of variation. In sectors where there is relatively more emphasis on the "long route" of accountability, the contractual relationship or other arrangements between Government and service provider are of great importance. On the other hand, the mechanisms for client participation and monitoring vis-à-vis service providers are important for strengthening the "short route" of accountability, and to be effective will require female involvement at community level. In both cases service delivery units need to be given greater scope and capacity to manage themselves, within an appropriate accountability framework. Finally, the desirable level of government oversight is at the sub-national level rather than in the central government. However, where contractual arrangements are being used to strengthen the long route of accountability (for example, for basic public health services), national government oversight of contracting is required in the case of provinces that have been "captured" by local interests and are not responsive to Government guidance.

Table 8.3. Institutions and Accountability in Selected Services in Afghanistan

	Public service			
	Elementary education	Basic health services	Water Supply and sanitation	Solid waste disposal
Main type of service provider	Government	Non-profit organizations	Public sector corporations	Private contractors
Main direction of accountability reforms	Short Route	Long Route	Long Route	Short Route
Desirable level of government oversight	Province	Provincial oversight of contracts (*)	Municipality	Municipality
Government-service provider relationship	Supervision and management	Competitive contracting	Regulatory	Contractual/ Regulatory
Role of cost recovery	No	No (minimal fees to ration demand)	Yes (with lifeline tariffs for poor)	Yes

(*) With central government contracting for "autonomous provinces" (chapter 3).

CHAPTER 9

Assisting the Poor and Vulnerable

A very large number of Afghanistan's people are poor by any reasonable definition (see Chapter 2), and some are extremely poor. Afghan households have been severely affected by drought, political and security instability, conflict, and natural disasters. These shocks have often led to deepening poverty or have reduced chances of escaping poverty. Furthermore, even non-poor households have experienced and continue to face multiple shocks, and are also vulnerable to fall into poverty as they deplete their assets—physical, human, social, and financial—to help smooth consumption. Divesting or mortgaging assets simply to survive, and also foregoing the building of assets (such as education), can have adverse implications for future productivity and broad-based economic growth, which are essential for sustained poverty reduction.

Yet, the people of Afghanistan are not on the brink of starvation, nor have they been in recent history, due mainly to widespread personal and private initiative. Afghans are a resourceful, resilient, creative, opportunity-seeking, and entrepreneurial people (as witnessed by the high incidence of labor migration, entrepreneurial activity wherever they are located, trading networks, and remittances). Their achievements in the face of adversity are noteworthy.

Building on the analysis of poverty in Chapter 2 and drawing on a forthcoming World Bank report (World Bank 2004b) which is based on the Government's recent household survey (Afghanistan Government 2003), this chapter focuses on issues and options related to social protection—the best way to help those among the poor who are least well-equipped and least likely to benefit directly and immediately from a growing economy (Chapters 1 and 3). Social protection is also intimately related to the capacity of the state (Chapter 4) and its delivery of services to the people (Chapter 8). The first section discusses the characteristics of the poor and vulnerable—key target groups, how people are coping through traditional mechanisms and private initiative, and the implications of these coping mechanisms. The second section assesses the Government's present approach and social protection programs. The final section puts forward key elements of a broad-based, effective, and sustainable social protection policy, which the Government is developing.

Poverty, Vulnerability, and Coping Mechanisms

Poverty and Vulnerability in Afghanistan

Building on the National Rural Vulnerability Assessment (NRVA; see Afghanistan Government 2003) and what is known about urban areas (see also Chapter 2), the following broad characterization of the population in terms of poverty and vulnerability seems appropriate. Around one-fifth of rural households (the lowest quintile) appear to be extremely poor. Roughly 50–60 percent of rural households (the middle three quintiles) are doing a little better, but most are still poor and vulnerable to falling deeper into poverty. The remaining households, the top quintile, while generally better off, in some cases do remain at risk of becoming poor in the event of being hit by shocks. It appears that the profile of the urban population is broadly similar. The essential characteristics of the three population groups, based on the NRVA data, are presented below and in more detail in Table 9.1.

Table 9.1. Essential Characteristics of Three Groups of Rural Households

	The extreme poor	The moderately poor or those at risk of becoming poorer	The better off
Share in NRVA sample (%)	+/–20	50–60	20–30
Adequate calorific intake	No	Yes	Yes
Problems meeting food needs year round	Yes	Sometimes	Rarely
Share of cereals (wheat) in diet (%)	70	60	50
Approximate % of hhs formally headed by women	13	6–7	4
Approximate % of households with literate hh head	18	24	32
Incidence of disability (% households)	22	12	9
Land ownership	High incidence of landlessness (40%); some sharecropping	Some landlessness (20–25%), some with land (including irrigated)	Mostly landowners of irrigated land; engage sharecroppers
Role of poppy	Grow own and provide labor to others	Grow own and provide labor to others	Grow, employ laborers

Table 9.1. Essential Characteristics of Three Groups of Rural Households (*Continued*)

	The extreme poor	The moderately poor or those at risk of becoming poorer	The better off
Employment patterns	On- and non farm unskilled labor, daily wages	Waged labor as well as self-employed (farm and non farm)	Self-employed farming & business, and regular wage based employment (some public sector)
Labor migration	Some, both domestic and abroad, but mainly reliant on short term opportunistic movements within provincial locality	Most prevalent, domestic and abroad	Some, predominantly abroad
Access to electricity (% households)	11	14	25
Access to potable water, modern sanitation	Rare	Rare	Rare
Access to primary school (within village)	About 50% of households	About 50% of households	About 50% of households
Use of health provider when sick	Occasionally, most likely traditional healer, rarely health center or private doctor	Occasionally, most often traditional healer and health center but private doctor for some	Often (but not always), most likely to use private doctor but also traditional healer
Coping strategies—what households do when a "shock" occurs	Reduce food intake, opt for cheaper calories; informal networks for food and credit; migration; poppy labor	Reduce food intake, opt for cheaper calories; mortgage and sale of assets; informal credit; migration; poppy cultivation	Reduce quality of diet, reduce other expenditures. Sale of assets, poppy cultivation
Approximate number of people (based on very rough estimate of total rural population)	3.5 million	10.5 million	3.5 million

Source: Afghanistan Government (2003) and staff estimates.

i. *The extreme poor*, who are food insecure all year round, and whose diet is primarily cereals, roots, and edible oil. These are often landless or very land-poor households, whose primary asset is their human capital and for whom wage employment (farm and non-farm, mainly informal sector) is central to their livelihood strategies.

Some may enter into share-cropping arrangements with landowners, which provide access to land and sometimes credit but can be highly exploitative. In some cases the extreme poor actually reside in the homes of landowners and provide labor services in return for accommodations and/or food. Children are less likely to attend school and often make an important income contribution. Households without members able to engage in gainful employment may have little choice but to depend on the charitable support of relatives and informal social networks. Extremely poor households are highly vulnerable to sickness and premature death but don't have the means to seek medical care when sick. They face volatile employment opportunities and are potentially at risk from fluctuating food prices. Years of shocks have eroded the asset base of these households, and they are reduced to daily survival strategies, living in a vicious cycle of indebtedness, very low wages, and exploitative relationships.

ii. *The moderately poor and those vulnerable to poverty*. These constitute the bulk of the rural and urban population and despite many differences, have a similar propensity to move up and down the welfare ladder. These households tend to have the most diverse livelihood patterns, often engaging in half a dozen or more activities through the employment of different household members. They are engaged in agriculture (their own small landholdings as well as laboring for others), non-farm wage employment, and labor migration. Their diverse portfolios can serve well as a buffer against the impact of any one shock but at the same time limit the scope for major gains. These households generally manage to maintain adequate calorific intake although chronic malnutrition is common duc to poor dietary diversity, high incidence of water-borne disease, and improper feeding practices of young children. Much of the time, they are able to manage risks and shocks without having to resort to extreme and degrading coping strategies. Welfare indicators for this category of households are better than for the extreme poor, but not by a large margin. The absence of schools, health facilities, potable water, electricity, and roads has an equally negative impact on the welfare of these households.

iii. *The better-off* (relatively speaking). These households enjoy greater stability in their consumption and are more likely to be food secure, both in calorific and nutritional terms. Consumption smoothing is possible due to household involvement in higher-value activities and their ability to divest assets when needed, as evident during the 1999–2001 drought. These households are typically land owners (85 percent), having access to irrigation water, capital to buy the necessary inputs, and employing outside labor. However, non-farm earnings (from wages or self-owned enterprises) represent a more significant form of employment than farm management. Remittances from family members working abroad may add to household income and asset accumulation. Services that can be procured privately, such as electricity from a generator and health services from private providers, are enjoyed by the better-off households. But these households remain exposed to many of the same risks and vulnerabilities as other rural households.

Another way of identifying the poor and vulnerable is by specific characteristics, such as people with physical disabilities, female-headed households, the nomadic kuchi, IDPs, returning refugees, and households farming only rain-fed lands. The NRVA collected information related to such groups (summarized in Box 9.1). These patterns confirm that

Box 9.1. Situation of Specific Vulnerable Groups

Returned refugees and IDPs have a slightly higher incidence of poverty compared to the overall NRVA sample, and the calorie intake gap is slightly higher, but all other indicators for this group are similar to the rural average. In fact, it is slightly better off in terms of land ownership, access to irrigated land, and literacy of household heads. Data on refugees and IDPs who have returned to urban locations rather than to their original rural homes (the majority) further confirm that these households are no worse off than others. Many returnees arrive with assets, including education and skills, existing social networks, and able-bodied men, and are well positioned to engage in economic activity and benefit from a growing economy.

Households with disabled people are visibly among the poorest along a number of dimensions: they have higher poverty rates and food gaps than average, and less land ownership and access to irrigated land. There is also a higher incidence of female headed households in this category. However, by no means are all households with disabled people poor. Depending upon the severity of the disability, how this impacts on both the individual as well as the household as a larger entity, the activities of non-disabled household members, and existing household assets including social capital, there is considerable variation in household well-being.

Female-headed households have the highest incidence of poverty of all vulnerable categories. They also have a high calorie intake gap (though the gap is less than for some other categories), suggesting that perhaps these households do better than some in meeting basic food requirement. This may well reflect targeting of female-headed households in humanitarian programs as well as intra-community charitable arrangements. Female-headed households also have a higher than average presence of disabled members. They are more likely to be landless, not to have access to irrigated land, and to have lower ownership of other assets, such as livestock. Female-headed households tend to have (i) restricted mobility outside the domestic compound and (ii) restricted formal entitlements/control with regard to productive assets.

Landless households have a high incidence of poverty, a very high calorie intake gap, and the lowest average daily calorie intake, suggesting a significant food insecurity problem. Owning no land (often the result of having to sell their land during the drought years) and little livestock, they are much more dependent on agricultural and non-agricultural labor, which are low-paid and precarious. A higher than average proportion of landless households are female headed (15%, nearly double the ratio for the sample as a whole), which may reflect the loss of formal asset entitlements by women to male relatives, after the loss of a husband.

Households farming only rainfed lands have the second highest poverty rate, although their food consumption patterns are about average. This may reflect significant livestock holdings for these households and extensive engagement in share-cropping and/or agricultural and non-agricultural labor. Households residing in rainfed zones are more likely to be female-headed and to include disabled persons.

female-headed households, some households with disabled members, the landless, and those farming small plots dependent on rainfall are indeed among the poorest and most vulnerable in rural Afghanistan. These groups are also less capable of protecting themselves against adverse shocks and are more likely to remain trapped in extreme poverty. While this is not an exhaustive list—there are, for example, extremely poor urban households and perhaps significant vulnerable elements within the Kuchi population—designing appropriate mechanisms to allow such groups to increase their income generating potential wherever possible and considering direct transfers as a measure of last resort are called for as an important policy direction. However, returned refugees appear not to be necessarily poorer or more vulnerable than other households.

With respect to the geographical location of the poorest and most vulnerable, insights from the NRVA and other information sources suggest that there is some regional variation, such as a greater concentration of the extreme poor in the west and north-west of the country, and less poverty in the north-east. However, there is significant heterogeneity in household welfare both within communities and across communities throughout the country. This poses a particular challenge for any form of geographical program targeting. By contrast, in urban areas location of residential area (insofar as it conditions employment opportunities, services, access to shelter, environmental, and sanitary conditions) is an important factor in identifying the poor and vulnerable. Stability of income source, social capital, and status of housing (owned or rented) are other proxy indicators of urban poverty/vulnerability.

Less is known about poverty and vulnerability in urban Afghanistan, but urban poverty is clearly as much a multi-dimensional phenomenon as rural poverty. The urban poor suffer from similar deprivations as their rural counterparts, such as lack of access to employment, adequate housing, and services. Personal security appears to be a greater concern in urban areas than in rural areas, although this could also be a reflection of the more qualitative assessments and enhanced intra-household research conducted with urban communities. The nationwide 2003 Multiple Indicator Cluster Survey (UNICEF and CSO 2003) collected information in both rural and urban areas and provides some interesting comparisons (shown in Table 2.1). The data show significant levels of poverty and vulnerability in both urban and rural Afghanistan. For several indicators, mainly relating to access to basic services, such as birth delivery in health facility, literacy and school enrollment (particularly for girls), access to safe drinking water and sanitation facilities, the situation in urban areas is slightly better than in the rural areas. While infant and child mortality rates not surprisingly are around 20 percent lower in urban areas than in rural areas, there is no significant variation as between urban and rural areas in diarrhea prevalence, the proportion of disabled children, the incidence of child labor, orphans, and fertility rates.

Traditional Safety Nets: How Well are They Faring?

As noted above, the remarkable resilience, responsiveness, and strength of the Afghan people is confirmed by the absence of any large-scale famine in the face of adverse circumstances over the last twenty five years. This would appear to be borne out by nutritional data from different parts of the country.[1] A key contributing factor is undoubtedly the diversity of economic activities across Afghanistan, within communities and even within most households, facilitating a wide range of private and informal risk management instruments, utilized by Afghans in the face of adversity.[2] Undoubtedly the rich fabric of community-based networks and institutions has also played a significant role in supporting households and individuals.

When faced with a multitude of risks and shocks, rural households in Afghanistan have for decades relied mostly on informal and private risk management instruments.

1. While the nutritional situation in Afghanistan is characterized by very high prevalence of chronic malnutrition (stunting), estimated at 45–59 percent, levels of acute malnutrition (wasting) remain relatively low, estimated at 6–10 percent. While severe stunting often is associated with a high incidence of chronic poverty characterized by food insecurity and poor health etc., low wasting may imply less probability of nutritional deterioration as a result of rapid shocks.

2. Analysis of a particular economic crisis resulting from a blockade by the Taliban in 1997/98 combined with a severe winter and rising grain prices concludes that households averted famine by employing a range of complex livelihood strategies including sale of livestock, increased labor migration, growing indebtedness, use of social support mechanisms, and access to distress foods. The overall impact of this severe shock was heightened impoverishment for many households, but not outright famine.

During the drought of 1999–2001, the worst drought in living memory, households adopted a number of *ex post* risk management strategies. These included the sale of assets (livestock, land, farm tools, and in the most extreme cases family members—for example, under-age child marriage), generation of additional household incomes through migration strategies, increased reliance on the labor of women and children, employment with local militias, and informal credit (both in cash and in kind). As reported in the NRVA, almost 40 percent of the rural households affected by drought reduced food consumption, another 25 percent decreased overall expenditure, 17 percent sold assets (such as livestock), while 9 percent relied on informal coping instruments (such as borrowing from family and friends). Similar patterns emerge in response to other shocks, such as health shocks.

While preventing starvation, the majority of the coping strategies employed by rural households have long-run adverse implications. Particularly when utilized by poorer households, decreasing food consumption lowers productivity in the short run and in the longer run has adverse health/nutritional consequences among children. Similarly, while asset depletion may be an appropriate smoothing mechanism for households that are relatively rich in assets, this may have major adverse implications for the ability of poorer households to generate income in the future. In addition to food consumption reductions, poorer households may have to rely on support from family and friends in the form of informal borrowing or transfers. This is frequently reported by rural households as a potentially damaging dis-investment in social capital and can incur a significant burden for household members (and may give rise to increased personal and psychological insecurity).

Opium poppy cultivation, and associated wage labor involving as many as two million people altogether, have emerged as a major mechanism helping poor rural households recover from the asset losses and other ill-effects of the drought. However, the burgeoning opium economy is profoundly damaging to state building, security improvements, political normalization, and other critical components of national reconstruction (see Chapter 7). Moreover, many of the rural poor have become increasingly mired in opium-denominated debt.

While the most severe coping mechanisms such as child labor, indentured labor, and giving up under-age daughters in marriage are less frequent in the NRVA sample, their utilization by some households reveals destitution and absolute lack of better risk management instruments. Such practices by all accounts continue, with tragic social consequences for children—a very vulnerable segment of the poor—and there are reports of sale or theft of children for organ transplant purposes as well. These extreme coping mechanisms which some of the poor are forced to resort to underline the critical importance of developing a broad-based social protection strategy focused on the extreme poor, to prevent such tragic outcomes.

Government Strategy and Programs

The Livelihoods and Social Protection Program

As discussed earlier in this report, poverty reduction through broad-based economic growth is at the core of the National Development Framework (NDF). Investments in physical infrastructure (especially roads, water systems, and electricity), agriculture, securing land and property arrangements, creating a healthy business climate with access to skills and capital, good governance, health, and education, will all be parts of a sound poverty reduction strategy.

The Livelihoods and Social Protection Public Investment Program (LSP PIP), part of the first pillar of the NDF, has been developed with a view to ensuring that the needs of poor and vulnerable people are addressed through both their direct (self-reliance) and indirect (targeted public transfers) inclusion in national development. The stated purpose of the LSP PIP is "to empower and support the poor and most vulnerable people in Afghanistan, thereby assisting individuals, households, and communities to better manage risks through both support to sustainable livelihood strategies and direct provision where people are unable to help themselves" (Afghanistan Government 2004b, LSP Technical Annex). The budget for the LSP PIP outlined six sub-programs, each consisting of a coherent set of priority interventions, including many not directly implemented by the Government. The total investment budget for 1382 was $250 million, 14 percent of the National Development Budget. In addition, food aid programs (300,000 million tons of food) costing around $150 million were planned for the same period. Significant achievements of 1382 are highlighted in Table 9.2, including major progress in implementation of the National Emergency Employment Program (NEEP), which generated more than eight million labor days of labor-intensive public works employment.

Table 9.2. LSP Significant Achievements in 1382 (FY 2003/04)

National Emergency Employment Program (NEEP)	The NEEP generated **8 million labour days** through establishment of a nationwide employment based safety net for the construction of rural infrastructure (including **5,000 km of rural roads**) using mainly cash payments
National Solidarity Program (NSP)	The NSP, Afghanistan's flagship intervention for community empowerment, provided resources through **block grants for community managed small-scale reconstruction and development in rural areas**, and promoted more participatory and inclusive decision making and governance at the village level. The target is to cover the country's approximately 20,000 villages over a four year period. As of May 2004, **4,600 village level community development councils** had been elected, 3,400 village development councils completed, and 2,350 sub-projects submitted to approval.
Comprehensive Disabled Afghan's Program (CDAP)	The delivery of **services to 30,000 disabled** people in Herat, Farah, Kandahar, Ghazni, Mazar and Takhar.
Community Based Rural Water Supply and Sanitation Program (CBRWSS)	The construction of over **12,000 water points** across the country with prioritization given to areas where pressure on host communities resulting from returning refugees and IDPs has resulted in particularly acute needs for safe water and sanitation facilities.
National Area Based Development Program (NABDP)	The formulation and implementation of **immediate recovery and development projects** in areas where the local economy has been particularly damaged, based on local resources and existing/historical skills and productive enterprises.
Micro-Finance Support Facility of Afghanistan (MISFA)	The **establishment of MISFA** following a National Micro-Finance Work shop in February 2003 to provide funds for the competitive contracting of specialist professional agencies to sustainably deliver financial services to poor Afghans. As of May 2004, **30,000 loans** had been disbursed to clients (90% of whom are women), and the repayment rate is 98%.

The Performance of Safety Net Programs

The Government introduced its support for labor-intensive public works (LIPW) programs as part of the LSP PIP in 2002. These interventions, most notably NEEP, are generally designed to (i) generate additional employment opportunities in rural areas at a minimum wage, as a safety net to as many people and in as short a time as feasible; and (ii) rehabilitate Afghanistan's basic infrastructure (rural roads and irrigation channels).

In addition to several multi-agency "cash for work" initiatives, the largest single LIPW initiative, the NEEP, was operational by the time the NRVA was carried out in the summer of 2003. The NRVA collected information on participation in cash-based LIPW initiatives (lumping together NEEP with other programs), and separately for two other programs: (i) food for work and (ii) relief food aid. Food-for-work, like cash-for-work programs (including NEEP), is designed with the dual objectives of creating rural infrastructure and providing short-term employment for some of the poor and vulnerable. Relief food aid, administered mainly by the World Food Program, has the objective of reaching food-insecure households. Further details on all three programs can be found in Box 9.2.

Box 9.2. Safety Net Programs

Labor Intensive Public Works Program (NEEP) (cash based): The total value of these initiatives, which were largely nationwide by March 2003, was estimated at over $130 million. Within provinces, the criteria for selection of project sites included areas of intense IDPs and returnee activity; drought-affected areas; areas severely affected by war; areas where existing NGO programs (often food-for-work) could be scaled up quickly; areas where few alternative employment opportunities existed; kuchi areas; and areas sufficiently stable and secure to be able to undertake works. Participation in the program was self-selected, predicated on the assumption that at a low wage of $2/day only the poor and needy would want to participate. In practice, work was spread fairly evenly among all those who wanted work, typically a wide cross-section of any community. Over time, however, at $2/day labor became scarce during the summer months while remaining plentiful during the winter months. Some barriers to participation of the extreme poor and vulnerable have been identified and include distance to project site, share-cropping and other arrangements binding labor to landlords, and traditional values vis-à-vis women's work.

Food for work/food for asset creation programs. These programs are similar to cash-for-work programs, except that payment is made in food commodities (wheat, flour, cooking oil). The main criterion for FFW targeting is areas of acute and very high food insecurity where households meet less than 50 percent of caloric requirements, as assessed by the WFP's vulnerability assessment methodology. Wages are set below casual labor rates so that FFW should be largely self-targeting and does not compete with other work. FFW activities involve community participation, allowing villagers, including women, to agree on projects to be supported and to determine who should participate. Food for work programs have been a feature of life in rural Afghanistan for many years.

Relief food aid, also under the umbrella of the WFP, consists of various programs to assist food-insecure households to meet basic food requirements, with particular attention to the most vulnerable (returning refugees, IDPs, malnourished children, TB patients). Major programs in 2002/03 included: (i) returning refugees—150 kg of wheat per family provided at place of return, with follow-on support for three months; (ii) IDPs—support for both returning to their homes (150 kg of wheat) as well as those remaining in camps; (iii) vulnerable rural households—households living in FFW communities but unable to participate, such as widows, orphans, households headed by elderly or disabled person, and households without income earners (rations provided for five months per year); and (iv) Assistance to TB patients and their families, mainly women (food rations for eight months per year). In 2002/03, Food for Work and relief food aid combined covered around 10 million people.

Figure 9.1. Program Participation by Quintile (percent)

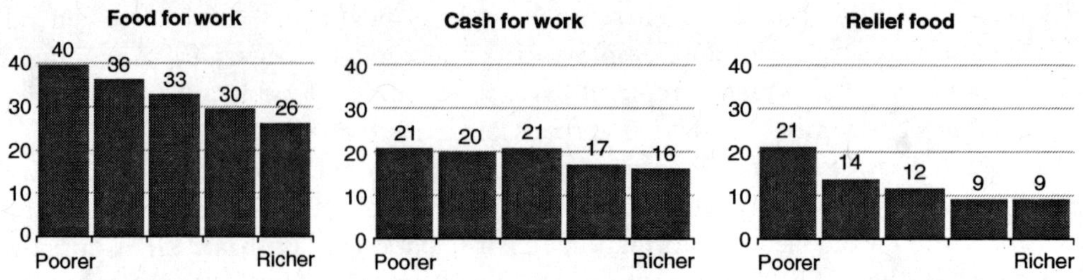

Note: Quintiles are based on per capita food expenditure.
Source: Afghanistan Government (2003).

The participation rates in these programs are quite high. More than one-third of rural households in the NRVA sample had participated in food-for-work in the year preceding the survey, almost 20 percent of households in cash-for-work programs, and 13 percent had received relief food aid.

Turning to the participation of different categories of rural households (extreme poor, moderately poor—further subdivided into the middle three quintiles of the sample—and better-off), of the three programs only relief food aid appears to be highly progressive in targeting the extreme poor households (see Figure 9.1). Food for work appears to be modestly progressive, and LIPW (cash-for-work) programs are reaching only slightly more of the extreme poor than of the rest of the rural population. Moreover, many of the extremely poor households are excluded from these programs altogether. On the other hand, households in the "better-off" category participate in all three programs, especially cash-for-work programs. While it is possible that some of these people were less well-off at the time of participating in the program (the data refer to the year preceding the survey) and may have been more eligible beneficiaries at that time, this seems unlikely. Indeed, insights gained from qualitative reviews of the LIPW programs suggest that at the community level the work is divided fairly evenly among all those in the community who are able to work.

Thus, there is an issue of targeting, especially in LIPW programs, and a considerable share of the resources devoted to all three types of programs seem to be going to relatively better-off rural households. These issues also relate to the objectives of the programs, in particular whether they are seen primarily as: (i) social protection mechanisms to alleviate the situation of the extreme poor; (ii) programs designed to inject purchasing power (in the form of cash or food) more generally into the rural economy, for example in the face of a massive shock like a drought; or (iii) rural infrastructure programs to build or repair physical assets that are of use to the poor, such as rural roads and small-scale irrigation facilities. The balance between these different objectives affects the importance of targeting issues. Finally, in making comparisons between the three categories of programs, cost-effectiveness

3. The payment of a monthly stipend to more than 250,000 war-related disabled persons and their families is an additional program on the operating budget of the government.

should be a primary consideration. For example, although as discussed above cash-for-work programs appear to be less well-targeted at the extreme poor, this would most probably be more than offset by the much higher overhead costs (especially food transport and handling costs) of food-for-work and relief food aid programs. Thus the total program costs required for LIPW programs to put a dollar into the hands of someone in the poorest 20 percent of the rural population might well be considerably less than in the case of the other two programs because of the much more reasonable overhead costs involved, even if food-for-work and especially relief food aid are somewhat better targeted at the poor.

In conclusion, additional information not collected in the NRVA is needed to fully evaluate these programs. The patterns outlined above, however, suggest that the programs are not proving very effective in reaching the poorest and most vulnerable. Steps need to be taken to improve targeting and selection criteria, and to help restructure and redesign some of the objectives and goals of existing and potential new programs. The detailed evaluation of one cash-for-work program (in Hazarajat; see Box 9.3) suggests some pointers for successful labor-intensive public works programs:

Box 9.3. Lessons from Oxfam's Cash for Work Program in Hazarajat

Background: The Oxfam cash for work program was funded by ECHO at a project site where Oxfam had been present since 1991. The intervention was focused on livelihood protection over the winter period when employment opportunities are reduced and to ensure avoidance of damaging coping mechanisms such as distress migration. Cash-based transfers were chosen since food-based transfers were frequently re-distributed, were often not perceived as a development activity for asset building by communities, and to minimize the potential adverse impact on agricultural activities.

Targeting and Activities: Targeting mechanisms were facilitated through the introduction of Oxfam developed criteria, but managed by communities to the extent possible. Where greater investment in shura/community participation had taken place, targeting problems were minimalized. Communities had clear ideas regarding the identification of the most vulnerable households including homeless; landless; small landowners; widows; and people with disabilities. Cash for work activities included construction of water reservoirs and river protection walls, protection against erosion, safeguarding irrigation channels, tree planting, vegetative propagation, fodder collection, and planting. A women's embroidery project component was also introduced, and Oxfam acknowledged that the identification of acceptable work for Hazara women was a challenge, given the inappropriateness of external manual labor. Traditional community safety net instruments were reinforced through the contribution by participants of cash transfers to the non-able bodied.

Payment: Half of the cash payments were distributed before winter and the other half at the end of winter, which coincided with the communities' greatest need for cash. Wage levels were around $2/day for unskilled labor and $4/day for skilled labor. Interestingly, although community representatives argued that other agencies were paying higher rates, local government supported the principle of greater self targeting through lower payments. Monitoring confirmed that participating households accessed 70 days work and that around 90 percent of wages were spent on food, much of it stocks for the winter season. Market traders responded well with additional food supplies. Despite the existence of high debts, money was not spent on debt repayment.

Impact: The household impact of the intervention included increased purchasing power; prevention of migration and distress asset sales; and creation of new community assets. Communities appeared most interested in the overall and longer-term impact of the infrastructure on livelihoods (particularly when these were located within the local vicinity) rather than the more immediate impact of the cash receipts on household well being. The quality of outputs, design, materials etc. was considered very important.

i. *Seasonality*—more activities in winter months when other income generating activities are fewer, with before winter and end winter payments (the most cash-needy times);
ii. *Types of activities*—activities which the extreme poor and vulnerable can help with (a particular challenge with regard to the inclusion of different groups of women and people with disabilities)—and location of activities, in or near to the village;
iii. *Duration of employment*—long enough to provide a significant cash injection and to provide a meaningful alternative to other less desirable short-term livelihood strategies;
iv. *Create quality and durable infrastructure*—this outcome should be considered as a more important objective of LIPW programs;
v. *Mode of payment*—preference for cash-for-work over food-for-work projects; and
vi. *Support traditional distribution mechanisms*—support communities to generate transfer instruments for less-able bodied households.

Toward a Broad-based, Effective, Sustainable Social Protection Policy

The challenge for Afghanistan's social protection strategy lies in effectively reaching the poorest and most vulnerable people in the short run while supporting effective risk management for the broader population over the medium term, all at an acceptable, sustainable fiscal cost. Thus far, social protection has proven more effective in reaching the broad population, and programs that were intended for the extreme poor have not been as successful in reaching them directly. This is not an unusual outcome—countries around the world that have much more institutional capacity than Afghanistan and better data on the poorest have great difficulty in reaching them through programs with low inclusion and exclusion errors (relatively few better-off people included in the programs, and relatively few of the poorest left out of them).

Many of the elements of good policy are already in place in Afghanistan's social protection strategy. These include favoring productive safety nets such as labor intensive public works and other labor-based activities over entitlement programs, strengthening livelihoods through skills development and micro-credit, and working with and through communities. In the immediate future the focus should be on ensuring that key programs are effectively implemented, with meaningful monitoring and evaluation providing insights for improved design. Above all, the challenge is to increasingly move beyond a fragmented project-driven approach to a more systematic national program, effectively drawing on analysis of poverty and vulnerability and carefully monitoring the impacts of interventions on different groups. Implementation can remain dispersed and in the hands of NGOs, local communities, and private individuals, if transparently and competitively conducted within the national social protection framework.

Government policy will need to build on and complement private and informal livelihood strategies and self-protection arrangements, revitalizing and supporting informal risk management instruments. The emphasis should be on productive and inclusive programs that:

i. Focus on the extreme poor in both rural and urban areas, but create safety nets for them only as a last resort;
ii. Take a labor-based approach to investments in rural infrastructure wherever possible (NEEP);

iii. Operate through communities and empower communities to manage their own resources (NSP);
iv. Promote sustainable financial service delivery to the poor through micro-finance (Microfinance Support Facility of Afghanistan—MISFA);
v. Promote sustainable provision of enterprise support (e.g. business development services);
vi. Enhance the health of rural and urban communities (National Water Supply and Sanitation Program);
vii. Provide rural and urban communities with services and infrastructure; and
viii. Further develop emergency response interventions which are also important for risk management (National Disaster Risk Management Program).

Direct social transfers (cash, in-kind) will be limited to the extremely poor and vulnerable who are not able to participate in asset-creating, income-generating programs. These include disabled people with the more debilitating disabilities; poor female-headed households; and destitute and displaced families (as identified in Chapter 2). The new National Vulnerability Program (NVP) will attempt to address the needs of these groups. However, the lack of formal institutions in Afghanistan, weak institutional capacity, and very limited fiscal resources, coupled with the fact that the extreme poor are scattered throughout a vast country with difficult physical access, mean that formal and market based options will be limited in the immediate future.

In conclusion, even if strong economic growth is sustained, the need for continued support for the extreme poor and most vulnerable groups in Afghanistan is clear. In many cases household assets of the poor have been depleted, employment opportunities remain limited, and land fragmentation and high population growth present challenges to both the rural and urban economy. The social protection strategy selected and associated national programs must be fiscally sustainable in the longer term. Hence, continuing research on the nature of vulnerability, linking findings to enhanced targeting of programs, will be key to increasing the efficiency and effectiveness of limited resources in a difficult delivery environment. Moreover, an important aspect of enhancing budget execution in the area of social protection is increased institutional capacity for both public and not-for-profit organizations. Priority civil service reforms also are required in key central Ministries and sub-national departments responsible for social protection.

CHAPTER 10

Priorities for Action, Challenges, Prospects, and Risks

Afghanistan has come a long way since emerging from major conflict in late 2001. As detailed in the earlier chapters of this report, good progress has been made in economic recovery, political normalization, macroeconomic stability, revival and initial reform of public administration, expansion of primary education, initiation of reconstruction, and structural reforms in trade and the financial sector as well as in other areas. Perhaps most important, the energy and initiative of the Afghan people, demonstrated under duress during the more than two decades of conflict, are now being channeled to securing livelihoods, rebuilding assets, restoring a credible state, and more generally reinvigorating the economy. Their efforts have been supported by Government leadership and by major assistance from the international community.

The challenge for the Afghan people, their Government, and international partners is to turn the recent economic recovery, and the promising progress in other respects, into sustained growth, poverty reduction, and social progress over the medium term, while building the state, improving security, and continuing to move forward with political normalization. As indicated in Chapter 1 and elaborated in the SAF report, the Afghan economy does have sources of growth potential, which can be unlocked to sustain growth through a good investment climate and availability of infrastructure and other support services for the private sector. Equally important, especially over the medium term, will be further unlocking the potential of the Afghan people through human resource development.

This challenge is complex and risk-laden. Adverse trends on the security and narcotics fronts constitute the most serious threats to the national vision of economic, political, and social development articulated in the *National Development Framework* and other Government documents. Worsening security in many parts of the country threatens to derail reconstruction, undermine state-building efforts, adversely affect elections and other political normalization, reduce private sector activity, and keep it in the informal/illicit economy. Closely related to insecurity is the problem of drugs—the burgeoning recovery of opium production during the past three years is an important driver of insecurity and funds interests strongly opposed to state building. Drugs, insecurity, "capture" of large parts of the country by illegitimate regional powerbrokers, and the weak capacity of the state all contribute to a self-reinforcing "vicious circle" that would keep the country insecure, fragmented politically, weakly governed, poor, dominated by the informal/illicit economy, and a hostage to the drug industry.

Breaking out of this vicious circle and moving toward a "virtuous circle" of state building, security, dynamic formal-sector economic activity, sustained growth and poverty reduction, and escaping from the opium economy will require simultaneous progress on several key fronts. Actions in any one area alone are unlikely to be effective given the forces at work to maintain the informal equilibrium. On the other hand, the Government has limited political capital and capacity and must focus on those aspects which really matter. There also needs to be a premium on implementing and completing reforms already underway rather than devising and starting new initiatives, which will use up limited capacity and high-quality human resources in the Government without achieving as much in the way of results.

With these considerations in mind, key priorities for action over the coming 1–2 years include:

i. *Enhance Security and Rule of Law, Respond to Drugs in a Coordinated Manner*: The continued existence of warlords and forces disloyal to the central government, funded in large part by drug money, undermines state building and other reconstruction agendas. Security sector reforms need to be given top priority, and administrative reforms in the Ministries of Defense, Interior, and Justice need to be urgently stepped up. The Afghanistan Stabilization Program (ASP) will need to support improved governance of security in provinces and districts. There are no easy answers on drugs, but it is clear that actions against the opium economy must be integrated within broader national objectives and particularly the security and state-building agenda to have any hope of success. The recent establishment of a Counter Narcotics Steering Group, chaired by the Government and including the main government and external agencies involved, is encouraging in this regard.

ii. *Pursue Political Normalization:* The upcoming Parliamentary elections will mark the completion of the political process mandated by the Bonn Agreement, but there is still a long way to go before the political landscape in Afghanistan approaches full normality. The key priority will be making Afghanistan's nascent political institutions—ranging from the new Cabinet to the new elected legislative bodies and the judiciary—fully functional and effective so that they can take on their Constitutionally-mandated roles.

iii. *Maintain Growth with Macroeconomic Stability:* This is essential but will face risks—drought, political instability, "poppy shock," "Dutch disease," and so forth—as well as other challenges (fiscal pressures, limited private sector supply response). The Government will need to monitor economic performance closely and make adjustments in response to shocks, while developing over time analytical capacity and conventional macroeconomic policy instruments.

iv. *Intensify Public Administration Reforms with Extension to the Provinces:* This is a critical part of the state-building agenda, and the Government will need to continue and accelerate current administrative and civil service reforms, including implementation of the PRR process, increasing revenue mobilization, and reducing vulnerability to corruption. It will be especially important to enable provinces to better interface with the public and deliver services, by ensuring timely payments of their employees and access to their non-salary budgets, strengthening their capacity through the ASP, and so forth.
v. *Accelerate Private Sector Development, Including Agriculture:* Priority should be given to implementation of ongoing reforms: adoption of key laws (Investment, Mining, and Petroleum Laws), acceleration of micro-credit schemes, and development of Industrial Parks. Irrigation, marketing, credit, and extension services need to be efficiently provided to Afghan farmers, relying on the private sector as much as possible to provide these services.
vi. *Poverty Reduction, Gender, and Social Protection:* The effectiveness of a poverty reduction strategy will largely depend on national ownership—requiring more extensive consultations with different stakeholders than has occurred hitherto. Enhancing the role of women requires addressing some of their main concerns, such as poor access to education, basic health services, and credit. Building on experience, the Government needs to continually improve existing programs to effectively target them at the poorest.

This is a daunting agenda, and in each area listed above strong, sustained, and well-coordinated assistance from the international community will be required. International security assistance will continue to be needed in the coming several years, and its further expansion outside Kabul would have a high pay-off. Maximizing assistance provided through budget channels is very important, so that Government institutions have a chance to work. Payments to non-legitimate authorities should be stopped. Technical Assistance can support the reconstruction agenda but needs to be coordinated and fully under Government leadership and supervision, with sensitivity to the problems created by the "second civil service." The international community needs to be prepared to respond to major shocks like a drought, by adjusting and accelerating assistance as needed to support appropriate macroeconomic policy responses.

Although Afghanistan's path forward will undoubtedly contain numerous pitfalls and detours, the experience so far gives ground for hope. Despite serious problems and risks, Afghanistan's position and prospects today far exceed what reasonably could have been expected in late 2001, let alone earlier during the protracted conflict. This is a tribute to the energy, initiative, and entrepreneurship of the Afghan people. The vast majority of them have demonstrated by their actions their keen desire for peace and prosperity, most recently manifested in the high voter turn-out for the Presidential election despite security threats. The Government has navigated a very difficult situation remarkably well in most respect. The international community has demonstrated its unity, commitment, and staying power with respect to Afghanistan. This all bodes well for concerted, sustained efforts in the future to tackle the most important constraints hindering further progress in national reconstruction.

Statistical Appendix

Data Availability and Quality

The analysis of the Afghan economy and of poverty in Afghanistan is hindered by severe data limitations: statistics on Afghanistan remain "wild guesses based on inadequate data," as Louis Dupree (1980) described them. But much has been learned about how the Afghan economy functions, and this report draws on the best available estimates, prepared, *inter alia*, by the Central Statistics Office (CSO), the Ministry of Rural Rehabilitation and Development (MRRD), the Ministry of Finance, the Central Bank, FAO, the IMF, UNICEF, and the World Bank.

Institutional Structure and Reform Program

Currently, the core of the statistical system in Afghanistan is the CSO, with branches in all provinces. In addition, there are statistical units in line ministries (and other agencies such as Da Afghanistan Bank) collecting data from administrative sources. The organizational structure and methods used emphasize central planning: CSO continues to use many statistical methods that are inappropriate and inherited from the previous era, and the organization focuses on collecting data for sectors relevant for planning on a complete enumeration basis. CSO and other Ministries and agencies responsible for the compilation of administrative and other data at the sector level have suffered greatly from the conflict and are confronted by serious human resource, material, and physical constraints. In the last two years, a number of NGOs and international agencies have mounted *ad hoc* data collection efforts, but with no or limited involvement of CSO.

A Statistical Master Plan has been prepared to develop the Government's statistical capacity and coordinate donor support (Chandar 2003). The Government is expected to gradually strengthen its institutional capacity to monitor and evaluate its development strategy, including public expenditures. According to this plan, a National Statistical Council will be constituted, with a large membership (statistics producers and users), to set priorities and review progress. The plan also involves reform of CSO (including preparation and implementation of the Priority Reform and Restructuring scheme for CSO). It programs improvements in most areas, including the design, implementation, and analysis of regular households surveys.

National Accounts

The official GDP estimate of $4 billion for 2002/03 produced by CSO, is based on expenditure categories (Table A.1). The traditional method, compiling value-added for different sectors and aggregating the sectoral figures, is simply not workable in the short term in Afghanistan.

Government consumption was easily estimated from the national budget. Investment was based on an estimate of investment in construction and imports of machinery and equipment (mainly for transportation). Exports included recorded exports (about $100 million), plus an estimate of $1.2 billion for opium exports, smuggling, and re-exports, and $300 million of non-factor services (expenditures by foreign embassies in Kabul and non-residents including foreign military, UN, NGOs, and other international consultants and missions). To recorded imports of $2.3 billion were added smuggling and some non-factor services (Afghan embassies abroad, Afghans visiting abroad especially Pakistan, students, and so on). Household consumption was based on a very rough survey of a few households in Kabul (consumption was estimated at 4,500 Afghanis per month per household, or approximately $200 per year per capita).

From this total estimate, CSO derived sectoral value added estimates by updating sectoral shares from estimates of the "Net Material Product" (a concept used for planning purposes in Soviet-style economic systems, with six main branches evaluated at constant 1978 prices).

The GDP estimate used in this report is based on the assumption used in the Government's SAF report, namely that the total income of the economy is calculated as the sum of the official GDP estimate and the value of opium production. Indeed, even though some opium exports appear to be included in the official data,[1] a large part of the opium economy is probably excluded and needs to be added to the official estimate.

Agriculture and Opium

Most estimates of agriculture production, by UNODC for drugs and by FAO/WFP for the rest, rely on satellite images to measure cultivated surfaces (Tables A.7–10). It is also necessary to estimate yields, which are based on surveys with possibly significant margins of error due to heterogeneity throughout the country. Very little agricultural price data is available, which makes the value of production difficult to measure.

1. In the CSO estimate, only $1.2 billion is included for opium exports (including smuggling and net value of re-exports), while the value of opium/opiate exports is estimated by UNODC at $2.5 billion.

For opium, surveying farm-gate prices combined with production estimates can be used to derive and estimate of the value of opium production at the farm level (estimated at $1.2 billion in 2002/03). But the total income from opium for Afghanistan should be evaluated at border prices, which are far more difficult to measure. UNODC roughly estimated total opium-related income at around $2.5 billion in 2002/03 (the base year for the national accounts estimates).

Household Data

The main source of household data is the National Risk and Vulnerability Assessment (NRVA), carried out in July-September 2003 by MRRD. It surveyed 1,850 rural villages in almost all districts in the country and collected data at the village, (subjective) "wealth group," and household levels (11,227 households). The survey estimated average rural expenditures at $165 per year per capita (as discussed at the end of the Statistical Appendix).

UNICEF conducted a Multi-Indicator Cluster Survey in 2003 (Table A.2). The survey covered more than 20,000 households and focused on health, education, and access to related facilities (including water and sanitation).

Another source of data is the labor market information survey conducted by IRC (2003). Although the sample design is rudimentary, this survey provides information on incomes, employment, and business constraints based on questionnaires completed by 992 families, 637 local businesses, and 77 local shuras (councils of village elders).

Government Finances

The Government has implemented an information system (Afghanistan Financial Management Information System). Even though there are still issues of quality, notably with regard to data from provinces, this system provides rich information on Government finances (Table A.3). Data on the civil service are difficult to interpret in the absence of a nominal roll, however. Data on projects directly implemented by donors (not through Treasury) suffer from inaccuracies. As a result, an integrated view of the budget (with financing) is subject to uncertainties (Table A.4).

Other Data

A Kabul Consumer Price Index (CPI) and foreign exchange rates are now officially recorded on a monthly basis (Table A.1). Price data collection has expanded from 50 to 202 items surveyed in four markets in Kabul. Plans are in place to extend the CPI to five other cities. However, the weights for the CPI are problematic, and this weakness is unlikely to be overcome until a full-scale household expenditure survey is completed.

The CSO, in collaboration with the IMF, has made an attempt to estimate the balance of payments. However, many flows (including smuggling and remittances, among others) are not adequately recorded.

Finally, population data also comprise rough estimates in the absence of a full Census or other reliable sources of information. The official estimate from CSO is 22.2 million in 2003, based on the preliminary phase of the Census conducted as part of the electoral process.

Analysis of Household Data

The analysis in Chapter 2, detailed in Tables A.3 and A.4, is based on a measure of welfare that was obtained as follows.

A vector of food consumption for 11,227 households was obtained from the NRVA household survey. This was then multiplied by a fixed vector of prices (a national median) to obtain a measure of expenditure on food that is the closest approximation to money metric utility available. Non-food expenditure on education, medicine, clothing, taxes, fuel, and oil was obtained from 5,559 wealth group surveys within villages. This was an estimate of the typical amount a household in one of three wealth groups in that village would spend on these items and was estimated by a gathering of household members from that wealth group (who for convenience were often later chosen as sample households). Therefore there were between two and three data points which had the same non-food expenditures in each village. A total expenditure measure was then calculated by summing food and non-food expenditure.

This was found to be the best measure when compared to food expenditures alone and expenditures calculated using locally weighted price indices. The method used was ascertaining which measure better fit (in R-squared terms) various dependent variables that are either strong indicators of poverty or are in themselves factors in poverty (for example, dietary diversity, troubles satisfying food need, and village wealth group).

Almost all the results shown are derived from data reported at the household level. Sometimes this is data for the household head only (for example occupation), which is clearly stated. The exceptions are debts and remittances and the priorities for the Afghan Government, which are obtained, as in the case of non-food expenditure, at the wealth group level.

Due to the lack of a comprehensive Afghan census, the weightings used only scale the results up to the sample population. The quintiles are weighted by individual as are all individual statements, while household statements are weighted by household weights.

For the regression analysis in Table A.4, data points containing missing observations were dropped and the top and bottom 5 percent tails were dropped to avoid the results being contaminated by clear outliers (for example, some individuals were apparently consuming more than 10,000 calories a day). The quintile regressions were done using STATA code, with standard errors being obtained from bootstrapping. Significance levels are likely to understate the significance for the normal regressions as the fact that the survey was implicitly stratified into wealth groups will tend to reduce variance although not to an easily quantifiable degree. This is not true of the quintile regression where the programming has not yet been developed to carry out such techniques taking into account survey factors such as clusters and strata.

Table A.1. Macroeconomic Indicators

	Afghanistan			Post-conflict countries[a]		Other countries (2002)[b]		
	1975	2002	2003	Year 1–3	Year 4–6	Neighbors	Sub-Saharan Africa	Low income countries
I. Level of Development								
Official GDP (US$ billion)	2.4	4.0[c]	4.6	—	—	36.8	7.1	16.8
Population (million)	14.0	21.8	22.2	—	—	49.4	15.8	39.0
GDP per capita ($)	169	186	207	—	—	746	446	430
GNI per capita, PPP ($)	—	—	—	—	—	3,200	2,050	1,617
Official annual growth (%)	3.0	29	16	9	6	7.6	3.0	3.2
Life expectancy	39.4	43.2	—	—	—	66.3	48.5	52.8
II. Structure of the Economy (% GDP)								
Agriculture	51	53	47	—	—	17	27	25
Industry	16	25	21	—	—	20	23	22
Services	34	22	29	—	—	62	51	52
Household consumption	86	107	110	—	—	52	69	62
Public consumption	6	8	9	—	—	10	14	11
Gross fixed capital formation	92	20	38	17	20	22	19	17
Exports of goods and services	13	3[c]	12	21	27	29	30	27
Imports of goods and services	14	38	69	41	41	31	41	38
Net trade	(2)	(35)	(56)	(20)	(14)	(2)	(12)	(11)
III. Prices								
Inflation (%)	6.6	(9)	36	179	13	8.8	14.7	12.9
Exchange rate (% increase)	—	(29)	18	—	—	—	—	—

(continued)

Table A.1. Macroeconomic Indicators (*Continued*)

	Afghanistan			Post-conflict countries[a]		Other countries (2002)[b]		
	1975	2002	2003	Year 1–3	Year 4–6	Neighbors	Sub-Saharan Africa	Low income countries
IV. External Balance								
Current account (US$ billion)	(0.1)	(0.1)	(0.0)	—	—	0.8	(0.0)	0.2
External debt (% GDP)	—	—	—	—	—	26	68	49
V. Monetary Indicators								
Domestic currency in circulation (growth %)	—	20.1	40.9	—	—	—	—	—
Gross foreign exchange reserves (US$ million)	—	426	731	—	—	—	—	—
VI. Government Finances								
Current revenues (% official GDP)	11.4	3.3	4.5	15	18	16	18	14
Total expenditures (% official GDP)	15.2	22.0	71.7	21	23	19	21	19
Current expenditures (% official GDP)	9.1[d]	8.6[d]	10.0[d]	—	—	16	16	14
Capital expenditures (% official GDP)	6.1[d]	13.4[d]	61.7[d]	—	—	3	5	5

a. Countries: Azerbaijan, Bosnia and Herzegovina, Myanmar, Cambodia, Congo Rep., Congo Dem. Rep., El Salvador, Ethiopia, Georgia, Lebanon, Liberia, Morocco, Mozambique, Nicaragua, Peru, Philippines, Rwanda, Sierra Leone, Serbia, Tajikistan, Uganda, and Yemen. Year 1 is the year the conflict ended.
b. Simple average of country statistics.
c. excludes export of opium.
d. For Afghanistan, current expenditures = ordinary budget and capital expenditures = development budget.

Source: CSO (2004); World Bank (2004f).

Table A.2. Millennium Development Goals

MDGs	Current level (indicators)	Target 2015 (indicators)
1. Eradicate extreme poverty and hunger	Poverty:[a] n/a Population below minimum level of Hunger:[b] n/a dietary energy consumption: n/a	Poverty: n/a Population below minimum level of Hunger: n/a dietary energy consumption: n/a
2. Achieve Universal Primary Education	Primary Gross Enrollment Rate (total): 54% (female 68%, male 40%) Adult Literacy rate: 36%	Primary net enrollment (total): 100% Adult Literacy rate: 56%
3. Promote Gender Equality and Empower Women	Female primary gross enrollment: 68% Ratios of girls to boys in primary education (1990): 0.52	Female primary net enrollment: 100% Girls Enrollment share: 50% Ratios of girls to boys in primary education: 1
4. Reduce Child Mortality	Under-five mortality rate: 172 per 1000 Infant mortality rate: 115 per 1000	Under-five mortality rate: 130 per 1000 Infant mortality rate: 55 per 1000
5. Improve Maternal Health	Maternal mortality ratio: 1,600 per 100,000	Maternal mortality ratio: 205 per 100,000
6. Combat HIV/AIDS Malaria, other diseases	Measles: 718 cases per/year Polio: 10 cases/year Malaria: 16% of population at high risk, 3 million cases/year Tuberculosis: 321 cases per 100,000; 91 deaths per 100,000 (65% of cases are women)	Measles: 0 cases per/year Polio: 0 per/year Malaria: 8% of population at high risk Tuberculosis: 48 cases per 100,000; 8 deaths per 100,000
7. Ensure Environmental Sustainability/ Access to safe drinking water and sanitation	Population without access to safe drinking water: 87%	Population without access to safe drinking water: 20%
8. Develop a global partnership for development	ODA (% of GDP): 48% GDP per capita (US$): 170 Billion Total GDP US($): 3.7 Billion	ODA (% of GDP): 20% GDP per capita ($): 450

a. Incidence of poverty (percentage) based on national poverty line. Official poverty estimates, on which corresponding MDG targets would be based, are not available at present.

b. Percentage of the hungry in total population; official estimates not available.

Source: Afghanistan Government (2004b), drawing on UN and other international agencies' reports.

Table A.3. Distribution of Characteristics Across Expenditure Quintiles, 2003

	Q1 (Poorer)	Q2	Q3	Q4	Q5 (Richer)	Total
Welfare (per capita)						
Total expenditure per year (US$)	66	116	151	193	301	165
Food expenditure per year (US$)	48	91	122	160	262	137
Non-food expenditure per year (US$)[1]	18	25	29	33	38	29
Overall situation compared to last year (worse = 0, same = .5, better = 1)	0.44	0.47	0.51	0.56	0.59	0.52
Household Characteristics						
Number of household members	8.2	8.1	8.1	8	7.5	8
Ages 0 to 5	1.2	1	0.9	0.9	0.8	1
Ages 65 and above	0.3	0.3	0.3	0.3	0.2	0.3
Female household head (%)	9.3	9.3	6	4.7	3.9	6.6
Disabled household head (%)	7.1	3.9	2.8	2	2.4	3.6
Migrated within country over last five years (household, head, %)	12.3	11.3	11.8	8.1	7.1	10.1
Returnees from abroad over last five years (household head, %)	8	11.6	10.8	11.4	10.5	10.5
Kuchi household (%)	5	3.3	6.2	4.4	3.6	4.5
Food and Nutrition						
Calories per day (minimum caloric requirement = 2100)	1,834	2,290	2,626	3,044	3,996	2,802
Problems satisfying food need (never = 0, always = 1)	0.62	0.59	0.49	0.4	0.34	0.49
Dietary diversity (number of food items consumed)	7.2	12.4	14.7	17.1	21.2	14.5
Calories from wheat (%)	69	63	59	55	48	58
Education						
Household head attended school (%)	20	24	27	33	37	28
Illiteracy of household head (%)	79	73	71	66	62	70
Housing						
Owns house (%)	76	83	85	91	93	86
Persons per room	3.8	3.5	3.1	2.6	2.3	3.1
Public Goods						
Electricity (%)	11	14	16	17	27	17
Access to: (more than 1 day travel = 0, in the community = 1)						
Drinking water	0.96	0.97	0.97	0.98	0.98	0.97
Permanent food market	0.62	0.65	0.68	0.67	0.69	0.66
Public transport	0.65	0.72	0.77	0.75	0.76	0.73
Primary school	0.74	0.79	0.78	0.76	0.81	0.78
Secondary school	0.35	0.47	0.48	0.51	0.55	0.47
Health facility	0.53	0.59	0.63	0.61	0.65	0.6

Table A.3. Distribution of Characteristics Across Expenditure Quintiles, 2003 (*Continued*)

	Q1 (Poorer)	Q2	Q3	Q4	Q5 (Richer)	Total
Employment (%)						
Employment rate for household head	78	83	85	82	82	82
Number of jobs held by household head	2.12	2.09	2.06	2.05	2.11	2.08
Self-employed household head in main occupation	60	63	69	71	70	67
Main occupation (16–64 year old):						
Agriculture	61	58	56	56	56	57
Construction	13	19	19	17	13	16
Trade	3	4	7	9	10	7
Manufacturing (textiles, crafts)	9	6	4	4	3	5
Transport	3	4	4	4	4	4
Education and Health	4	3	4	5	5	4
Administration	1	2	3	2	5	3
Others (Mining, industry, hunting and gathering)	5	4	3	3	4	4
Total	**100**	**100**	**100**	**100**	**100**	**100**
Method of payment in main occupation (16–64 year old):						
Self-employed	37	43	48	52	54	47
Casual daily wage	49	43	40	35	30	39
Regular salary	8	9	10	11	14	10
Payment in kind	6	5	2	2	1	3
Unpaid work	1	1	0	1	1	1
Total	**100**	**100**	**100**	**100**	**100**	**100**
Farming and Livestock						
Own some land (%)	78	85	85	90	92	86
Irrigated land owned (ha)	1.38	1.32	0.76	1.45	1.01	1.18
Rainfed land owned (ha)	0.66	0.43	0.39	0.42	0.54	0.48
Engaged in sharecropping (%)	22	16	10	8	6	12
Livestock owned (US$)	538	542	636	783	1358	769
Poppy Cultivation						
Cultivate opium (%)	3.6	3.4	4.4	4.7	7.8	4.8
Area of opium cultivated (ha)	0.16	0.20	0.24	0.25	0.31	0.24
Farming Constraints: (% reporting as one of top 3 constraints)						
Lack of irrigation water	53	61	65	69	63	62
Lack of seeds	53	54	58	60	59	57
Lack of fertilizers	42	47	51	55	54	50
Lack of oxen/traction power	50	36	33	30	32	36
Lack of farming land	35	34	32	23	26	30

(*continued*)

Table A.3. Distribution of Characteristics Across Expenditure Quintiles, 2003 (*Continued*)

	Q1 (Poorer)	Q2	Q3	Q4	Q5 (Richer)	Total
Lack of credit/cash	31	30	25	21	18	25
Lack of rainfall	20	25	24	26	24	24
Lack of farm labour	3	3	3	5	12	5
Reduced access due to landmines	1	1	1	1	1	1
Conflict and insecurity	1	1	1	2	2	1
Shocks (% suffering in last 12 months)						
Insecurity/violence	6	4	4	5	7	5
Influx of returnees	4	5	4	3	3	4
Human disease	41	30	27	30	23	30
Reduced water	58	58	59	60	54	58
Crop disease	42	37	38	40	38	39
Livestock disease	38	34	35	40	39	37
Late frosts	34	27	28	27	30	29
Debts and Remittances						
Household food debt (kg wheat)	55.2	51.7	48.4	33.9	28.6	45
Household cash debt (US$)	97	125	118	105	90	108
Households receiving remittances (%) from:	10.5	10.1	12.8	18.3	23.2	15.2
Pakistan/Iran (%)	35	32	32	28	27	31
Other (%)	65	68	68	72	73	69
Amount of remittances per capita (receiving households, US$)	19	28	33	38	47	34
Participation in Social Programs: (%)						
Food-for-work	39	34	33	31	26	32
Cash-for-work	19	22	20	18	16	19
Food relief	17	13	11	9	8	12
Demand for Development Projects (% reporting as one of top 3 priorities)						
Health facility	63	68	73	74	69	70
Education facility	50	53	55	55	62	55
Rehabilitation of irrigation system	37	45	47	46	46	44
Improved drinking water quality/ quantity	36	34	34	35	35	35
Construction or repair of rural roads	19	19	20	24	26	22
Micro-credit schemes	31	24	21	17	15	21
Employment opportunities	26	22	18	14	11	18
Others	32	31	30	32	33	32

1. Non-food expenditure includes spending on medicine, education, clothes, taxation, fuel and oil.
Note: Local prices in Afghans converted at exchange rate of Afs 45/US$1.
Source: Afghanistan Government (2003).

Table A.4. Determinants of Rural Poverty, 2003[1]

Variables	Coefficient	t-statistic
Household Characteristics		
Numbers of household members	–0.032***	–7.69
Ages 0 to 5	–0.028***	–4.63
Ages 65 and above	–0.042***	–3.47
Female household head	–0.135***	–4.88
Numbers of household members disabled	–0.018	–1.55
Age of household head	0	0.32
Number of female members/ household size	0.028	0.6
Internally displaced over last five years	–0.066***	–3.14
Returnees from abroad over last five years	–0.013	–0.72
Kuchi household	0.149***	3.05
Education		
Literate household head	0.072***	4.86
Public Goods		
Electricity (yes = 1)	0.036**	2.19
Access to: (more than 1 day travel = 0, in the community = 1)		
Clean water	0.004	0.05
Food market	–0.018	–0.47
Public transport	0.038	1.44
Primary school	–0.033	–1.35
Secondary school	0.085***	4.57
Health facility	–0.004	–0.16
Employment (household head)		
Employed	–0.04*	–1.83
Self-employed in main occupation	0.027	1.63
Main activity of employed: (Agriculture omitted)		
Construction	–0.11***	–5.38
Trade	0.067***	2.87
Education and health	0.047	1.3
Administration	0.039	1.11
Farming and Livestock		
Own some land	0.083***	4.17
Engaged in sharecropping	–0.137***	–7.03
Agricultural laborer (main job of household head)	–0.116***	–7.43
Cultivate opium	0.078***	2.9

(continued)

Table A.4. Determinants of Rural Poverty, 2003[1] (*Continued*)

Variables	Coefficient	t-statistic
Shocks from: (suffering in last 12 months)		
Insecurity/violence	–0.037	–1.15
Influx of returnees	0.013	0.29
Human disease	–0.031**	–2.07
Reduced water	–0.006	–0.49
Crop disease	0.017	0.94
Livestock disease	0.065***	3.71
Late frosts	–0.012	–0.75
Debts and Remittances		
Probability of receiving remittances	0.093***	7.08
Region (Southern Region omitted)		
Central	–0.162***	–3.87
East-Central	–0.074***	–3.61
Eastern	–0.115***	–6.14
North-Eastern	0.022	0.66
Northern	–0.054**	–2.09
Western	–0.287***	–10.14
Memo: Number of observations[2]	5916	
R-Square	0.189	

Note: Regression also includes a constant and a date of household interview variable (not reported).
* significant (difference from 0) at 10% level, ** significant at 5% level, *** significant at 1% level.
1. Dependent variable: Log of per capita total expenditure.
2. Missing observations and the 5% tails of the distributions dropped.
Source: Afghanistan Government (2003); staff analysis and estimates.

Table A.5. Government Expenditures and Employment

Solar year[a]	2002/03 Budget	2002/03 Estimate	2003/04 Budget	2003/04 Estimate	2004/05 Budget
Ordinary Budget (US$ million)					
Location[b]					
Center		193.1	391.7	269.7	418.4
Provinces		155.8	158.3	183.1	190.2
Total	**460.3**	**348.9**	**550.0**	**452.9**	**608.6**
Economic classification[c]					
Wages	190.4		274.8	243.5	348.8
Pensions	15.6		1.1	3.6	14.5
Debt service	6.6		6.7	4.4	5.6
Goods and services	131.0		179.1	125.0	144.3
Transfers	4.0		22.4	15.0	22.5
Contingencies	74.1		28.3	—	27.8
Capital expenditures	38.7		37.5	61.3	45.1
Total	**460.3**	**348.9**	**550.0**	**452.9**	**608.6**
Functional classification					
General Public Services	14.2		42.2	46.2	34.1
Defense	115.5		128.5	122.3	119.1
Public Order and Safety	93.5		82.0	111.0	124.9
Economic Affairs	61.2		41.0	45.3	58.7
Housing and Communal Services	0.4		1.3	2.5	1.3
Health	27.9		28.0	21.7	25.3
Recreation, culture, and religion	16.0		13.4	10.0	12.5
Education	61.6		133.0	77.0	127.3
Social Protection	4.9		7.2	16.9	8.5
Reserves	65.1		73.4	—	97.0
Total	**460.3**	**348.9**	**550.0**	**452.9**	**608.6**
Development Budget (US$ million)[d]					
General Public Services		7.2	120.0	158.8	517.2
Defense		129.6	445.8	694.1	678.8
Public Order and Safety		77.7	173.6	190.5	494.9
Economic Affairs		109.2	403.7	591.3	1,315.3
Housing and Communal Services		2.9	35.5	89.8	78.3
Health		7.2	212.9	153.5	289.4
Recreation, culture, and religion		18.6	30.0	19.0	34.3
Education		3.5	84.7	109.9	277.0
Social Protection		185.6	448.4	365.8	539.6
Reserves					299.5
Total		**541.5**	**1,954.5**	**2,372.7**	**4,524.3**

(continued)

Table A.5. Government Expenditures and Employment (*Continued*)

Solar year[a]	2002/03 Budget	2002/03 Estimate	2003/04 Budget	2003/04 Estimate	2004/05 Budget
Employment ('000)[e]					
General Public Services			11.5	9.3	9.9
Defense			100.0	100.0	66.7
Public Order and Safety			78.7	77.2	88.3
Economic Affairs			43.1	29.7	34.4
Housing and Communal Services			1.1	0.8	1.0
Health			26.3	18.9	20.6
Recreation, culture, and religion			16.3	11.9	12.5
Education			172.2	129.9	166.9
Social Protection			6.1	5.5	5.9
Total			**455.3**	**383.2**	**406.1**
Memorandum Item					
Exchange rate (Af/US$)	34.0	44.5	44.8	49.0	49.8

a. Afghan solar year 2002/03 = March 21, 2002–March 20, 2003.
b. 2002/03 based on IMF report. 2003/04 budget: based on first quarter allotment.
c. Based on GoA's chart of accounts (differs from IMF's GFS). Wages include PRR allocation.
d. 2002/03 and 2003/04 estimates = disbursement estimate.
e. Budget = employment ceilings. 2003/04 Actuals = Mid-Year Review.
Source: Data provided by Ministry of Finance, Government of Afghanistan.

Table A.6. Government's National Budget

	2002/03	2003/04
A. Domestic Revenues	**163**	**208**
B. Expenditures (B1+B2)	**891**	**1,514**
B. 1. Ordinary Expenditures	349	452
B. 2. Development Expenditures	542	1,062
Through Treasury	—	190
Directly by Donors[a]	—	872
C. Budget Deficit (A-B)	**–728**	**–1,306**
D. Financing (D1+D2+D3)	**728**	**1,306**
D. 1. External Assistance through Treasury	**709**	**463**
ARTF	79	217
LOTFA	17	36
Other Grants and Loans	207	210
D. 2. External Assistance Outside Treasury	511	872
D. 3. Other Financing[b]	**–86**	–29

a. Disbursements.
b. Other financing reflects changes in the balance of GoA's account at DAB.
Note: These are estimates as the Government's accounts have not been finalized.
Source: Data and estimates provided by Ministry of Finance; staff estimates.

Table A.7. Regional Distribution of Geographical and Arable Land, 2002

Region	Percentage distribution of geographical area	Percentage distribution of arable land	Percent arable land to geographical area
North	12	35	35
Northeast	12	21	21
West	20	17	10
West-Central	9	3	5
Central	4	3	11
South	8	6	9
East	4	2	6
Southwest	31	12	5
Total	**100**	**100**	**12**

Source: Maletta and Favre (2003); Afghan Web Directory (www.afghana.com)

Table A.8. Cropwise Distribution of Area Cultivated, 2002

Crop	Area cultivated (ha)	Percent area cultivated
Wheat	2,486,730	68.3
Other cereals (Barley, Rice, Maize, Millet)	573,470	15.7
Pulses	69,377	1.9
Oilseeds	68,787	1.9
Cotton	17,509	0.5
Clover (fodder)	137,073	3.8
Fruits	80,000	2.2
Vegetables	73,000	2.0
Poppy	74,000	2.0
Others	62,401	1.7
Total Area Cultivated	**3,642,347**	**100**

Source: Maletta and Favre (2003); Afghanistan Government (2004b); UNODC (2003b).

Table A.9. Area, Production and Yield of Cereals in Afghanistan: 2001–03

	Area ('000 ha)			Production ('000 tonnes)			Yield (Kg/ha)		
Regions	**2001**	**2002**	**2003**	**2001**	**2002**	**2003**	**2001**	**2002**	**2003**
North		608	1,034	355	753	1,367		1,239	1,322
North-East		565	716	419	958	1,576		1,696	2,200
West		406	409	218	630	722		1,551	1,765
East-Central		106	95	19	150	102		1,415	1,074
Central		120	139	115	281	467		2,342	3,360
South		48	105	156	93	325		1,938	3,095
East		106	114	289	243	267		2,294	2,344
South-West		254	206	397	482	547		1,898	2,656
Total Cereals	**2067**	**2,213**	**2,819**	**1,968**	**3,589**	**5,372**	**951**	**1,622**	**1,906**

Note: Cereals consist of Wheat, Barley, Maize and Milled Rice; Regional break-up for Area and Yield in 2001 is not available.

Source: FAO/WFP (2001, 2003).

ORPHAN HOLD
DO NOT SHIP

H1 – 000000000688

ISBN 9780821360958

Afghanistan – State Building, Sustaining Growth, and Redu...

CLIENT	Alternate Sourcing
STATION	TPP Receiving Station 03
HELD	2026 – 10 – 13 07:39

SHELF

If its order arrives, scan this label at a receiving station.

Table A.10. Area under Wheat and Wheat Yields by Regions in Afghanistan (1997–2003)

	Area ('000 ha)							Yield (Kg/ha)						
Region	**1997**	**1998**	**1999**	**2000**	**2001**	**2002**	**2003**	**1997**	**1998**	**1999**	**2000**	**2001**	**2002**	**2003**
Wheat Irrigated														
North	292	280	274	265	254	260	217	1599	1500	1401	1102	929	1727	2525
North-East	197	200	200	188	173	204	224	1701	1600	1600	1101	1491	2216	3263
West	183	190	184	176	174	170	139	1798	1900	1902	1000	1057	2106	2554
Central	71	69	70	77	75	74	107	2000	1696	1600	1247	1520	2405	3598
East	71	75	72	66	77	57	63	1901	1707	2097	1803	2156	2193	2238
South	95	95	92	95	95	44	103	1495	1505	1402	905	1568	1977	3117
South-West	254	270	260	274	280	186	170	1799	1700	1900	1099	1400	2011	2765
West-Central	61	55	44	48	28	50	35	1197	1309	1091	1104	536	1740	1829
Total	**1224**	**1234**	**1196**	**1189**	**1156**	**1045**	**1059**	**1699**	**1637**	**1662**	**1118**	**1310**	**2019**	**2849**
Wheat Rainfed														
North	220	250	225	260	245	269	670	700	900	702	200	102	669	907
North-East	260	260	260	250	156	180	314	600	700	500	200	199	950	1535
West	210	230	220	220	142	180	204	800	1000	800	100	99	944	1137
Central	20	20	5	3	3	3	5	800	900	200	333	333	0	800
East	10	10	5	4	4	0	0	800	900	400	250	500		
South	40	42	10	8	8	0	1	800	810	400	125	125		1000
South-West	90	90	66	55	50	30	3	800	900	500	109	100	800	0
West-Central	50	50	40	40	15	35	39	500	700	200	200	333	886	462
Total	**900**	**952**	**831**	**840**	**623**	**697**	**1235**	**701**	**855**	**616**	**167**	**133**	**826**	**1089**

(continued)

Table A.10. Area under Wheat and Wheat Yields by Regions in Afghanistan (1997–2003) (*Continued*)

	Area ('000 ha)							Yield (Kg/ha)						
Region	**1997**	**1998**	**1999**	**2000**	**2001**	**2002**	**2003**	**1997**	**1998**	**1999**	**2000**	**2001**	**2002**	**2003**
All Wheat														
North	512	530	499	525	499	529	887	1213	1217	1086	655	523	1189	1303
North-East	457	460	460	438	329	384	538	1074	1091	978	587	878	1622	2255
West	393	420	404	396	316	350	343	1265	1407	1302	500	627	1509	1711
Central	91	89	75	80	78	77	112	1736	1517	1507	1213	1474	2312	3473
East	81	85	77	70	81	57	63	1765	1612	1987	1714	2074	2193	2238
South	135	137	102	103	103	44	104	1289	1292	1304	845	1456	1977	3096
South-West	344	360	326	329	330	216	173	1538	1500	1617	933	1203	1843	2717
West-Central	111	105	84	88	43	85	74	883	1019	667	693	465	1388	1108
Total	**2124**	**2186**	**2027**	**2029**	**1779**	**1742**	**2294**	**1276**	**1296**	**1233**	**725**	**898**	**1542**	**1901**

Note: Regional groupings of provinces are as follows—**North** (Faryab, Juzjan, Sar-i-pol, Balkh, Samangan); **Northeast** (Bughlan, Kunduz, Takhar, Badakhshan); **West** (Herat, Farah, Badghis); **West-Central** (Ghor, Bamyan); **Central** (Kabul, Parwan, Kapisa, Logar, Ghazni, Wardak); **South** (Paktya, Paktika, Khost); **East** (Nangarhar, Kunar, Laghman, Nooristan); **Southwest** (Kandahar, Helmand, Zabul, Nimroz and Uruzgan).

Source: FAO/WFP (2002, 2003).

Table A.11. Wheat Production across Regions, 2003

Region	Production ('000 tonnes)	Percent production (%)
North	1156	27
North-East	1214	28
West	587	13
Central	389	9
East	141	3
South	322	7
South-West	470	11
East-Central	82	2
Total	**4361**	**100**

Source: FAO/WFP (2003).

Table A.12. Average Yield and Comparative Gross Income of Horticulture Crops as Compared to Other Crops

Crop	Average yield (Kg/ha)	Average gross income (USD/ha)	Comparative income wheat = 100
Wheat	2170	440	100
Maize	3360	517	118
Rice	2275	792	180
Cotton	1645	642	146
Almonds	2415	3179	723
Apple	10325	1814	412
Apricot	8890	1423	323
Grape	9065	1628	370
Pomegranate	9730	1424	324
Melon	11690	725	165
Onion	12845	1109	252
Potato	14175	1943	442
Tomato	10710	1024	233
Watermelon	14350	792	180
Opium poppy	70	3535	803

Source: ICARDA (2003).

References

Afghanistan Government. 2002. *National Development Framework.*

———. 2003. *National Risk and Vulnerability Assessment* (NRVA).

———. 2004a. *Constitution of Afghanistan.*

———. 2004b. *Securing Afghanistan's Future: Accomplishments and the Strategic Path Forward.* Transitional Islamic State of Afghanistan and international agencies. http://www.af/recosting/index.html

———. 2004c. Security Sector Reform in Afghanistan. Paper presented by the Transitional Government at the Berlin International Conference, March 2004.

ALMP. 2001. *Meeting Employment Challenges in the Global Economy: Overview of ALMP Evaluation Results.*

Alston, J.M., M.C. Marra, P.G. Pardey, and T.J. Wyatt. 1998. "Research Returns Redux: A Meta-Analysis of the Returns to Agricultural R&D." EPTD Discussion Paper No. 38. April.

AREU. 2004. "Understanding Markets in Afghanistan: Case Studies on the Markets in Construction Materials, Raisins, and Carpets." Processed.

AREU and an NGO Consortium (CARE, Mercy Corps, MEDAIR and ACTED). 2003. *One Hundred Households in Kabul: A Study of Winter Vulnerability, Coping Strategies and the Impact of Cash for Work.*

Asian Development Bank. 2003a. *Key Indicators of Developing Asian and Pacific Countries.*

———. 2003b. *Rebuilding Afghanistan's Agricultural Sector.*

Batra, G., D. Kaufmann, and A.H.W. Stone (2000). *Voices of the Firms 2000: Investment Climate and Governance Findings of the World Business Environment Survey.* World Bank. http://www.worldbank.org/wbi/governance/pdf/voicesfirms2k_fulltext.pdf

Bhatia, M., J. Goodhand, with H. Atmar, A. Pain, and M. Suleman. 2003. "Profits and Poverty: aid, livelihoods and conflicts in Afghanistan." HPG report background paper, February.

Binswanger, H., and S.A. Swaminathan. 2003. "Scaling Up Community-Driven Development: Theoretical Underpinnings and Program Design Implications." World Bank Policy Research Paper.

Chandar, R. 2003. *Afghanistan: A Statistical Master Plan.* Report prepared by a joint inter-agency mission composed of the World Bank, ADB, IMF, and DFID at the request of the Government.

Cohen, D., and M. Soto. 2002. "Why are some countries so poor? Another look at the evidence and a message of hope." OECD Development Centre Technical Paper, 197.

Coke, A. 2004. "Wheat Seed and Agriculture Programming in Afghanistan: its Potential to Impact on Livelihoods." AREU Case Studies Series, March.

CSO. 2004. *Statistical Yearbook 1382.*

DACAAR. 2003. "Survey of Three Villages in Alingar, Laghman: Understanding Rural Livelihoods Undertaken as part of the EC funded AREU Livelihoods Monitoring Project."

De Soto, H. 2000. *The Mystery of Capital: Why Capitalism Triumphs in the West and Fails Everywhere Else.* ILD.

Dercon, S. 2003. "Insurance Against Poverty." United Nations University WIDER Policy Brief.

Department for International Development, UK Government. 2003. "Development of Alternative Livelihoods in Afghanistan."

DRN. 2003. "Assistance to the Transitional Authority of the Islamic State of Afghanistan to Elaborate Policy Guidance Regarding Food Aid Utilization in Afghanistan."

Dupree, L. 1980. *Afghanistan.* Princeton, New Jersey: Princeton University Press.

Ensminger, J. 1997. "Changing property rights: reconciling formal and informal rights to land in Africa." In J. Drobak and J. Nye, eds., *The Frontiers of the New Institutional Economics.* New York: Academic Press.

Evans, A., N. Manning, Y. Osmani, A. Tully, and A. Wilder. 2004a. *A Guide to Government in Afghanistan.* Kabul and Washington, D.C.: AREU and the World Bank.

———. 2004b. *Subnational Administration in Afghanistan: Assessment and Recommendations for Action.* Kabul and Washington, D.C.: AREU and the World Bank.

FAO. 2003a. *Afghanistan: Survey of the Horticulture Sector.*

———. 2003b. *National Livestock Census, Interim Report.*

FAOSTAT. 2003. *Agricultural Production Indices Data.* www.faostat.fao.org/faostat accessed in March.

FAO/WFP. 2001. *FAO/WFP Crop and Food Supply Assessment Mission to Afghanistan.* June.

———. 2002. *FAO/WFP Crop and Food Supply Assessment Mission to Afghanistan.* August.

———. 2003. *FAO/WFP Crop and Food Supply Assessment Mission to Afghanistan.* August.

Fan, S., L. Zhang, and X. Zhang. 2002. "Growth, Inequality and Poverty in Rural China: The Role of Public Investments." Research Report 125, International Food Policy Research Institute.

Favaro, E. 2004. "Managing Volatility in Small States." Processed.

Friedman, E., S. Johnson, D. Kaufmann, and P.Z. Lobatón. 2000. "Dodging the Grabbing Hand: The Determinants of Unofficial Activity in 69 Countries." *Journal of Public Economics.* June.

Goodhand, J., and A. Pain. 2002. "Afghanistan: Current Employment and Socio-Economic Situation and Prospects." Infocus Programme on Crisis Response and Reconstruction Working Papers, 8.

Grace, J. 2004. "Gender roles in agriculture: case studies of five villages in northern Afghanistan." AREU Case Studies Series, March.

Greif, A. 1997. "On the interrelations and economic implication of economic, social, political, and normative factors: Reflections from two late medieval societies." In J. Drobak and J. Nye, eds., *The Frontiers of the New Institutional Economics.* New York: Academic Press.

Guimbert, S. 2004. "Structure and Performance of the Afghan Economy." *World Bank South Asia Working Paper Series,* No. 1.

Hakimi, E., N. Manning, S. Prasad, and K. Prince. 2004. "Heroic Reforms: Agency-Level Reforms in the Afghan Civil Service." Draft discussion paper.

Human Rights Research and Advocacy Forum. 2003. *Speaking Out: Afghan Opinions on Rights and Responsibilities.* Kabul. http://www.reliefweb.int/library/documents/2003/care-afg-19nov.pdf

ICARDA (International Center for Agricultural Research in Dry Areas). 2003. *Needs Assessment on Horticulture in Afghanistan.*

IMF. 2003. *Afghanistan Country Report: Rebuilding a Macroeconomic Framework for Reconstruction and Growth.* Country Report No. 03/299.

———. 2004. *Islamic State of Afghanistan: Staff-Monitored Program.* Country Report No. 04/110.

IOM. 2004. "Trafficking in Persons: An Analysis of Afghanistan." January.

IRC. 2003. "Afghanistan: Labor Market Information Survey." Processed. September.

Kerr-Wilson A., and A. Pain. 2003. *Three Villages in Alingar, Laghman: Understanding Rural Livelihoods.*

Klein, M. 2003. *Ways Out of Poverty: Diffusing Best Practices and Creating Capabilities.*

Leipziger, D. and others. 2003. *Achieving the Millennium Development Goals: The Role of Infrastructure.* World Bank.

Maimbo, S. 2003. *The Money Exchange Dealers of Kabul.* World Bank Working Paper No. 13. Washington, D.C.

Maletta, H. and R. Favre. 2003. "Agriculture and Food Production in Post-War Afghanistan: A Report on the Winter Agricultural Survey 2002–03." Ministry of Agriculture and Animal Husbandry. August.

Mani, R. 2003. "Ending Impunity and Building Justice in Afghanistan." AREU.

Molla, D. 2003. "Food Aid, Wheat Prices and Poppy Cultivation in Afghanistan: Is there a link?" Processed.

Pain, A. 2004. "Understanding Village Institutions: Case Studies on Water Management from Faryab and Saripul." AREU Case Studies Series. March.

Pain, A., and S. Lautze. 2002. "Addressing Livelihoods in Afghanistan." AREU Issues Paper Series. September.

Rivera, W. M., W. Zijp, and G. Alex. 2000. "Contracting for Extension: Review of Emerging Practice." AKIS Good Practice Note, AKIS Thematic Team. World Bank.

Rodrik, D. 2003. "Growth Strategies." Processed.

Rubin, B. 2000. "The Political Economy of War and Peace in Afghanistan." *World Development,* 28.

———. 2002. *The Fragmentation of Afghanistan.* Princeton, New Jersey: Princeton University Press.

Schütte, S. 2004. "Urban Vulnerability in Afghanistan: Case Studies from Three Cities." AREU. May.

Sedra, M., and P. Middlebrook. 2004. "Afghanistan's Problematic Path to Peace: Lessons in State Building in the Post-September 11 Era." Silver City, New Mexico and Washington, D.C.: Foreign Policy In Focus. March.

Sheladia Associates. 2004. *Final Report for Framework of Water Resources Management & Draft Report on Proposed Water Resources Development Strategy, Afghanistan.* February.

Thomas, J.J. 1992. *Informal Economic Activity.* LSE Handbooks of Economics. London: Harvester Wheatsheaf.

UNDP. 2001. *Disaster Profiles of the Least Developed Countries.*

———. 2003. *Human Development Report: Millennium Development Goals: A Compact Among Nations to End Human Poverty.*

UNEP. 2003. "Strategy Paper on Integration of Environmental Management and Recovery in the National Development Plan for Afghanistan."

UNICEF and CSO. 2003. *Multiple Indicator Cluster Survey.*

UNODC. 2003a. *Afghanistan Opium Survey 2003.*

UNODC. 2003b. *The Opium Economy in Afghanistan: An International Problem.*

UNODC. 2004. *Afghanistan Opium Survey 2004.*

Ward, C. 2004. "Afghanistan's Opium Economy: A Preliminary Overview and Analysis." Draft discussion paper. March.

WFP. 2002. "Vulnerability Analysis Mapping."

Wily, L.A. 2003. *Land Rights in Crisis: Restoring Tenure Security in Afghanistan.* AREU.

———. 2004. "Presentation: Rural Land Conflict and Peace in Afghanistan." AREU. April.

Williams, M. 2004. "The role of the private sector in the provision of infrastructure services in Afghanistan." Processed.

World Bank. 1978. *Afghanistan: The Journey to Development.* Washington, D.C.

———. 2000. *World Development Indicators.* Washington, D.C.

———. 2001a. "Afghanistan Border States Development Framework Approach Paper." November 12.

———. 2001b. *World Development Report 2000/2001: Attacking Poverty.* Washington, D.C.

———. 2002. *World Development Indicators.* Washington, D.C.

———. 2003a. *Breaking the Conflict Trap.* World Bank Policy Research Report. Washington, D.C.

———. 2003b. *The Contribution of Social Protection to the Millennium Development Goals.* Washington, D.C.

———. 2004a. *Agriculture Investment Sourcebook.* Washington, D.C.

———. 2004b. *Poverty, Vulnerability, and Social Protection in Afghanistan.* Forthcoming.

———. 2004c. *Program Document for Programmatic Support for Institution Building: The Islamic Republic of Afghanistan.* Washington, D.C.

———. 2004d. *Trade and Regional Cooperation between Afghanistan and its Neighbors.* Washington, D.C.

———. 2004e. *Transitional Islamic State of Afghanistan: Mining as a Source of Growth.* Washington, D.C.

———. 2004f. *World Development Indicators.* Washington, D.C.

———. 2004g. *World Development Report 2004: Making Services Work for Poor People.* Washington, D.C.

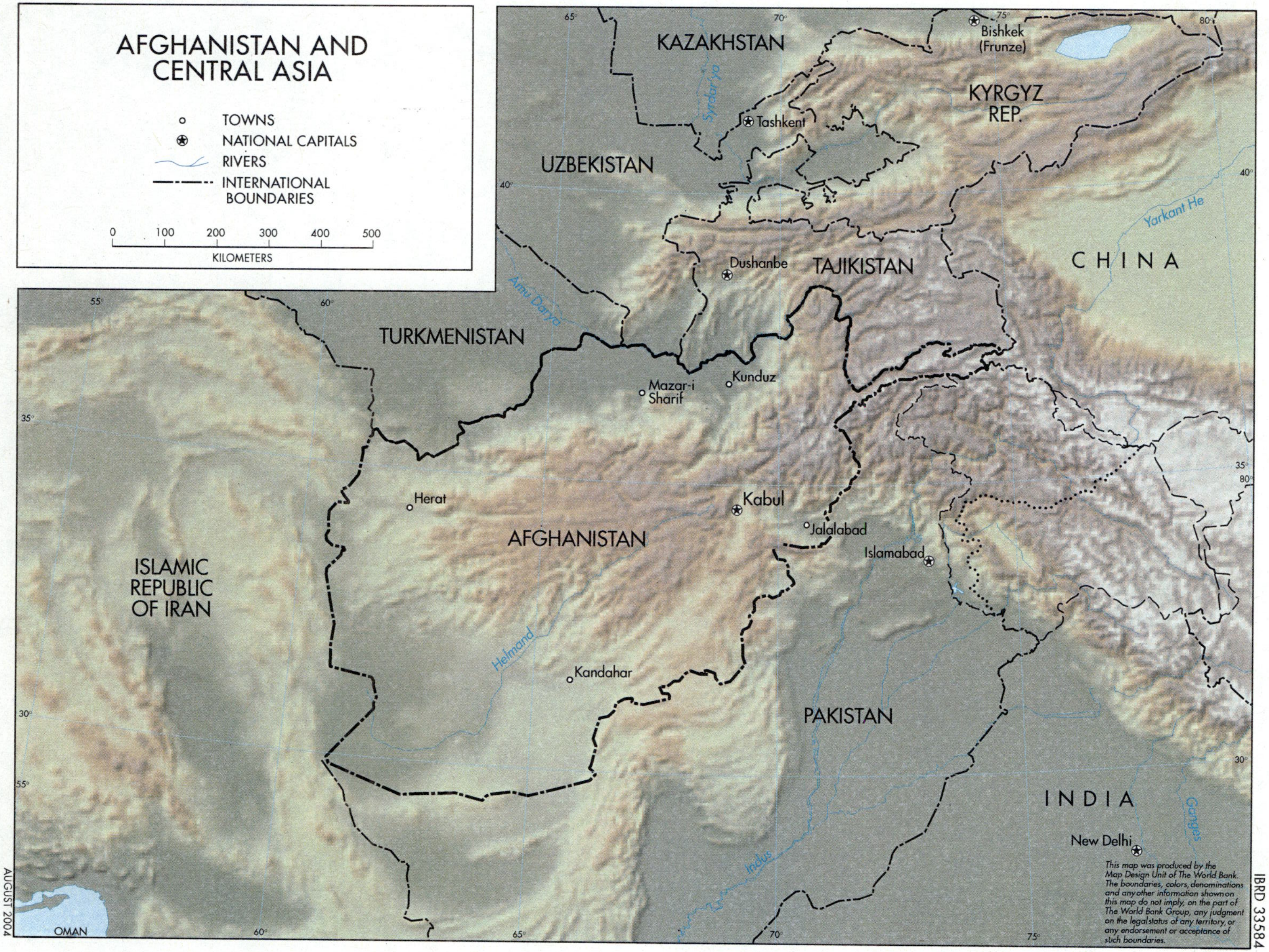

AUGUST 2004

IBRD 33584